SOTHIS PRESS

Sothis Press aims to completely reimagine the public domain book with an emphasis on universal access to captivatingly designed print editions. We believe that technology will enable every single book ever published to be perpetually accessible in beautiful print form. Sothis is beauty in ubiquity.

www.sothis.press
1 Waterhouse Square, London, ECIN 2ST

A Summary of the Law of Set-Off

With an Appendix of Cases Argued
and Determined in the Courts of Law
and Equity Upon That Subject

Basil Montagu

SOTHIS PRESS

ISBN 978-1-83548-668-9

This edition is published by
Sothis Press © 2023. The company
is registered in England and Wales.
The Company Number is 14900389.

A

SUMMARY

OF

THE LAW OF SET-OFF:

WITH

AN APPENDIX OF CASES

ARGUED AND DETERMINED

IN THE

COURTS OF LAW AND EQUITY

UPON THAT SUBJECT.

BY BASIL MONTAGU, ESQ.
Of Gray's Inn, Barrister at Law.

NEW-YORK:

PRINTED BY AND FOR I. RILEY & CO.
Lexitypographic Press.
1806.

3

2

TABLE OF CITED CASES.

[The figures which immediately follow the names refer to the Summary, and those which stand in the column refer to the Appendix.]

TABLE OF CONTENTS.

Set-off. [2]

. At Law. [5]

I. At Comm

II. By Statut

II. In Equity. [61]

ANALYSIS.

- 'e the subjects of Set-off. [2]
- f set-off. [3]
  - I. At Law. [5]
    - I. At Common Law. [5]
    - II. By Statute. [15]
      - I. In General. [15]
        - I. Requisites to enable a person to give a set-off in evidence. [17]
          - I. There must be mutual debts. [17]
            - I. The demand of each party must be a *debt*. [18]
              - I. The demand of the plaintiff. [18]
              - II. The demand of the defendant. [20]
            - II. The debt of each party must be *due in his own right*, except in the case of Executors and Administrators, when it must be due between the testator or intestate and the other party. [22]
              - I. Joint and several debts. [23]
              - II. Trustees. [27]
              - III. Principal and Agent. [29]
              - IV. Husband and Wife. [33]
              - V. Executor and Administrator. [34]
          - II. The debt must be due at the commencement of the action. [35]
        - II. Of a person's option to waive or to avail himself of his right to set-off. [37]
        - III. Of the pleadings and of the mode of setting-off debts. [39]
          - I. Of the defendant's option either to plead or to give notice; and which mode is to be preferred. [40]
          - II. Of the nature of the notice and of the pleadings. [41]
            - I. The Notice. [41]
            - II. The Pleadings. [42]
              - I. The Plea. [42]
              - II. The Replication. [44]
        - IV. The Judgment. [45]
      - II. In particular Cases. [46]
        - I. In Bankruptcy. [46]
          - I. By the particular Statute in the case of bankruptcy. [46]
            - I. Requisites for a balance of accounts. [47]
              - I. Mutual debts or credits. [47]
                - I. The demand on either side must be a debt or a credit. [47]
                - II. The demand must be due to the bankrupt and to the creditor in their own rights respectively. [47]
              - II. The debt must be due or the credit exist between the parties before the bankruptcy. [52]
                - I. It must exist *before the bankruptcy*. [52]
                - II. It must exist *between the parties* before the bankruptcy. [55]
            - II. Modes of balancing the accounts. [56]
          - II. By the general Statutes of Set-off. [58]
        - II. In insolvency. [59]
  - II. In Equity. [61]

ımary.)

SET-OFF.

INTRODUCTORY CHAPTER.

WHEN there are opposite demands between two persons, and the accounts are *connected* by originating in the same transaction, or by any subsequent agreement, the balance is the debt, and is the sum recoverable by suit. When the accounts are *unconnected* by originating and by continuing in distinct transactions, each demand is a legal debt, and recoverable by a separate action;(*a*) but such accounts may be balanced by setting off one debt against the other, either at law or in equity.

(*a*) In Green v. Farmer, 1 Blackst. Rep. 651, 8 G. III. Lord Mansfield. "The justice of allowing cross-demands is supported by natural equity: the balance only is really due in such cases. But the common and established forms of law have in general directed separate remedies to be mutually had by different actions: and though, where the nature of the transaction consists in a variety of receipts and payments, the law allows the balance only to be the debt; yet, where the mutual debts stand unconnected with each other, the *law hath said*, they shall not be set-off: and courts of equity have followed this rule, merely because it was the law." So in Burr. 2221, Lord Mansfield says, the statutes of set-off seem to refer only to mutual unconnected debts: for at common law, where the nature of the employment necessarily constituted an account of receipts and payments, debts and credits, the balance only was the debt.

Dale v. Sollet, 4 Burr. Rep. 2133. A. D. 1767. Action for money had and received—non-assumpsit:—issue. The defendant, a ship-broker, was the plaintiff's agent in suing for and recovering a sum of money for damages done to the plaintiff's ship; and did recover and receive 2000*l.* for the plaintiff's use, and paid him all but 40*l.* which he retained for his labour and service therein, which the witness (Mr. Fuller) swore he thought to be a reasonable allowance; and the jury were of opinion, "that the defendant ought to retain 40*l.* as a reasonable allowance;" consequently the plaintiff was not entitled to recover. The plaintiff objected at the trial, "that the defendant could not give *evidence* in this manner, of this labour and service; but *ought to have pleaded it by way of set-off*, or at least have given *notice* of it as a

The law relating to the balancing of *unconnected* accounts is called the law of set-off.

---

set-off." A verdict was found for the plaintiff, subject to the opinion of the court; and if the court should be of opinion against him, then judgment to be entered as upon a nonsuit—Accordingly Mr. Dunning moved, on behalf of the defendant, "that judgment might be entered against the plaintiff, as upon a nonsuit," and had a rule to shew cause. Lord Mansfield had no doubt of the defendant's being at liberty to give this evidence. This is an action for money had and received to the plaintiff's use. The plaintiff can recover no more than he is in conscience and equity entitled to, which can be no more than what *remains after deducting* all just allowances, which the defendant has a right to retain *out of the very sum demanded.* This is not in the nature of a *cross* demand or *mutual* debt: it is a *charge* which makes the *sum* of money received for the plaintiff's use so much *less*. The two other judges concurred. Per curiam. Judgment for the defendant, as on a nonsuit.

Dobson, assignee of Patrick, v. Lockhart, 5 Ter. Rep. 135. A. D. 1793. (Appendix 1.) Action for goods sold and delivered. General issue and set-off, "That the defendant, before the bankruptcy, had executed two bonds as surety for the plaintiff, on agreement (inter al.) that the defendant should retain such money as should at any time be due from the defendant to the bankrupt, in respect of any dealings between them in trade, until the two first bonds should be satisfied; and that the defendant should, out of the money which should be due from him to the bankrupt, retain and set-off so much money as he should at any time pay on the two first bonds; that, after the bankruptcy, the defendant paid part of the money for which he was surety; that the money due from the defendant to the bankrupt was due on account of dealings between them in the course of trade, &c. &c." Lord Kenyon nonsuited the plaintiff, with liberty to move to enter up a verdict for him, if the court should be of opinion that he was entitled to recover. Upon a motion for this purpose,

Lord Kenyon. The defendant had various transactions with the bankrupt; among others, he became surety for him in two several sums of money, and, at the time of becoming such security, the latter engaged that the defendant should not be called upon to pay for the goods, until he was indemnified against those bonds. The agreement is valid and a good defence, under the general issue, to this action.

Ashhurst, J. This case falls within the stat. 5 Geo. II. c. 30. § 28.

Buller and Grose, Justices, of the same opinion with Lord Kenyon.

Sturdy v. Amand, 3 T. R. 599. A. D. 1790. (Appendix 4.) Action on bond by the assignees of a bankrupt for securing the payment of an annuity at certain times in the year: before the first instalment became due the obligor lent to the obligee 200*l.* and, in order to secure the repayment, the obligor was authorised, by an instrument under the hand of the obligee, to retain the payments of the annuity from time to time, till the 200*l.* and interest was paid. The obligee became a bankrupt before the 200*l.* was repaid. The assignees brought debt on bond for the arrears. The obligor pleaded the agreement. The plaintiff replied the bankruptcy of the obligee before either

This summary of the law of set-off is divided into two books; the first is appropriated to "*Set off at Law;*" the second contains a few decisions upon "*Set-off in Equity.*" The first

---

of the quarterly payments became due. Demurrer and joinder. The court were clearly of opinion that, without any relation to the law of lien or set-off, the demurrer was valid. Judgment for defendants.

James v. Kynnier, 5 Ves. Jun. 108. A. D. 1799. (Appendix 5.) In 1789, Rice James and Richard Beckford, partners, borrowed 19,000*l.* on their joint and several bonds, and on the assignment of a mortgage. Of the money borrowed 2,500*l.* was advanced by Mure & Co.

In May 1790, an agreement was entered into for the sale of James's interest in the partnership to James Keighley, for 30,500*l.* payable by instalments. A sum of money was deposited by Keighley, and the securities were to be changed. In October 1793, the Mures applying for payment of their bond, Beckford said it was not then convenient; upon which they requested that they might be accommodated with such sum of 2,500*l.* as a loan, to be repaid at a future period. Keighley offered to lend part of the money deposited by him in pursuance of the agreement for the purchase of James's share in the partnership, if James would consent. Robert Mure accordingly, upon the 21st of October, wrote to James, stating their want of money—the application to Beckford to relieve them—"by an application to Mr. "Keighley to take up your debt to us secured upon William Beckford's "estate, either wholly, or to accommodate us with the amount upon our engaging to repay it at a future period: this latter mode Beckford told me "would be most agreeable to him; and that he would mention it to Keighley." The letter proceeded to state that Keighley had no other money disengaged but what is lying at the banker's to be paid to James upon the signature of the deeds; but professes himself ready to accommodate them, provided James will give his consent to his appropriating so much of the money to that purpose.

Upon this letter James came to London, and received from Keighley 2,500*l.* which he immediately, upon the 24th of October 1793, delivered to the Mures; and he received from them a promissory note for that amount, payable to him three months after date. Upon the 31st of December 1793, the Mures became bankrupt. Since 1793 the interest upon the debt to the Mures was paid up to 1797, by Beckford and Keighley, or by Keighley after the death of Beckford.

The bill was filed by James, praying that it may be declared, that the sum of 2,500*l.* paid by the plaintiff to the Mures, was a payment or part payment of the debt then owing to them from the plaintiff and Beckford; or that the plaintiff is entitled to have such payment set off against such debt; that an account may be taken, &c.

Lord Chancellor. Is there any doubt, that, where there are upon account mutual credits between two parties, though they cannot set-off at law, yet it is the common ground of a bill? If James had brought an action against Mure upon the note, supposing no bankruptcy had taken place, I should have stopped that action while he was a debtor upon the bond. When there comes book is subdivided into two sections; the first section relates to "*Set-off at Common Law;*" the second to "*Set-off by Statute.*"

---

a case of bankruptcy, it is much stronger; between solvent persons, there might be a ground to say, indulgence was given, the credit extended, and therefore that credit ought to be continued. But the moment a bankruptcy comes the account is to be settled. They might sue Beckford's executors at law, but I should stop the action. Therefore there is a clear mutual credit.

Lord Chancellor. I have not a particle of doubt upon this case, which is the clearest I ever heard.

At the time of this transaction the Mures had not accepted Keighley, nor given up the particular bond. The transaction of the change of the partnership was not then a completed transaction. Under these circumstances Keighley, going on with the purchase, had money applicable to the settlement of that transaction, when the business could be finished. The application was made to James, that he would agree, that that money should go to the relief of the Mures, creditors of the partnership. The mode in which he does it is by taking this note. The transaction going on between Keighley and him, I never would let him proceed upon that note. The fact is beyond a doubt, that the partnership effects of Beckford and James have paid this debt to the Mures. The decree must be according to the prayer of the bill.

BOOK I.

SET-OFF AT LAW.

SECTION I.

SET-OFF AT COMMON LAW.

IF one of two persons, between whom there have been mutual dealings, for the purpose of arresting the other, swear to the sum due to him, without deducting the sum for which he knows himself to be *indebted*, it is an evasion: and, if not ground enough to support an indictment for perjury, will, at least, entitle the defendant to an action for a malicious proecution.(*b*)

If different parties to different actions on policies of insurance enter into the rule to consolidate, the interlocutory costs of one action may, upon motion, be set-off against the interlocutory costs of the other.(*c*)

(*b*) Tyd. K. B. 35.—In Barclay v. Hunt, 4 Burr. 1996. 7 Geo. III. which was a question, whether the assignees of a bankrupt could hold to bail upon an affidavit in these words—" as appears to these deponents, by the last examination of the bankrupts, and as these deponents verily believe." Lord Mansfield, in delivering the opinion of the court, said to an observation of Sir Fletcher Norton's, " that bills may have been paid after the last examination." If that were really the fact, it would not save the person who should swear in the evasive manner that this affidavit would, in such case, be expressed, either from losing the security of bail, or from criminal observation: he might surely be indicted for perjury, upon such an evasive oath, as it would upon that supposition be. In Dr. Turlington's case, he swore to the sum due upon one side of the account only, without regarding the other side of it; but that was a mere evasion, and so treated. So in a case from Plymouth, there was a like manner of swearing: and it was considered as a gross evasion; for the balance is the point in question, and neither side of the account can be taken of itself without the other.

Barker v. Braham, 2 Blackst. 869. 3 Wils. 396. H. T. 13 G. III. (Appendix 8.)—Blackstone, J. says, the courts have been gradually extending this equitable remedy. In the outset of a suit they compel the plaintiff to make a set-off in the affidavit to hold to bail, and will not suffer him to swear to one side only of the account.

(*c*) Nunez v. Modigliani, 1 H. Blackst. 217. A. D. 1789. In Easter term 1788, the plaintiff brought several actions against the defendant, and the other

Opposite demands arising upon judgments may upon motion,(*d*) be set-off against each other,(*e*) whenever such set

---

underwriters, on two policies of insurance; the first effected in the year 1784, on a homeward-bound ship of the intestate's; the second in 1785, on the same ship, outward-bound. The same parties underwrote both the policies. The actions on each being respectively consolidated, *Nathan Modigliani* was made defendant in the former, and *Hannanel Modigliani* in the latter.—When the first came on to be tried, on an application from the defendants' attorney, it was put off to a future time, on his consenting to pay the plaintiff the costs of the day; and an order of nisi prius for that purpose was afterwards made a rule of court. The action on the second policy was to have been tried at the sittings after Hilary term; but the plaintiff withdrew the record, and thereby became, though an administrator (Cont. 2 Comp. Prac. 476) liable to pay the costs of the action. The costs of the first action having been taxed, and allowed to the plaintiff—A rule was granted to shew cause why the prothonotary should not review his taxation, and why the costs, which should be taxed and allowed to the defendant in the second action, should not be set-off against those taxed and allowed to the plaintiff in the first. The court said it was consistent with justice to allow the set-off, as the defendant *Nathan Modigliani* was a party to both actions; in one, being made defendant on the record; in the other, being within the rule to consolidate.—Rule absolute.

(*d*) Previous to the year 1791, it seems to have been supposed, that this right to set-off judgments depended upon the statutes of set-off. In Nunez v. Modigliani, 1 H. Bl. 217. A. D. 1789. Bond and Le Blanc, Serjeants, urged, that the costs in one action could not be set-off against those in anothar, where there were different defendants. If the defendant had been the same in both, it would alter the case; but costs due from A. to B. shall not be set-off against those due from A. to C. This would not be authorised by the statutes of set-off: and the court will not interfere and create a set-off, which those statutes do not allow. There is the same species of argument in O'Connor v. Murphy, 1 H. Bl. 1791. A. D. 1791; but in Mitchell v. Oldfield, 4 Term Rep. 123. A. D. 1791, (Appendix 13) Bearcroft observing, that this was not such a debt as could be set-off under the statute, Lord Kenyon, C. J., said, that this did not depend on the statutes of set-off, but on the general jurisdiction of the court over the suitors in it: that it was an equitable part of their jurisdiction, and had been frequently exercised.

(*e*) This equitable practice seems not to have been permitted before 24 Geo. II. In H. T. 4 Geo. II. in K. B. Butler v. Innys & Ux. 2 Str. 891.—The plaintiff sued, as a pauper, and was nonsuited; after which he brought a second action and recovered; and Strange moved on behalf of the defendants, that the costs in the first action might be deducted out of the recovery in the second; but it was refused. In E. T. 12 Geo. II. in C. B. Ford v. Miles et e contra, stated in Clenlow and Lowe, Barnes 130. The court of Common Pleas denied to set costs against costs. In T. T. 16 Geo. II. in C. B. Goodtitle on demise of Clenlow and Wife v. Lowe and Lowe, and Lowe v. Lowe (q. if not Clenlow) in case 2 Barnes 130. Rule obtained on the motion of Clenlow, upon affidavit of Lowe's insolvency, to shew cause why the costs off is equitable,(*f*) though the judgments are in different courts, (*g*) and though the parties to the different records are not the same.(*h*)

---

recovered by Clenlow in one of these actions should not be set off against the costs recovered by Lowe in the other action. Ware, attorney for Lowe, shewed for cause that the parties in the two causes were different; and that, by this means, Clenlow, who was in good circumstances, would be discharged, and Ware would have no remedy for his costs, Lowe being insolvent. The rule was discharged: (and it is to be noted that in this court the attorney's lien is only subject to the equitable claims of the parties; post, note *t*) so that upon that supposition this decision must have been upon the ground either that the parties were different, or that costs were never set off against costs. In H. T. 17 G. II. in K. B. Duthy v. Tito & al. Tito v. Duthy, Strange 1203. In both causes the verdict was for the defendants: and now Tito, one of the defendants in the first cause, moved that the costs he was to pay to Duthy in the second cause might be set against the costs Duthy was to pay in the first. Sed, per curiam, it cannot be done: there was forced to be an act of parliament in the case of mutual debts: besides, how can we prefer Tito, who is but one defendant out of five, when the plaintiff in that action may pay the costs to either of the others? In 23 Geo. II. in C. B. Mordecai v. Nuting, et al. Bull. Ni. Pri. 336. In an action of trespass against four, three were acquitted, and motion, on their behalf, that their costs might be deducted out of what the fourth defendant was to pay, upon an affidavit, that the plaintiff was a travelling Jew—denied. The same decision is reported in Barnes 145. saying that the court declared the motion to be unprecedented.

Since 23 Geo. II. all the cases, except that of Powel v. Smith, et e contra. T. 25 Geo. II. Bull. Ni. Pri. 336. uniformly allow demands arising upon opposite judgments to be set off against each other. The following are the cases: Wills v. Crabb, E. 24 Geo. II. Bull. Ni. Pri. 336. A plaintiff being nonsuited, the defendant took out a fi. fa. and levied part of the costs, and, at the same time, took out a ca. sa. for the rest, and took the plaintiff in execution; which being irregular, the court set it aside with costs: the defendant moved that the proceedings against him on account of these costs should be stayed, upon his entering up satisfaction upon the judgment obtained by him for the sum at which the costs for the irregularity were taxed, and upon shewing cause the rule was absolute. Powel v. Smith, et e contra, T. T. 25 Geo. II. Bull. N. P. 336. In cross actions of assault, each party being nonsuited, S. had his costs taxed at 9*l.* 10*s.* and P. his at 13*l.* 10*s.* whereupon he moved to be at liberty to deduct the 9*l.* 10*s.* out of the 13*l.* 10*s.* paid by him unto the sheriffs: rule to shew cause, but the defendant not consenting, the court said they could not do it. In Scoffin v. Robinson, in trespass, E. T. 26 Geo. II. C. B. cited 2 Blackst. 826. plaintiff, at the last assizes for Kent, recovered a verdict against defendant; and, at the same assizes, in an ejectment on the demise of Robinson (defendant in this action) plaintiff recovered a verdict. Robinson applied to have the costs he was entitled to deducted out of the costs to be allowed Scoffin. Rule for that purpose made absolute. Thrustout, on demise of Barnes v. Crafter, 2 Blackst. 826. T. T. 12 Geo. III.

Costs may be set-off against costs only, or against debt and costs.(*i*)

Barnes the lessor of the plaintiff had a judgment last Michaelmas term, for 40*l*. 5*s*. against the defendant for his debt and costs on an action for the use and occupation of the premises, but was nonsuited in the present cause, the costs of which are taxed at 12*l*. 5*s*. for non-payment of which, an attachment is taken out against the plaintiff. The demands arising upon each judgment were set-off against each other. The court said that the point had been settled by the cases which had been cited by the counsel, viz. Terlo v. Lowe, 16 Geo. II. 1 Barn. 102, (I cannot find this case) Scoffin v. Robinson, Roberts v. Biggs, Roberts v. Mackroul, T. T. 9 Geo. III. This doctrine is now finally settled. Vide the following notes.

(*f*) Glaister v. Hewer, 8 T. R. 69. 39 Geo. III. (Appendix 9) It is stated by the counsel, and acceded to by the court, that applications of this nature are to the equitable jurisdiction of the court; and that, in attending to them, they will be guided by the rule adopted in a court of equity, that he who asks equity must do equity. Vide O'Connor v. Murphy, 1 H. Bl. 659. A. D. 1791. (App. 10) where the court proceeded solely on equitable principles.

(*g*) Barker administratrix v. Braham, 2 Blackst. 896. 3 Wils. 396. 13 Geo. III. (Ap. 8) The sum of 102*l*. 18*s*. 1*d*. was due from the plaintiff as administratrix of her husband, on a judgment recovered in the King's Bench, in Hil. Ter. 1769. The plaintiff in the same right as administratrix, brought this action in the Common Pleas against the defendant, for a debt due to the intestate, and had a verdict for 106*l*. 9*s*. 6*d*. last T. T. On motion that these judgments might be set-off against each other: De Grey, C. J. No mischief can follow from allowing it: no devastavit can happen, unless the plaintiff knows of any superior debt; and, if she know it, she might disclose it, and shew it for cause. The same answer may be given to the strange supposition of the debts being satisfied by executing a void ca. sa. for which Barker had been amply repaid in damages. If it had been so determined, she might have shewn that for cause: I am therefore for allowing the present motion, but desire it may be remembered, that this is the case of one judgment against another, both in the same right: and must be distinguished from setting off private debts, not in suit, and upon which no judgment has been obtained.—The other judges of the same opinion.

Hall v. Ody, 2 P. and B. 28. A. D. 1799. (Ap. 12) Cockell Serj. this day shewed cause against a rule nisi for setting-off the costs of an action of ejectment recovered in the K. B. by the defendant against the plaintiff, against the costs of an action of trespass in this court, in which the plaintiff had recovered a verdict; and insisted that in all the cases where a set-off of this kind had been allowed, both actions had been in the same court. But the court overruled the objection, saying that a set-off had even been allowed between costs in a court of equity, and costs in a court of law. And Heath, J. observed, that he remembered a case where an ejectment having been brought in the K. B. and afterwards a formedon in this court, proceedings were stayed in the latter until the costs of the former were paid.

(*h*) Previous to 27 Geo. II. this practice seems not to have been permitted. In Duthy v. Tito et al. and Tito v. Duthy, Str. 1203. H. T. 17 Geo. II.

The judgments may be after verdict, or upon a nonsuit, or by default.(*k*)

(ante, note *e*) the defendant Tito moved to have the judgments set-off against each other; but per curiam, how can we prefer Tito, who is but one defendant out of five, when the plaintiff in that action may pay costs to either of the others, and in Goodtitle on demise Clenlow et Ux. v. Lowe and Lowe, and Lowe v. Lowe (q. Clenlow) in case T. T. 16 Geo. II. 2 Barnes 130, (ante, note *e*) the court of C. B. would not permit the opposite judgments to be set-off against each other, the parties in the two causes being different, and Lowe's insolvency defeating the attorney's lien for his costs: the modern practice in the C. B. (post, note *r*) being to allow the attorney's lien only to extend to the balance between the parties: this decision, if the practice were then in existence, must have been founded solely on the ground that the parties were different. Roberts v. Biggs, 27 and 28 Geo. II. Barnes 146. and Bull. Nisi Pr. 336. where Roberts had brought an action against Biggs and others, and Biggs had brought a cross action against Roberts, the court of C. B. ordered that upon Biggs's acknowledging satisfaction on the record, in the cause in which he was plaintiff, the plaintiff in the other cause in which he (Biggs) and others were defendants should be restrained from taking out execution. And in Mitchell v. Oldfield, 4 Ter. Rep. 123. A. D. 1791. (Appendix 13) The plaintiff recovered a judgment against the defendant for 182*l.* 10*s.* but the defendant having also recovered in another action against this plaintiff and another, obtained a rule to shew cause why the debt and costs in the latter should not be set-off against the judgment in the former action; suggesting among other reasons, that Mitchell had absconded.—Bearcroft (shewing cause on behalf of Mitchell's attorney in the first action) hinted that perhaps the court would not interfere at all: inasmuch as one debt was due to the plaintiff alone, whereas the other was the joint debt of the plaintiff and another to the defendant; and he observed that this was not such a debt as could be set-off, under the statute. Lord Kenyon, Ch. J. said that this did not depend on the statutes of set-off, but on the general jurisdiction of the court over the suitors in it: that it was an equitable part of their jurisdiction, and had been frequently exercised. Rule absolute, on the defendant's allowing the lien, and on his entering a remittitur in the cause in which he was plaintiff. Vide Nunez v. Modigliani, 1 H. Bl. 217. ante, note *c*.

(*i*) Thrustout v. Crafter, 2 Blackst. 826. 12 Geo. III. (Appendix 7.) To a rule obtained to shew cause why costs in ejectment should not be set-off against debt and costs in an action for use and occupation: it was stated by counsel, that there was a difference in the nature of executions: one being for debt as well as costs, for which an action would lie on the judgment, the other for costs only, to be recovered by contempt. But the court made the rule absolute.

(*k*) *Upon a nonsuit* Thrustout v. Crafter, 2 Blackst. 826. 12 Geo. III. (Appendix 7.) O'Connor v. Murphy, 1 H. Bl. 656. A. D. 1791. (Appendix 10.) *by default* Glaister v. Hewer, 8 T. R. 69. 29 Geo. III. (Appendix 9.)

Though the judgment on one side existed at the commencement of the action, and might have been pleaded, it may be set-off.(*l*)

When there are opposite demands arising upon judgments, and the party on one record is indebted to the other party, on a consideration distinct from the judgment, it seems that the court will not permit such debtor to set-off his demand arising upon the judgment without taking the other debt into account; but the court will not prevent judgments being set-off against each other when there are many parties to one of the actions, because one of these persons does not take into the account a separate debt due from him to the party on the other record.(*m*)

In an action against several defendants, of whom some are entitled to receive, and the others are liable to pay costs; the defendants cannot balance their respective costs, and pay the difference to the plaintiff upon the suspicion of his insolvency;(*n*) but the court will permit the plaintiff to set-off the costs which

---

(*l*) Barker v. Braham, 2 Bl. 869. 3 Wils. 396. A. D. 1746. (Appendix 8.) There being due to the defendant 102*l*. 18*s*. 1*d*. from the plaintiff, on a judgment recovered in the K. B. in H. T. 1769, the plaintiff brought an action against the defendant in the C. P. and had a verdict for 106*l*. 9*s*. 6*d*. last T. T. The defendant moved to have these judgments set-off, which (without taking notice that the judgment might have been pleaded) was alllowed.

(*m*) Glaister v. Hewer and A. and B. et Hewer and A. and B. v. Glaister. } 8 Term Rep. 69. 39 Geo. III. (App. 9.) Gibbs and Park shewed cause against a rule, obtained by Hewer, and the two other defendants A. and B. for setting-off these judgments against each other: they contended that the defendants were not entitled to set-off their judgment against that which the plaintiff recovered against them, because the plaintiff had another demand against Hewer, saying that this was an application to the equitable jurisdiction of the court, who would therefore be guided by the rule that is adopted in a court of equity, that he who asks equity must do equity: the court thought that this would be carrying the rule too far; for that the effect of discharging this rule would be to subject the two other defendants to the payment of a separate debt of Hewer.—Rule absolute.

(*n*) Mordecai v. Nuting and al. B. N. P. 326. 23 Geo. II. in C. B. In an action of trespass against four, three were acquitted, and motion, on their behalf, that their costs might be deducted out of what the fourth defendant was to pay, upon an affidavit that the plaintiff was a travelling Jew—denied: the same decision is reported in Barnes 145, saying that the court declared the motion to be unprecedented.

he is to pay, against the costs which he is to receive, when the defendant, to whom he is to pay, is the principal party to the suit, and has undertaken to pay costs and damages.(*o*)

One of several defendants, against whom a judgment has has been recovered, may, upon suspicion of the plaintiff's insolvency, set-off a demand arising upon a separate judgment, which he has obtained against the plaintiff, though the plaintiff has offered not to take out execution against such defendant, because he is not the principal party to the suit.(*p*)

A person who is equitably entitled to a judgment, may set-off such judgment, though his name is not upon the record.(*q*)

(*o*) Schoole v. Noble and two others, viz. S. & B. 1 H. Bl. 23. (App. 11.) The plaintiff brought trespass against the defendants for breaking and entering his house, &c. Defendants S. and B. had suffered judgment to go by default: Noble went on to trial, and obtained a verdict. Damages were assessed against S. and B. at one half-penny each; on which Runnington, Sergeant, obtained a rule to shew cause why the costs which might be taxed against S. and B. on the judgment by default, and the damages assessed, should not be deducted out of the costs taxed to Noble on the postea, and allowed to the plaintiff, and, in the mean time, execution against them stayed. This was moved on an affidavit, stating that the defendants S. and B. had acted under the authority of Noble, who had undertaken to pay the damages and costs.—Rule absolute.

(*p*) Dennie v. Elliot, Hill and others, 2 H. Bl. 587. A. D. 1795. (App. 12.) Dennie obtained judgment against the present defendants; Hill obtained a rule to set off a judgment which he had obtained against Dennie, on an affidavit that Dennie appeared to be insolvent, that his goods were all distrained for rent, and that he was not to be met with. This was opposed on an affidavit of Dennie's, stating that Hill had told him that Elliott, one of the other defendants, was to indemnify Hill, as having acted under his orders, and that the plaintiff had offered not to take out execution against Hill. But the rule was made absolute.

(*q*) O'Connor v. Murphy, 1 H. Bl. 659. A. D. 1791. (App. 10.) There were two causes, (Murphy v. O'Loughlin, and O'Connor v. Murphy) and nonsuits in each. The first was an action of trover for a ship, which was the property of O'Connor and one O'Sullivan (who were partners in trade,) and of which O'Loughlin was master. The second action was by the indorsee against the maker of a promissory note. A motion to set-off arising upon these judgments, was made on the ground that the action against O'Loughlin was defended at the joint expense of O'Connor and O'Sullivan, and that O'Sullivan was interested, together with O'Connor, in the promissory note, on which the present action was brought. Lord Loughborough said that, without any regard to O'Sullivan's interest in the promissory note, O'Connor was equitably entitled to the costs of the nonsuit in the action of trover against O'Loughlin; and therefore he ought to be permitted to set them off, as far as they would go against the costs in the present action.—Rule absolute.

It is the settled practice of the Court of King's Bench,(*r*) that the attorney's lien upon the judgment of his client shall,

---

(*r*) Cases in K. B.—Mitchell v. Oldfield, 4 T. R. 123. A. D. 1791. (App. 13.) Mitchell had absconded; upon an application by Oldfield to set-off opposite judgments, Bearcroft shewed cause on behalf of Mitchell's attorney, contending, as he was not concerned as attorney in the other action, he had a lien for his costs on the judgment obtained by his client.

Lord Kenyon thought it right that the attorney in this case should be satisfied his costs before the defendant was allowed to make the set-off.

Buller, J. Though this court have said that they will not interfere on the behalf of the attorney, and prevent the plaintiff's settling his own cause without first paying the attorney's bill; yet, when the adverse party, against whom a judgment has been obtained, applies to get rid of that judgment, the court will take care that the attorney's bill is satisfied.

Rule absolute, on the defendant's undertaking, inter alia, to pay the attorney's bill.

Randle v. Fuller, 6 T. R. 456. A. D. 1793. (Appendix 14.) A rule obtained by the defendant to shew cause why a judgment obtained by him against the plaintiff should not be set-off against a judgment obtained by the plaintiff in this action, was opposed by the plaintiff's attorney, claiming a lien upon the judgment obtained by his client; and stating that the plaintiff had absconded, and that he had no other security for his bill than the judgment.

The court, understanding that, by the practice in the C. P. the attorney's lien only extended to the defendant's residue upon balancing the accounts, desired the matter to stand over—and, after deliberation,

Lord Kenyon, C. J. said, "It has been expressly determined in Mitchell v. Oldfield, that the attorney had a general lien on the costs and damages recovered, without any such restriction as was now endeavoured to be put upon it: and that, upon the reason and justice of the case, he could find no reason to impose such a restriction. That, whatever might be the practice in the court of C. P. he was glad to find that his opinion was warranted by the settled practice of this court.

The law on this head is considered as settled in Glaister v. Hewet, 8 T. R. 69. 3 Geo. III. (Appendix 9.)

Morland and Hammersley v. Lashley; Same v. Lashley and Ux. B. R. A. D. 1795. in notes, 2 H. Bl. 441. Both these causes were tried at the sittings Trin. 34 Geo. III. The first was an action upon the separate bond of the defendant: the second upon the joint bond of the defendant and his wife. In the first, the plaintiff obtained a verdict, and in the second was nonsuited. In the same term Henderson on the part of the plaintiff obtained a rule to shew cause, why the costs of the nonsuit should not be deducted from the sum given by the verdict in the first cause.

Palmer shewed cause contending on the authority of Mitchell v. Oldfield, 4 T. R. B. R. 123. that the attorney for the defendants had a lien on the judgment for his costs. In support of the rule Henderson cited Barker v. Braham, 3 Wils. 396. and attempted to distinguish the present case from Mitchell v. Oldfield, because there were different attornies in the different causes in that case, but here the attorney was the same in both. But upon his application,(*s*) be first satisfied, before the opposite party is permitted to set-off any judgment which he has obtained, whether there are the same or different attornies in the

---

Lord Kenyon said that circumstance made no difference between the cases, and, as to the case in Wilson, it did not there appear that any application was made on the part of the attorney. That an attorney had a lien on the judgment for his costs which it would be unjust in the court to take from him. The rule, therefore, was made absolute, with a reservation of the attorney's lien. But as his costs were equal to the costs of the nonsuit, the rule was afterwards abandoned.

The following are cases in C. P.

Roberts v. Figgs, 28 Geo. II. 2 Barnes. Suppl. 12. cited by counsel in Thrustout v. Crafter, C. P. 2 Blackst. 826. T. T. 12 Geo. III. A rule to shew cause why 13 guineas costs taxed against the plaintiff in a former cause, should not be set-off against 16 guineas costs recovered against the defendant in this cause: it was shewn for cause that the plaintiff was insolvent: and that his attorney had a lien upon these costs for his bill: but it was held by Wilmot, C. J. et cur. that the attorney's lien was only upon what the plaintiff was entitled to have, viz. the difference.

Thrustout v. Crafter, 12 Geo III. 2 Blackst. 826. (App. 7.)

Schoole v. Noble and others, 1 H. Bl. 23. A. D. 1788. Application to set-off judgments.

The court held that the attorney can only have such a lien on the costs, as is subject to the equitable claims of the parties in the cause.

Nunez v. Modigliani, 1 H. Bl. 217. A. D. 1789. (ante. note *e*.) An application to set-off costs.

Lawrence, Serjeant, was stopped by the court, who said that it had been decided in the case of Schoole v. Noble and others, in this court, that an attorney had only such a lien on the costs, as were subject to the equitable claims of the parties in the cause.

Vaughan v. Davies, 2. H. Bl. 440. A. D. 1795. (App. 11.) This was an application by the defendant to set-off judgments.

Adair, Serjeant, shewed cause, on the part of the attorney for the plaintiff, on affidavits, stating that he had no fund to resort to but the sum recovered by the plaintiff for the payment of his bill, the plaintiff himself being insolvent: the set-off therefore ought not to be allowed, till the attorney's bill was satisfied. He said that the court would protect an attorney who was their officer, who would otherwise be without remedy; and that in the court of King's Bench the equitable right of setting-off the sum recovered in one action against that recovered in another, was always subject to the attorney's lien for his bill; for which he cited Mitchell v. Oldfield, 4 T. R. B. R. 123. and Morland v. Lashley, B. R. Trin. 34 Geo. III. But

On this day, after consideration, the court said that the attorney's lien did not extend to prevent the parties in the cause from having the benefit of the set-off, which was applied for in this case, and therefore made the rule absolute.

Buller, J. mentioned that a similar decision had taken place this term in the Court of Chancery, in a case of Barton v. Etherington.

different causes.(*t*) In the Court of Common Pleas the attorney's lien extends only to the difference upon balancing the judgments; but this practice seems not to be finally settled.(*u*)

Denie v. Elliott, Hill and others, 2 H. Bl. 589. A. D. 1795. (App. 12.) In this case a rule was granted to shew cause why a judgment obtained by the defendant should not be set-off against the plaintiff's judgment in this cause.

In opposition to the rule Le Blanc, Serjeant. The attorney for the plaintiff made an affidavit that he had no security for his costs, which the plaintiff was unable to pay, and which he verily believed he should lose, if the set-off were allowed, as he had no chance of recovering them, but out of the damages and costs to be received under the judgment for the plaintiff.

Le Blanc also relied on the practice of the court of King's Bench, and cited Mitchell v. Oldfield, 4 T. R. B. R. 123. and Randle v. Fuller, 6 T. R. B. R. 456.

In support of the rule, Bond, Serjeant, insisted on the known practice in this court, that the attorney's lien for his costs was subject to the equitable claims of the parties in the cause, which, he said, was settled in the cases of Schoole v. Noble, ante vol. i. 23. Nunez v. Modigliani 217. O'Connor v. Murphy 659. and Vaughan v. Davies, vol. ii. 440.

The court held the practice here to be clearly established by these cases, whatever might be the rule in the King's Bench; and therefore that it was not now to be disputed.—Rule absolute.

Hall v. Ody, 2 P. and B. 28. A. D. 1799. (App. 12.) A rule was obtained by the defendant for setting-off judgments.

Cockell, Serjeant, stated, that he opposed the rule on the part of the plaintiff's attorney, who had not been paid his costs, and represented that the plaintiff himself was now in prison. He cited Mitchell v. Oldfield, 4 T. R. 123. to shew that the attorney has a lien on the judgment for the amount of his costs.

Shepherd contra relied on Denie v. Elliot: when it was held, that whatever might be the rule in the King's Bench, yet according to the practice of this court, the lien of the attorney was subject to the equitable claims of two parties.

Lord Eldon, C. J. Finding it to be the practice of this court, that an attorney shall not take his costs out of the fund, which by his diligence he has recovered for his client, where the opposite party is entitled to a set-off, it does not become me to say more than that I find it to be the settled practice with much surprise, since it stands in direct contradiction to the practice of every other court as well as to the principles of justice. In the Court of Chancery the same parties are often concerned in many suits, and I never knew the idea entertained of arranging the funds till the respective attornies were paid their costs. However, as the attorney in this case has acted with a knowledge of the settled practice of the court, he can have no right to claim the advantage of a more just principle: and it will only remain for the court to consider, whether the practice of the Court of King's Bench should not be adopted here for the future.

Heath, J. I have no objection to have the practice reconsidered.

SECTION II.

OF SET-OFF BY STATUTE.

Set-off by Statute relates 1st, to Set-off in General; and, 2d, to Set-off in the particular Cases of Bankrupts, and of Insolvent Debtors.

CHAPTER I.

OF SET-OFF BY STATUTE IN GENERAL.

WHEN there are mutual debts between the plaintiff and the defendant at the time of the commencement of the action; or if either party sue or be sued as executor or administrator, where there are mutual debts between the testator and intestate, and the other party; one debt may be set against the other, either by being given in evidence upon the general issue, or by being pleaded in bar; except where either of the debts accrues by reason of a penalty contained in a specialty; when the debt intended to be set-off *must be pleaded in bar*, and the plea must state how much is truly and justly due on either side; but, in all cases where the general issue only is pleaded, notice must be given, at the time of pleading, of the particular sum or debt intended to be set-off, and upon what account it became due: and, if the plaintiff recover in any suit or action where a set-off is given in evidence, judgment must be entered for no

---

Rooke, J. There can be no objection to reconsidering the practice, but it does not appear to me to be unfair as it stands at present. The attorney looks in the first instance to the personal security of his client, and if beyond that he can get any further security in his hands, it is a mere casual advantage. Rule absolute.

(*s*) Vide Morland v. Lashley, note *r*.

(*t*) Vide note *r* Morland v. Lashley.

(*u*) Vide note *r*.

more than appears to be due to him on the balance of accounts.(*v*)

(*v*) 2 Geo. II. ch. 22. sect. 13. And be it further enacted by the authority aforesaid, That where there are mutual debts between the plaintiff and defendant, or if either party sue or be sued as executor or administrator, where there are mutual debts between the testator or intestate, and either party, one debt may be set against the other; and such matter may be given in evidence upon the general issue, or pleaded in bar, as the nature of the case shall require, so as at the time of his pleading the general issue, where any such debt of the plaintiff, his executor or intestate is intended to be insisted on in evidence, notice shall be given of the particular sum or debt so intended to be insisted on, and upon what account it became due, or otherwise such matter shall not be allowed in evidence upon such general issue.—8 Geo. II. ch. 24. sect. 4. And whereas the provision for setting mutual debts one against the other, is highly just and reasonable at all times, be it therefore enacted by the authority aforesaid, That the said clause in the said first recited act, 2 Geo. II. ch. 22. 'for setting mutual debts one against the other, shall be and remain in full force for ever.' Sect. 5. And be it further enacted and declared by the authority aforesaid, That by virtue of the said clause in the said recited act contained, and hereby made perpetual, mutual debts may be set against each other, either by being pleaded in bar, or given in evidence under the general issue, in the manner therein mentioned notwithstanding that such debts are deemed in law to be of a different nature, unless in cases where either of the said debts shall accrue by reason of a penalty contained in any bond or specialty: and in all cases where either the debt, for which the action hath been or shall be brought; or the debt intended to be set against the same, hath accrued or shall accrue by reason of any such penalty, the debt intended to be set-off, shall be pleaded in bar, in which shall be shewn how much is truly and justly due on either side; and in case the plaintiff shall recover in any such action or suit, judgment shall be entered for no more than shall appear to be truly and justly due to the plaintiff, after one debt being set against the other as aforesaid.

Opinions upon the statutes considered together.—1. The provision for setting mutual debts one against the other is highly just and reasonable at all times. 8 Geo. II. ch. 24. sect. 4.——2. At common law, before these acts, if the plaintiff were as much or even more indebted to the defendant, than the defendant was indebted to him, yet the defendant had no method to strike a balance: he could only go into a court of equity, for doing what is most clearly just and right to be done. The statutes of set-off were made to remedy this defect. Lord Mansfield, Burr. 1230—3. The meaning of these acts of parliament was, that in all cases of mutual debts, the less sum should be deducted out of the greater, if the defendant desire it. Burr. 1230.—4. The statutes only say, that the defendant may set-off the debt due to him from the plaintiff, but do not compel him to do so. Burr. 823.—5. Where there are mutual debts unconnected, the law said they should not be set-off, but each must sue: and courts of equity followed the same rule, because it was the law; for, had they done otherwise, they would have stopped the course of law, in all cases where there was a mutual demand. The natural

This subject is divisible into four parts.(*w*)

1. The requisites to enable a person to give a set-off in evidence.

2. Of a person's option to waive or to avail himself of his right to set-off.

3. Of the pleadings and of the mode of setting-off debts.

4. The judgment.

SECTION. I.

The requisites to enable a person to give a set-off in evidence.

These requisites are two.—1. There must be mutual debts.—2. The debts must be due at the commencement of the action.

---

sense of mankind was first shocked at this, in the case of bankrupts, and it was provided for by 4 Ann. ch. 17. sect. 11. and 5 Geo. II. ch. 30. s. 28.—Where there was no bankruptcy, the injustice of such setting-off (especially after the death of either party) was so glaring, that parliament interposed by 2 Geo. II. ch. 22. and 8 Geo. II. ch. 24. But the provision does not go to goods, or other specific things wrongfully detained: and therefore neither courts of law nor equity can make the plaintiff, who sues for such goods, pay first what is due to the defendant, except so far as the goods can be construed a pledge; and then, the right of the plaintiff is only to redeem. Lord Mansfield, Burr. 2221. *Opinions upon the statutes considered relatively and separately.*—1. The cause in 8 Geo. II. ch. 24. is extremely beneficial to the subjects. Lord Mansfield, Burr. 823. 2. The 2 Geo. II. ch. 22. enacts generally, "that where there are mutual debts between the parties, one "debt may be set against the other," upon which act of 2 Geo. II. doubts have arisen about the different natures of debts; by the 8 Geo. II. ch. 24. there is a general provision without exception. Lord Mansfield, Burr. 826. 3. The former act is general, that mutual debts may be set one against the other, upon which there was a doubt, and a difference of opinion, between this court (K. B.) and the court of Common Pleas, concerning setting off debts of different natures: the 8 Geo. II. ch. 24. allows notwithstanding the debts are deemed in law to be of a different nature. Burr. 1025. 4. The day after the last act passed, the Lord Hardwicke, Ch. J. delivered the opinion of the court of King's Bench, that a debt by simple contract might, by the former act, have been set off against a specialty debt. Bull. Ni. Pri. 179.

(*w*) This is obvious from observing that the following divisions of the foregoing section in the text, correspond respectively with the four parts into which the subject is divided. 1. When there are mutual debts between the plaintiff and the defendant at the time of the commencement of the action, &c. 2. One debt *may* be set against the other. 3. By being given in evidence, &c. 4. And, if the plaintiff recover in any suit or action, &c. judgment must, &c.

I. There must be mutual debts, *that is,*

1. The demand of the plaintiff and the demand of the defendant must be a *debt, and*

2. The debt of each party must be due in his *own right,* except in the case of Executor or of Administrator, where the debts must be due between the testator or intestate, and the other party in their own rights respectively.

I. The demand of the plaintiff and of the defendant must be a debt.

1. *As to the demand of the plaintiff.*

A set-off cannot be pleaded to any action upon a tort; not to trespass; to case; to replevin, or to detinue.(x)

(x) Absolom v. Knight, Bull. Nisi Pri. 181. In replevin the avowant justified under a distress for rent: the plaintiff at nisi prius insisted, that there was more due to him than the rent amounted to, and Denison, J. refused the evidence, and, upon motion for a new trial, the court held that 2 Geo. II. did not extend to the case of a distress; for that is not an action, but a remedy without suit: they likewise declared that it did not extend to detinue, and the like actions of wrong. Vide Barnes 450. Laycock v. Tuffnell, E. T. 27 Geo. III. MS. Replevin for taking plaintiff's goods.— Avowry for rent. Plea of set-off. General demurrer. The avowry stated the rent payable half yearly, and avowed for half a year's rent. The case of Graham v. Fraine, B. R. H. T. 24 Geo. III. was cited, where it was held a set-off could not be pleaded in an action of replevin, it being an action for a tort: and so held by Buller. J. that a set-off in this case could not be pleaded to an avowry for rent. Sapsford v. Fletcher, 4 T. R. 511. H. T. 32 Geo. III. (Appendix 14.)

Replevin for taking goods in the plaintiff's dwelling house. Avowry for rent. Plea that the defendant was tenant to the Duke of Portland, and that one Brookes was the occupier of the premises; that, upon Fletcher's refusing to pay the rent, the Duke distrained upon Brookes for the value: and so the plaintiff said that nothing of the said rent was in arrear to the said Fletcher. General demurrer. Chambre, in support of the demurrer, urged that the plea in bar was no answer to the avowry: for, though it was not pleaded in form as a set-off, it was so in effect: and it has been held that the statutes of set-off do not extend to a replevin. (Absolom v. Knight, Bull. Nisi Pri. 181.) Lord Kenyon, C. J. The general principle that has been relied on in the argument, that a set-off cannot be pleaded to an avowry for rent, is not questioned: it is much to be lamented that it should have been so decided: however, for the sake of certainty in the law, we must submit to these decisions till the legislature alter the law. Buller, J. and Grose, J. of the same opinion, that a set-off cannot be pleaded to an avowry for rent: but verdict for plaintiff, the plea being good on other grounds.

A set-off cannot be pleaded to debt on bond conditioned for the performance of covenants, where damages are to be assessed by a jury: nor to an action for general damages in covenant or assumpsit: but a set-off may be pleaded to an action of debt, covenant or assumpsit, for a sum certain.(*y*)

In an action of damages for the breach of a special agreement, the defendant cannot avail himself of a set-off unless the plaintiff is obliged to have recourse to the common counts.(*z*)

(*y*) Hutchinson v. Sturges, Willes Rep. 261. H. T. 14 Geo. II. Bull. Nisi Pri. 179. (Appendix.) Defendant to the plaintiff, one of the bearers of the virges of the King's household, and an officer and minister of the King's court of his palace at Westminster: the condition of the bond was for the appearance of S. Daniel before the judges of the King's court of his palace at Westminster at, &c. to answer T. S. in a plea of trespass on the case—Plea of set-off. Judgment for the plaintiff, that a set-off could not be pleaded to this action. Vide note (*z*) and (2*f*) page 21.

(*z*) Colson & al. Assignees of Hunter, a bankrupt, v. Wesh, 1 Esp. Cases, Nisi Pri. 378. A. D. 1793. This was an action on the case. The declaration stated, that Hunter, the bankrupt, on the 14th of May, 1793, then being the owner of 40 barrels of pork, which were in the possession of one Atkinson, a wharfinger; and Hunter being indebted to the defendant in the sum of 80*l*. and to Atkinson in the sum of 50*l*. it was agreed by and between Hunter and the defendant, that Hunter should give to the defendant an order upon Atkinson, to deliver the 40 barrels of pork to the defendant at and after the price of 65*s*. per barrel; and that the defendant should pay himself 40*l*. of his debt, the 50*l*. to Atkinson, and pay over the remainder to Hunter, to wit, the sum of 40*l*.; and that in consequence of this agreement, the pork was delivered to the defendant; he paid the 50*l*. to Atkinson; but, contrary to his agreement, after receiving 40*l*. himself on his own account, refused to pay over the remainder to Hunter, or the assignees, since his bankruptcy. This action was brought by the assignees for the purpose of recovering that residue. The defendant pleaded the general issue, and gave notice of set-off, of a large debt due from Hunter to him. The plaintiff proved the agreement, as laid in the declaration, and an express promise by the defendant to pay over the remainder, only deducting the discount; and that there should no attachment issue on it, or deduction be made. Erskine for the plaintiff insisted, 1. That this was a description of action, in which a set-off could not be allowed; but 2. That if it was an action in which a set-off could be allowed, the defendant had precluded himself from taking the benefit of it, by his own agreements, he having thereby waved every benefit of that sort by promising to pay over the residue of the price of the pork, after deducting the sums of 40*l*. and 50*l*. without any further deduction whatsoever. Lord Kenyon, said, he was of opinion that evidence of set-off was inadmissible; that the declaration was very ingeniously drawn, and was on the face of it not an action for a debt, but for damages for breach of an

A set-off may be pleaded to an action for the arrears of an annuity.(2a)

2. *As to the demand of the defendant.*

If a debtor is discharged out of execution, though upon terms with which he does not afterwards comply, the debt is extinguished, and cannot be set-off.(2b)

A debt barred by the statute of limitations cannot be set-off.(2c)

It is said to have been ruled at Nisi Prius that, if the de-

---

agreement; that the statute of set-off went only to cases of mutual debts: if therefore the plaintiff had been forced to have had recourse to the common count for money had and received, in such case the set-off would be admissible; but not in the present case, where the plaintiff had proved the special count a ground of action. The plaintiff recovered. In the next term, a new trial was moved for, but the court refused a rule to shew cause. Vide Lechmere v. Hawkins, and Atkinson v. Elliott, postea.

(2a) Collins v. Collins, 2 Burr. 820. A. D. 1759. (Appendix.) Debt on bond: the condition appeared upon oyer to pay the plaintiff an annuity of 10*l.* a year during his life: and likewise to maintain him in meat, drink, washing, and lodging in the dwelling-house at Arundal-end for and during his life. As to the payment of the annuity of 10*l.* per annum there was a plea of set-off, viz. that only 60*l.* is due to the plaintiff on account of the said annuity; and that the plaintiff owes him more than 60*l.*; and after the most mature deliberation, the court were unanimously and clearly of opinion that the plea was valid.

(2b) Jaques v. Withy, 1 Term Rep. 557. A. D. 1787. (Appendix.) Assumpsit. Set-off 340*l.* upon a judgment recovered in Trin. Term in the 22d year, &c. by the defendant against the plaintiff, which is still in force and unsatisfied. The facts were that the plaintiff, being in execution under this judgment, was liberated on consideration of his undertaking, by bond and warrant of attorney, to satisfy the judgment by instalments or by an annuity; and the present defendant was afterwards obliged to deliver up this bond and warrant to be cancelled by reason of a mistake, informality and irregularity in the memorial. The court were clearly of opinion that the plea was bad. Per Buller, J. The case of Vigo v. Abdich goes the whole length of this; for it shows that if a defendant has been once discharged out of execution upon terms which are not afterwards complied with, the plaintiff cannot resort to the judgment again, or charge the defendant's person in execution: so here if the defendant has neglected to avail himself of the advantage of the security, it is his own fault, and he must take the consequences. Judgment for plaintiff.

(2c) If a debt barred by the statute of limitations be pleaded as a set-off, the plaintiff may reply the statute: if it be given in evidence on a notice of set-off, it may be objected to at the trial. Bull. Nisi Pri. 180. The same doctrine is allowed in Cranch. Extrin. v. Kirkman and others, Peake's Cases. 121. A. D. 1791. (Appendix.)

mand of the plaintiff and the demand of the defendant be both upon bills of exchange for their mutual accommodation; and these bills are of the same date and given in the same transaction, and of above six years standing; and, if the operation of the statute against the demand of the plaintiff be prevented by issuing process within six years, the defendant's demand, though no such process has been issued, may be set off.(2*d*)

If a tradesman make goods according to order, but refuse to deliver them till the vendor, who is insolvent, procures some person to join him in giving a security for the payment, it seems that the price of the goods is a debt, and may be set-off.(2*e*)

Unliquidated damages cannot be set-off, but liquidated damages may be set-off.(2*f*)

(2*d*) Ord. v. Ruspini, 2 Esp. Cases, 569. T. T. 37 Geo. III. (App. 16.) The plaintiff's demand arose on a bill of exchange due in the year 1784, which he had kept alive by suing out process within the 6 years—the set-off consisted of bills and notes of the plaintiff, of the same date, which the defendant had taken up or paid on the plaintiff's account: but they had not been kept alive by issuing any process: Upon an objection to their inadmissibility, Lord Kenyon said, that, as the transactions between the plaintiff and the defendant were all of the same date, and as the bills seemed to have been given in the course of these transactions, and for their accommodation, it would be the highest injustice to allow one to have an operation by law and not the other, and that he would therefore hold the latter to be good as well as the former, and suffer them to be set-off; and upon proof of their payment, they were set-off, and the defendant had a verdict.

(2*e*) Dunmore v. Taylors. Peake's Cases, Nisi Pri. 41 H. T 31. Geo. III. Assumpsit for goods sold and delivered—Set-off for goods sold and delivered, and also for goods bargained and sold. On the cross-examination of the plaintiff's witness, it appeared that the defendant had made a waggon for the plaintiff, but had refused to deliver it unless the plaintiff would get some person to join him in giving a security for the balance which the delivery of the waggon would make in his favour: the plaintiff was then insolvent.—It was objected that this contract, being only executory, could not be made the subject of a set-off—Buller, J. thought it could be set-off as goods bargained and sold. When the cause had proceeded further, it appeared that it was afterwards agreed that the plaintiff should not have the waggon, but that the defendant should keep it. Upon which the plaintiff had a verdict. Note, after the cause was over, Mr. J. Buller said, that he thought an indebitatus assumpsit would lie in this case, but that there was some nicety in the question.

(2*f*) Nedriff v. Hogan. E. 32 Geo. II. Bull. Nisi Pri. 180. To assumpsit for 40*l*. lent, &c. the defendant pleaded articles of agreement with mutual covenants in a penalty of 200*l*. for performance, and showed a breach where-

II. To constitute mutuality of debts it is also necessary *that the debt of each party be due in his own right: except in the case of Executor or Administrator, where the debt must be due between the testator and intestate and the other party in their own rights respectively.*

---

by the penalty became due, and offered to set-off: on demurrer, the court held this plea not within the statutes of set off, for there may not be 5*l.* justly due to the defendant on the balance.——Freeman v. Hyett, 1 Black. Rep. 394. M. 3 Geo. III. This action was for money due for a parcel of cloth. Dunning moved to stay the trial of the cause in order to send a commission into Portugal to establish a fact by way of set-off; viz. that in a former parcel of cloths sent to Portugal, and bought of the same plaintiff, it appeared on opening the bale, that they were burnt in the pressing, which had greatly lowered their value.—Norton, Solicitor General, objected that the set-off was not maintainable—You might as well set-off the damages which you are entitled to recover for a battery: you shall bring your special action on the case. And of that opinion was the court, and denied the motion. Howlet and others v. Strickland, Cowp. 56. E. 14 Geo. III. (App. 17.) This was an action of covenant. The defendant pleaded that he had sustained greater damages by reason of the breaches committed on the part of the plaintiff than the value of the damages sustained by the plaintiff on account of the breaches alleged in the declaration: all the breaches assigned in the plea were for non-delivery of allum in due time. The plaintiff demurred, and for special cause assigned that it was not competent to the defendant to plead the damages by way of set-off.—Lord Mansfield. I take this plea to be merely for the purpose of delay. The act of parliament and the reason of the thing relate to mutual debts only. These damages are no debts, and indebitatus assumpsit could not be brought for them. Mr. J. Ashhurst. Debts to be set-off must be such as an indebitatus assumpsit will lie for. Mr. J. Aston. Clearly an unliquidated demand or uncertain damages cannot be set-off. Judgment for plaintiff. Weighall v. Waters, 6 Term. Rep. 488. A. D. 1795. (App. 18.) To an action of covenant for half a year's rent, 27*l.* 10*s.* due at Christmas 1794, for a house demised by the plaintiff to the defendant for 21 years from Christmas 1788, the latter pleaded, that by the said indenture (on which the action was brought) he, the defendant, covenanted to repair and to surrender to the plaintiff at the end of the term the same premises well and sufficiently repaired, "casualties by fire and tempest excepted;" that before the 24th of June, 1794, a violent tempest arose, and threw down with great force and violence a stack of chimneys belonging to the house on the roof of the house, &c. and damaged the house so much that it would soon have become uninhabitable if he (the defendant) had not immediately repaired it; that he was obliged to lay out in the repairs 30*l.* which the plaintiff became liable to repay to him; that that sum is still due to the defendant, and exceeds the damage sustained by reason of the breach of covenant assigned; and that he is ready to set off that 30*l.* &c. according to the statute: to this plea there was a general demurrer assigning these causes; that it is not alleged in the plea that the plaintiff had any notice of the tempest or of the damage thereby

Cases on this head relate to

Joint debtors and several debtors:—principal and agent:—trustees:—husband and wife:—executors and administrators, &c.

AS TO JOINT AND SEVERAL DEBTS.

A joint debt and a separate debt cannot be set-off against each other. (2g)

Separate debts between partners may be set-off against each other. (2h)

---

done to the house, nor that he was requested to repair the same before the defendant made the repairs stated in the plea, &c. The court said that the plea could not possibly be supported, and that it did not admit of any argument. Lord Kenyon, Ch. J. The objection to the plea is, that it does not set-off any certain debt, but uncertain damages. I do not indeed see by what covenant the landlord is bound to repair damages occasioned by fire or tempest; the exception was introduced into the lessee's covenant for his benefit, and to exempt him from particular repairs. But if the defendant can maintain any action against the plaintiff, (his landlord) the sum to be recovered is uncertain; it must be assessed by a jury: and there is no pretence to say that those uncertain damages may be set-off to the present action. If the defendant has fairly laid out money in repairing what he was not bound to repair, perhaps a court of equity will give him relief. Vide note (2c)

Fletcher v. Dyche, 2 Term Rep. 32. A. D. 1787. (App. 21.) Assumpsit—Plea of set-off—that the plaintiff was bound to the defendant in the sum of 236*l.* on a condition which stated that the defendant had contracted with a Committee for repairing the Parish Church of St. Mary le Bow, to repair the same: and that the plaintiff had contracted with the defendant to perform the smith's and ironmonger's work within a certain time, or to forfeit 10*l.* a-week for every week after the expiration of the time till the completion of the work; that such smith's and ironmonger's work was not completed within the limited time, but continued unfinished for 4 weeks after its expiration: by which 40*l.* became due to the plaintiff, which he offered to set-off—The court were clearly of opinion that the 40*l.* was in the nature of liquidated damages, and that it might be set-off.

(2g) This is evident, and may be collected from all the decisions on set-off in the case of joint debts and several debts. Vide the four following notes.

(2h) Smith v. De Silva. A. D. 1776. Cowp. 469. D. Lord Mansfield.—The consequence on a bankruptcy between partners is, that they are entitled, as against each other, to the balance of accounts: and so it was settled in the case of Skipp v. Harwood (1 Vez. 239.) before Lord Hardwicke in Chancery.

Smith v. Barrow, 2 Term. R. 476. A. D. 1788. The plaintiff and Robert Smith his father had been in partnership together, during which time one Keate became indebted to them in 531*l.* Robert Smith died, leaving the plaintiff his sole executor. After the death of his father the plaintiff took

A debt on a partnership account becomes, upon the death of all but one of the partners, a debt to the survivor in his own

---

the defendant into partnership, and Keate became indebted to those two in the further sum of 30*l.*; he afterwards became involved, and his effects were transferred to certain trustees for the benefit of his creditors. Two payments were made in the course of distribution at different times. The first which was made to these parties (the plaintiff and the defendant) was divided between them according to their several proportions; that is, the proportion of the former debt of 531*l.* to the plaintiff's separate use, and the proportion of the 30*l.* in moieties between them. After this the trustees transmitted a bill of exchange to the plaintiff and defendant in their joint names, and the defendant alone received the money under the title of Smith and Barrow. The plaintiff's proportion of this second dividend, so far as related to his original debt, was 79*l.* 14*s.* 6*d.* for which this action for money had and received was brought. A rule was obtained to show cause why the verdict which had been given for the plaintiff should not be set aside, and a non-suit entered, on two grounds; first, that the action ought to have been brought by the plaintiff as executor, or surviving partner: 2dly, that the remittance being made to Smith and Barrow, it appears to have been received on a partnership transaction, and one partner cannot maintain this action against another, because a receipt by one is a receipt by both. Buller, J. I am of opinion not only that the action is properly brought, but that it could not have been brought in any other form. In what character was the money received by the defendant? The former dividend was received and divided according to the proportions of the respective debts of the plaintiff and defendant as partners: then on the receipt of the second dividend by the defendant, it should have been divided into two parts bearing the same proportion to each other, as the separate demand of the plaintiff on Keate's estate, and the joint demand of the plaintiff and defendant. The plaintiff would have been solely entitled to the first, and must have shared the other part with the defendant as due to the partnership account. So that the first part of the sum was money specifically received by the defendant to the plaintiff's use. And if the action had been brought by the plaintiff as surviving partner, it would have been necessary for him to have shown that he and the deceased partner had a cause of action against this defendant; but they never had any such cause of action; and it is immaterial to look back to see how third persons were concerned, if as between the plaintiff and defendant the latter has received a sum of money for the use of the former. Then it has been said, that there could not be a set-off in this case; but I am of a different opinion: for this is an action for money had and received, in which the plaintiffs can only recover what is in justice due to them. Therefore supposing any debts were due from the plaintiffs to the defendant, it was for the advantage of the latter to bring the action in this form:—With regard to the sum of 30*l.* due to this partnership, I agree that this action cannot be maintained. One partner cannot recover a sum of money received by the other unless on a balance struck that sum is found due to him alone. But this objection does not apply to the larger sum in this case, which is the one in dispute. Rule discharged.

right, and may be set-off against his separate debt. (2i)

A debt on a joint and several bond may be set-off to an action brought by only one of the obligors. (2k)

A debt on a bond purporting to be a joint and several bond, but executed only by one of the obligors, may be set-off to an action commenced by the obligor who has executed it. (2k)

French, Assignee, v. Fenn, T. T. 1783. Cooke, Bank. Laws (App. 19.) Action for money had and received. General issue and set-off. Verdict for plaintiffs on a case. "On the 24th of January, 1778, Cox, Holford and Fenn agreed to purchase a row of pearls for an adventure in trade, and that Fenn should advance the money: the profits and loss to be equally divided in thirds: and Cox and Holford were to pay Fenn interest, till the pearls were sold, for the money advanced by him on their account. In November 1778, Cox became a bankrupt: after which the defendant sent the row of pearls to China, where it was sold for 6000*l.* and, the net produce thereon being 5000*l.* was remitted to the defendant." The question for the consideration of the court was, "Whether the defendant was entitled to set-off the sums owing to him from the bankrupt in bar of the action brought by the assignees for a third of the profits of the sale."—And the court was clearly of opinion that the set-off was allowable.

(2i) Slipper, assignee of Lane, v. Stidstone. 1 Esp. Cases, N. P. 47. A. D. 1793. 5 Term Rep. 493. (App. 20.) This was an action of assumpsit for goods sold and delivered. Plea of the general issue, with notice of set-off. The set-off was, a debt due by the bankrupt to the defendant and one Abbot, who had been in partnership with him; but Abbot the partner was dead before the bringing of the present action. Lord Kenyon allowed the set-off. In the following term, Law obtained a rule to shew cause why there should not be a new trial, on the supposed misdirection of the judge; but he afterwards abandoned the rule, it being understood that the Court of K. B. concurred in opinion with the Chief Justice; and he, on being asked, admitted the point not to be maintainable.

French v. Andrade, 6 T. R. 582. A. D. 1796. (App. 21.) This was an action upon promises: to which the defendant pleaded that the plaintiff and one John Newton, who died before the commencement of the action, were indebted to the defendant in divers sums of money, &c. for work and labour, money paid, &c. that those sums remained unpaid at the death of John Newton, and at the time of commencing this action were and still are due from the plaintiff to the defendant, and that they exceed the sum due from the defendant to the plaintiff, against which sum the defendant is willing to set-off. To this plea there was a general demurrer. Per curiam. It is perfectly clear that the debt due from the plaintiff as surviving partner may be set-off against the demand he has in his own right on the defendant. Judgment for defendant.

(2k) Fletcher v. Dyke. 2 T. R. 32. A. D. 1787. (App. 21.) Assumpsit. Set-off of a joint and several bond which was, in fact, executed only by the plaintiff. General demurrer. Per Ashhurst, J. The parties have entered into a joint and several bond; it becomes the separate debt of both,

If a firm be carried on in the name of only one person, a separate debt from that person may be set-off either to an action commenced in his own right, or to an action commenced by the partners. (2*l*)

If a person give a note to his bankers on account of a debt due to them, and the bankers indorse the note to another firm consisting of some of the partners to the banking house: the maker of the note may set-off any debt due to him from his bankers to an action commenced against him on the note, by the firm who hold it. (2*m*)

---

and therefore may be set-off against either:—It is sufficient to say that there is a separate as well as a joint debt. Buller, J. The plaintiff's counsel then objected to this set-off, because there was no mutuality: but that depends on the question whether the debt is due from the plaintiff and another person, or from, the plaintiff alone. If the former, the debt cannot be set-off: but it appears that the bond was executed by the plaintiff alone. No debt can arise upon the bond from the other party who did not execute. The plaintiff therefore alone can be sued upon the bond; so that there is mutuality. Grose, J. of the same opinion.

(2*l*.) Stacey, Ross, and others v. Decy. 2 Esp. Cas. 269. M. T. 1789. 7 T. R. 359. (App. 30.) Assumpsit for goods sold. Set-off. The plaintiffs were partners: Ross's was the only name that appeared. In an action by the partners, the defendant offered to set-off a debt due to him from Ross. Lord Kenyon was of opinion that the set-off was good, that the plaintiffs had subjected themselves to it by holding out false colours to the world, by permitting Ross to appear as the sole owner: that it was possible the defendant would not have trusted Ross only, if he had not considered the debt due to himself as a security against the counter demand. The other part of the proposition, viz. that to a debt in his own right there may be a set off, is indisputable.

(2*m*) Puller v. Roe and others, M. T. 34 Geo. III. Peake 197. (App. 24.)

Caldwell, Smith, Forbes, and Gregory, were partners in Liverpool.

Caldwell, Smith, Roe, and Co. were partners.

Forbes and Gregory were partners in London.

Caldwell, Smith, Roe and Co. kept a banking account with Caldwell, Smith, Forbes and Gregory at Liverpool: and being indebted to the firm in Liverpool, Caldwell, Smith, Roe and Co. gave a note for the debt; which note the Liverpool firm indorsed to Forbes and Gregory in London for a sum due to that house.

In this action by the assignees of Forbes and Gregory against Caldwell, Smith, Roe, and Co. upon this note, the defendant insisted upon a right to set-off various sums due from Caldwell, Smith, Forbes, and Gregory in Liverpool.

Lord Kenyon. This note was given to Caldwell and Co. as a banking-house, and constitutes an article in the accounts between the defendants and them. They cannot, as between themselves, raise a distinct account, though they might indorse to a third person. The affairs of the company are

As to Trustees.

A debt from the cestuy que trust may be set off to an action commenced by the trustee in right of the trust. (2*n*)

The director or trustees of any company cannot set-off a debt to them as individuals against a demand upon them in their corporate capacity for stock. (2*o*)

---

in presumption of law, known to all the partners, and all are equally liable. The defendants send this bill to Caldwell and Co. to cancel part of the debt due to them. Can they, by any act between themselves, divert this money to another purpose, and leave the whole of the defendant's debt outstanding? The plaintiffs had a verdict for the balance. A motion was made for a new trial, but the court refused to grant a rule to shew cause.

(2*n*) Winch v. Keeley, 1 Term Rep. 621. A. D. 1787. Lawrence, in arguing, said: In the case of Bottomley v. Brook, (M. 22 Geo. III. C. B.) which was debt on bond, the defendant pleaded that the bond was given for securing 100*l.* lent to the defendant by one E. Chancellor, and was given by her direction to the plaintiff, in trust for her; and that E. Chancellor, before the action brought, was indebted to the defendant in more money than the amount of the bond: to this there was a demurrer, which was withdrawn by the advice of the court. The authority of this case was afterwards recognized in that of Rudge v. Birch (M. 25 Geo. III. B. R.) in this court, where, to debt on bond, the defendant pleaded that the bond was given to the plaintiff in trust for A, for a debt due from the defendant to A; and that A, at the time of exhibiting the plaintiff's bill, was indebted to the defendant in more money. The plaintiff demurred, and the court, on the authority of the case of Bottomley v. Brook, held this to be a good plea. It has likewise been since recognized in Webster v. Scales (M. T. 25 Geo. III. B. R.) Ashhurst, J. The cases which have been cited by the plaintiff's counsel go a great way in determining this question. It is true that formerly the courts of law did not take notice of any equity or trust: but of late years, as it has been found productive of great expense to send the parties to the other side of the hall, wherever this court have seen that the justice of the case has been clearly with the plaintiff, they have not turned him round upon this objection. Then, if this court will take notice of a trust, why should they not of an equity? It is certainly true that a chose in action cannot strictly be assigned: but this court will take notice of a trust, and consider who is beneficially interested, as in Bottomley v. Brook, where the court suffered the defendant to set-off a debt due from Mrs. Chancellor in the same manner as if the action had been brought by her.

(2*o*) Gibson v. Hudson's Bay Company, 1 Str. 639. M. T. 12 Geo. III. The plaintiff, as assignee of the effects of Evans a bankrupt, brings his bill against the Company to oblige them to suffer him to transfer stock. The Company insist, that Evans was their banker, and greatly indebted to them; and that, upon the clause in the bankrupt act, which directs the commissioners to state the account between mutual dealers, they shall be allowed to hold the stock, and account only for the balance, if any shall appear against them, and decreed accordingly. But, in Meliorucchi v. Exchange Assu-

If there is an express bye-law to subject the stock of each member to a satisfaction of the debt which he owes to the company, such bye-law is reasonable, and the debts may be set-off. (2p)

A debt from the sheriff cannot be set-off to an action commenced by him on a bail bond: but, if the bond be assigned and an action commenced upon it by the assignee, a debt from the assignee may be set-off. (2q)

---

rance, 1 Eq. Abr. 9. (App. 28) it was held that the case then before the court differed from that of the Hudson's Bay Company, because in that case there was an express bye-law to subject the stock of each member to satisfy the debts he should owe to the Company; which case (App. 28.) was as follows. The plaintiffs were assignees, and brought their bill to compel the defendants to assign some stock to which the bankrupt was entitled.—The defendants insisted that the bankrupt was one of the directors of their Company, and that, after his purchase of the stock, the Company lent him a sum exceeding the value of the stock, which they insisted they had a right to set-off. But the court would not allow the set-off; the claim of stock being against the trustees in their corporate capacity; and the loan to the bankrupt by the trustees being a loan by them as private persons.

(2p) I insert this in consequence of the explanation of Gibson v. Hudson's Bay Company, in Meliorucchi v. Royal Exchange, in the last note; though I am aware that there is scarcely any necessity for making it a separate article.—Because it seems that, 1st, a debt to the *whole company* may be set-off against a demand for stock; and, 2dly, a debt to the trustees, or to any individuals, on condition that the stock shall be liable to the payment of that debt, (which condition will be manifested by the bye-law,) may clearly be opposed to each other, the accounts being connected by the nature of the contract. Vide Introductory Chapter, page 1.

(2q) Hutchinson v. Sturges, Willes' Rep. 261. T. 14 Geo. II. C. B. in note (App. 40.) Lofting v. Stevens, M. 1733. Bull. N. P. 179. In debt upon bond the defendant pleaded a greater debt in bar, upon which the plaintiff prayed to have the condition of the bond inrolled which was to appear at Westminster, and demurred: and it was holden that this bond was not within the 8 Geo. II. for that statute relates only to bonds conditioned to pay money, and not to bail bonds; and it was not within the statute 2 Geo. II. because the plaintiff did not bring the action in his own right, but as trustee for another; (for he was an officer in the palace court) but if it had been given to the sheriff, and by him assigned to the other party, it might be otherwise, and then the penalty would have been considered as the debt, because it would have depended upon the 2 Geo. II. The distinctions between the two statutes, as stated in the foregoing reports, may possibly confuse and mislead: neither of the statutes relate to any bonds, except bonds conditioned for the payment of money, and both statutes require that the action should be brought in the right of the plaintiff, and not in the right of another.

As to principal agent.

A debt arising upon the contract of an agent who deals as principal, may be set-off against any demand between the agent and the debtor. (2*r*)

The debts between the agent and debtor may respectively be set-off against each other : and the debtor may set off a debt to him from the agent to a demand by the principal. (2*r*)

[2*r*] The cases on this subject of contracts by factors are divisible into three classes. 1st. *Where the agent actually receives payment.* 2dly. *Where the debtor of the agent insists upon a right to set-off a debt due to him from the agent, which is either to an action by the principal or to an action by the agent.* 3dly. *Where the agent insists upon a right to set-off.*

1st. *Where the factor actually receives payment.*

Scrimshire v. Alderton, 2 Str. 1183. H. T. 16 Geo. II. The plaintiff, who was a farmer, sent oats to his factor in London. The custom of the trade appeared to be, that, formerly, factors had 4*d.* per quarter for selling them, and gave immediate notice to the farmer of the name of the buyer and the price : but, this being inconvenient to farmers at a distance, it had for many years past been customary for the farmer to allow 2*d.* per quarter more, upon the factors' taking the risk of the debts : since which they had ceased to inform the farmers of the buyers. The goods in the present case were sold : but, the factor failing, the plaintiff before actual payment gave notice to the defendant (the buyer) not to pay the factor, which he did notwithstanding : and thereupon this action was brought. The C. J. Lee was of opinion that this new method had not deprived the farmer of his remedy against the buyer, provided there was no payment to the factor.—And the only reason of advancing 2*d.* per quarter was, to have both at stake : and here being notice before actual payment, there could be no harm done. And therefore he directed the jury in favour of the plaintiff. They went out and found for the defendant. They were sent a second and third time to reconsider it, and still adhered to their verdict : and being asked, man by man, they separately declared they found for defendant. Upon this a new trial was moved for : and, no cause being shewn, was accordingly granted ; and at the sittings after term it came on again before a special jury : when the C. Justice declared that a factor's sale does, by the general rule of law, create a contract between the owner and buyer. But, notwithstanding this, the jury found for the defendant : and, being asked their reason, declared that they thought from the circumstances no credit was given as between the owner and buyer, and that the latter was answerable to the factor only, and he only to the owner. Vide Escot v. Milward, (in this note,) where this case is considered as law.

Drinkwater and others, assignees of Dowding, v. Goodwin, Cowp. 251. A. D. 1775. Assumpsit. General issue. Verdict for plaintiffs on a special case.

J. Dowding, the bankrupt, was a clothier, and employed Jeffries a factor, who sold to the defendant the goods in question marked I. DOWDING : the clothes were sold by Jeffries, as factor, and the defendant knew him to

If an agent have a commission del credere, it is presumptive proof that he dealt as principal. (2s)

---

be so, in the usual course of his business, and in his own name. The money was paid by the defendant to Jeffries, after notice to him from the assignees not to pay it. Jeffries was a creditor of Dowding's to a greater amount than the value of the goods.

After hearing the argument, Lord Mansfield—" Jeffries sold these goods to the defendant Goodwin in his own name, and without any reference to the principal, or without even making the principal creditor for them. But the goods are marked I. DOWDING; therefore the defendant must have known he was the principal, and that was the reason of making that fact a part of the case." A few days after, his Lordship, in delivering the opinion of the court, said,

" We think that a factor who receives clothes, and is authorised to sell them in his own name, but makes the buyer debtor to himself, though he is not answerable for the debts, yet he has a right to receive the money: his receipt is a discharge to the buyer; and he has a right to bring an action against him to compel the payment, and it would be no defence for the buyer in that action to say, that, as between him and the principal, he the buyer ought to have that money, because the principal is indebted to him in more money than that sum: for the principal himself can never say that, but where the factor has nothing due to him: there is no case in law or equity where a factor, having money due to him to the amount of the debt in dispute, was ever prevented from taking money for clothes in his hands.

Ex parte Murray, 1783. Cooke B. Laws, 400. One Murray of Belfast in Ireland, in 1782, consigned a quantity of linens to B. and H. of London, to be disposed of by them as his factors, upon a del credere commission, B. and H. sold the linens for 192*l.* 14*s.* and, before they received the money, became bankrupts. The assignees afterwards received the money, which Murray demanded of the assignees, who refused to pay it, insisting that Murray might come in as a creditor under the commission. Murray petitioned that the assignees might be ordered to pay him the money his linen sold for, after deducting the commissions and charges, and a small sum due from Murray to the bankrupts on another account.

His Lordship, after hearing the point of law argued, was clearly of opinion that, the purchaser not having paid for the linens previous to the bankruptcy, Murray the consignee was entitled to receive the price of the linen, and accordingly ordered the assignees to pay him the money.

Scott v. Surman, Willes 400. A. D. 1743. (Appendix.) The assignees, after the bankruptcy of the factor, received some bounty money due to the principal for having imported some goods. In an action by the principal against the assignees, the court, on a case reserved, were unanimously of opinion that the plaintiff was entitled to recover.

2dly. *Where the debtor of the agent insists upon a right to set-off a debt due to him from the agent.*

Scott v. Surman, Assignees of Scott, A. D. 1742. (Appendix) Willes 100. Assumpsit. Verdict for plaintiff for 358*l.* 10*s.* subject to the opinion of the court on a case in substance as follows. The plaintiff abroad consigned some

It has been decided that if a factor is authorised to sell goods

---

tar to Scott his factor in England; who received and sold it to be paid for in notes at four months date, after deducting 31*l.* due from the factor to the vendees The factor became a bankrupt. The sum of 358*l.* 10*s.* consisted of the proceeds of the tar actually received by the asignees from the vendees, and of the 31*l.* The court were unanimously of opinion that judgment should be entered for the plaintiff for 329*l.* 10*s.* the balance remaining after deducting 31*l.* from 358*l.* 10*s.*

Rabone v. Williams, cited 7 T. R. 360. (App. 29.) Action for goods sold to the defendant by means of the house of Rabone and Co. at Exeter, factors to the plaintiff. The defendant, the vendee of the goods, set off a debt due to him from Rabone and Co. the factors, upon another account, alleging that the plaintiff had not appeared at all in the transaction, and that credit had been given by Rabone and Co. the factors, and not by the plaintiff. Lord Mansfield, Ch. J. Where a factor, dealing for a principal, but concealing that principal, delivers goods in his own name, the person contracting with him has a right to consider him to all intents and purposes as the principal; and though the real principal may appear and bring an action upon that contract against the purchaser of the goods, yet that purchaser may set-off any claim he may have against the factor in answer to the demand of the principal — This has been long settled. In Bailey v. Morley, London sittings after Michaelmas 1788, Lord Kenyon recognised the law of this case. The case of George v. Clagget, 7 T. R. 359. (App. 29.) was decided upon the authority of this case. Escot v. Milward, Cooke, and in George v. Clagget, 7 Ter. Rep. 359. (App. 29.) Sittings after Michaelmas Term 1793. This action was tried at Guildhall before Mr. J. Buller, in which it appeared the plaintiffs were merchants in London, and in June 1783, had a quantity of wheat consigned to them from Ostend, the sale of which they intrusted to one Farrer as their factor. The factors in the corn trade, like those in the linen trade, receive a del credere commission, besides their factorage, and never communicate the names of the purchasers to the owners, except in case of the factor's failure. Farrer, on the 9th June 1783, sold 211 quarters of the plaintiff's wheat to the defendant Milward. On the 16th June, Farrer being about to stop payment, gave up the wheat under his care to the plaintiffs, and sent them the names of the buyers. On the 20th June Farrer stopped payment, and a short time afterwards his creditors executed a deed of composition. On the 21st June, the plaintiff delivered the defendant, Milward, a bill of parcels of the wheat sold to him by Farrer as their factor, and desired him to accept a bill, at a month, for the amount; which he refused, insisting that he had a right to set-off a debt due to him from Farrer, against the price of the wheat. Mr. J. Buller, in his charge to the jury, declared the doctrine laid down by Lord Ch. J. Lee, in Scrimshire v. Alderton, 2 Str. Rep. 1168. to be law; but as the factor was insolvent for some time before, had avoided all dealings for a month, had desired that there might be no buying in his name, and had not dealt with the defendant for a year before, but was then in his debt, there was a verdict for the plaintiff on the ground of fraud.

In George v. Claggett, 2 Esp. Cases, 557. E. 37 Geo. III. 7 Term Rep.

in his own name, and he make the buyer debtor to himself, he deals as principal: though the goods, when sold, are marked

---

359. A. D. 1797. (App. 29.) Action for goods sold to the defendants by Messrs. Rich and Heapy, who were the plaintiff's factors, with a commission del credere, and who dealt as principals. The plaintiff claimed a right as principal to recover the price from the buyer, the money not having been actually paid over to the factors before the commencement of the action. The defendant claimed a right to set-off a debt due to him from Rich and Heapy. Lord Kenyon ruled that the defendants were entitled to hold the goods; and that the defendants, having dealt with Rich and Heapy as principals, should not be turned round by the plaintiff's setting up himself as principal, and considering them only as factors: that he had in a case before him adopted a similar principle founded on a determination of Lord Mansfield, viz. that where a factor deals for a principal, but which principal does not appear, and the factor delivers the goods in his own name, if the person dealing with the factor on his own account has any demand against the factor, he has a right to consider the factor as the principal: and to set-off any demand he may have against the factor, against the value of the goods so sold, and that such would be a good answer to any action brought by the principal for the price of the goods. His Lordship therefore ruled that the defendant was entitled to a verdict, which was so found by the jury. There was a motion for a new trial. The court were clearly of opinion that the directions given at the trial were right; and that this case was not distinguishable from that of Rabone and Williams.

3dly. *Where the agent insists upon a right to set-off.*

Grove v. Dubois, 1 T. R. 112. A. D. 1786. (App. 25.) Assumpsit by assignees of Bankrupt. Set-off. Verdict on a special case, "that the bankrupt, being an underwriter, subscribed policies filled up with the defendant's name for his foreign correspondents who were unknown to the bankrupt; that losses happened on the policies before the bankruptcy; that the defendant paid the amount of the losses to his foreign correspondents after such bankruptcy; that the defendant had a commission del credere from his correspondents, was made a debtor by the bankrupt for premiums, and always retained the policies in his hands." The court, saying that the whole turned on the nature of a commission del credere, were of opinion, that the defendant was entitled to set-off the money due on the policies to this action brought against him by the assignees of the bankrupt.

Bize v. Dickason, 1 T. R. 285. A. D. 1786. (App. 27.) The plaintiff, who had a commission del credere, was indebted to the bankrupt in the sum of 1356*l.* 0*s.* 3*d.* The bankrupt, an underwriter, had subscribed policies filled up with the plaintiff's name upon which losses had happened, and upon which there was due 661*l.* 9*s.* 10*d.* The plaintiff, taking for granted that he was not entitled to set-off the 661*l.* 9*s.* 10*d.* paid his whole debt of 1356*l.* 0*s.* 3*d.* to the assignees; but afterwards, discovering his mistake, he brought an action for money had and received: and, upon a case stated for the opinion of the court, recovered the sum of 661*l.* 9*s.* 10*d.*

Wilson, assignee of Fletcher, v. Watson and Creighton, M. 23 Geo. III Esp. Nisi Pri. 274. The defendants were insurance-brokers; and the bank with the name of the principal: and the factor sell as factor in the usual course of his business, and the buyer know him to be factor.(2t)

To a demand of an agent who deals as principal, the buyer cannot set-off a debt to him from the principal.(2v)

As to husband and wife.

A debt due to a man in right of his wife cannot be set-off in an action against him on his own bond.(2x)

A debt of the wife's, dum sola, cannot be set-off against a claim made by the husband alone; unless after marriage, he make the debt his own.(2y)

---

rupt before his bankruptcy, had underwritten for them several policies on the goods, the property of others, which had been losses, and for which the bankrupt was liable: to an action brought against the defendants for money due to the bankrupt, they pleaded a set-off of these losses: but it was held that the losses being on goods the property of others, the debts were properly to them, not to the brokers, and therefore could not be set-off to a demand against the broker himself.

(2s) Vide Escot v. Milward, Cooke 400. 7 T. R. 359. George v. Clagget, 7 T. R. 359. Grove v. Dubois, 1 T. R. 112. Bize v. Dickason, 1 T. R. 285. in the last note.

The case of Escot v. Milward, and common sense, seem to show that the del credere commisson is only presumptive proof.

(2t) Drinkwater v. Goodwin, Cowp. 251. in note (2r).

(2v) D. Lord Mansfield in Drinkwater v. Goodwin, Cowp. 251. in note (2r).

(2x) Ex parte Walker, C. B. E. 4 Geo. III. B. N. P. 179.

(2y) Wood v. Akers, 2 Esp. Cases, N. P. 594. M. T. 38 Geo. III. This was an action of assumpsit for money and goods sold and delivered. Plea non-assumpsit with notice of set-off. The articles contained in the set-off were three several sums of money which were stated to have been paid by the defendant for plaintiff, aud by his direction. One of them was a sum of six guineas, stated to have been paid to a Mrs. Grundy, which the plaintiff's wife, who was a sister of the defendant, owed her for lodging before her intermarriage with the plaintiff. The counsel for the plaintiff objected to the allowance of this sum in the present action, on the ground that this was an action by the husband alone, and the debt attempted to be set-off was a debt due by the wife before the marriage, for which the action should be against husband and wife. It was answered that the husband having ordered the money to be paid, had thereby made the debt his own. Eyre, Ch. J. said, that for a debt of the wife *dum sola*, the action must be against husband and wife, and therefore could not be set-off against a claim made by the husband alone, and for which the action was brought: but if it appeared that the husband, after the marriage, had ordered the debt to be paid, he thereby made it his own, and that it could be set-off. The defendant proved that the

As to executor or administrator.

A debt from an executor in his own right cannot be set-off against a debt to the testator(2z) even though the executor is residuary legatee.(3a)

A debt which accrued in the life-time of the testator cannot be set-off against a debt that accrues to the executor after the death of the testator.(3b)

---

husband had done so, and was allowed the sum in his set-off: but the plaintiff had a verdict for the residue of his demand.

(2z) Bishop v. Church, 3 Atk. 691. A. D. 1748. The plaintiff was the residuary legatee, and surviving executrix of her husband, to whom Church and one Owen had given a joint bond. Church, one of the obligors died, and the plaintiff was indebted upon her own private account to Owen, who was a bankrupt. Lord Chancellor said, it was admitted this could not be set-off at law, nor did he know of any instance here. The debts are due in different rights: the act of 2 Geo. II. does not comprehend this case, nor is it within 5 Geo. II. [postea,] for here was no mutual credit between the parties, and this had been before determined in Ex parte Hope.

(3a) This may be collected from the foregoing case of Bishop v. Church in the last note: but, query whether equity would not interfere where there was a residuum. Vide Lanesho' v. Jones, 1 P. W. 3250, &c. postea—(and vide Set-off in Equity, postea.)

(3b) Shipman v. Thompson, Bull. N. P. 180. A. having been appointed by B. his attorney, to receive his rents, did, after his death, receive rents in arrear in B's life-time: B's executrix brought an action for the money in her own name; the defendant gave notice to set-off a debt due to him from the testator which was not allowed at the trial, because the testator never had any cause of action against the defendant, for the money was not received till after his death. The same case is reported in Ch. J. Willes' Rep. 103. A. D. 1738. C. B. (App. 30.) This came before the court on a case reserved at the trial before Mr. Baron Fortescue. The plaintiff's late husband by his will made the plaintiff and Dr. Morgan (since deceased) his executors: in his life time he had appointed the defendant his steward by letter of attorney, who, after the testator's death, received of several tenants several sums of money due to the testator in his life time. The plaintiff brought this action in her own name, not naming herself executrix, for the money so received. The defendant gave notice to set-off several sums due from the testator to him, which the judge would not permit the defendant to set-off. The questions reserved were, 1st. Whether the plaintiff should not have declared as executrix: 2dly. Whether the defendant ought not to have been permitted to set-off the money due to him from the testator. The court, after argument, gave judgment for the plaintiff. The reasons given by the Court of Common Pleas do not appear in Lord Ch. J. Willes' papers: but the same case was referred to the opinion of Mr. Baron Fortescue, before whom the cause was tried, who, after hearing the cause argued, gave the following judgment in favor of the plaintiff. "As to the set-off: we cannot consider the convenience or the inconvenience on one side, or the other, but must go according to the act:

II. The next requisite to enable a person to give a set-off in evidence is, that "*the debts be due at the commencement of the action.*"(3c)

---

for the statute 2 Geo. II. ch. 22. s. 13. says, or *if either party sues or is sued as executor or administrator*, where there are mutual debts between the testator or intestate, and either party, one debt may be set-off against the other; so that it is confined by the statute expressly to cases where the suit is as executor or administrator. And therefore, in the present case the suit not being as executor, I think it is not within the statute, and that the debts due from the testator to the defendant cannot be set-off against the plaintiff in an action brought by her in her own name and not as executor. And supposing this to be so, it was urged as one reason why the action here ought to have been brought by the plaintiff as executrix: but this statute will not alter the law as to that point from what it was before; and if the statute has not remedied all the inconveniences, we must take it as it is, and cannot, I think, extend it further. So the postea must be delivered to the plaintiff, and she must have her judgment." To the above Mr. B. Fortescue afterwards added this note: " N. B. The Court of C. B. on a case made, were of the same opinion, as to both points." The same point, relative to the set-off, has been since determined in the Court of King's Bench in two cases, Kilvington v. Stevenson, E. T. 1768, on demurrer; and Teggetmeyer v. Lumley, T. T. 25 Geo. III. on a motion for a new trial.—Teggetmeyer v. Lumley, T. 25 Geo. III. MS. Action of covenant by executors for rent due in the life-time of the testator and also since his death. Plea of set-off for money due from the testator. Verdict for defendant. Erskine moved for a new trial on the ground that the defendant could not set-off a debt from the testator to an action for rent since his death, and cited the cases of Ridout and another, assignees, v. Brough, Cowp. 133. and Shipman v. Thompson, Buller's Ni. Pri. 180. He also cited a note-book of Mr. J. Yates of the case of Kilvington v. Stephenson, where it was held on demurrer that a debt from the testator could not be set-off against an action for goods sold by executors, as it would disturb the course of administration.—Cowper shewed cause—They have sued as executors, and as such protect themselves from costs, and have united both demands. The balance between the parties in the general account is the justice of the case. The case last cited is only a demand for a debt subsequent to the death, without any prior demand, and the reason that presses is the disturbance of assetts. The anwswer to that is, it is the executor's fault. Lord Mansfield said he was satisfied on the authority of the cases cited, and made the rule for a new trial absolute. Reported in Willes' Reports 261, in note (App. 40.)

(3c) Reynolds v. Beering B. R. M. 25 Geo. III. Douglas' Rep. 112. n. where it was determined on a demurrer, that a judgment obtained by the defendant against the plaintiff, after the declaration was delivered and before the plea pleaded, may be pleaded as a set-off; and *that*, although it did not appear that the cause of action on which the defendant's judgment was obtained was prior to the commencement of the plaintiff's action. But in Evans v. Prosser, B. R. E. 29 Geo. III. 3 Term Rep. 186. (Appen. 41.) it

A judgment recovered by the defendant after the commencement of the plaintiff's action cannot be set-off in that action.(3c)

A judgment recovered by the defendant before the commencement of the plaintiff's action may be set-off, though a writ of error is pending on the judgment.(3c)

An attorney may set-off his bill, though it was not delivered a month before the commencement of the action: it ought, if possible, to be delivered time enough to be taxed; but it seems that it must be delivered time enough to prevent the plaintiff's being surprised at the trial.(3d)

---

was determined that a plea of set-off that the plaintiff was indebted to the defendant at the time of the plea pleaded is bad; and that it should state that he was indebted at the commencement of the action. On the day after the judgment was given in Evans v. Prosser, Buller, J. said, he had looked into the case of Reynolds v. Beering, and found that it could not be supported. One question which arose there was, whether a judgment could be pleaded by way of set-off pending a writ of error: which the Court were of opinion might be done; and so far the judgment was right. On the other point there ruled, namely, that a judgment recovered after the action was brought, and before plea pleaded, might be pleaded by way of set-off—perhaps the Court did not consider the strict law so much as the justice of the case. But this point cannot be supported: on which judgment was given for plaintiff.

(3d) Martin v. Winder, note in Doug. Rep. 195. Law moved, on the part of the defendant, who was an attorney, for a rule to shew cause why the proceedings should not be staid till his bill should be paid, or till a month from the delivery of it should expire, that he might be enabled to set it off: the Court held that, though an attorney cannot bring an action on his bill till it has been delivered a month, that circumstance is not necessary to enable him to set-off—he must not produce it at the trial by surprise; but it is sufficient, in such case, to deliver it to the plaintiff time enough to have it taxed before the trial. Upon hearing this opinion of the Court, Law withdrew his motion as unnecessary.

Bulman v. Burkitt, 1 Esp. Cases, N.P. 449. H.T. 36 Geo. III. Assumpsit for goods sold and delivered. Plea of the general issue and a set-off.—The action was brought to recover the amount of a tailor's bill. The set-off was, for business done for the plaintiff as an attorney. It became a question whether the party was bound to deliver a bill, under the statute 2 Geo. II. in the same manner as if he had been plaintiff in the action. Lord Kenyon. The rule is, that when an attorney means to avail himself of his bill for business done, and to give it in evidence, he must deliver in a bill signed to the plaintiff; but it is not necessary that a month's time should intervene between the delivery and the action. The cause was referred.

Hooper v. Till & Ux. Doug. 199. A. D. 1779. Motion to make a rule absolute for taxing an attorney's bill after judgment: Lord Mansfield absent.

SECTION II.

Of a person's option to waive or to avail himself of his right to set-off.

It is optional with the defendant whether he will waive or avail himself of his right to set-off.(3*e*)

A set-off reducing the plaintiff's demand under forty shillings does not affect the jurisdiction of the superior court.(3*f*)

Buller, J. read a note of a case, where Lord Mansfield and the Court had refused to permit a bill to be referred to the master to be taxed, because it had been read in evidence at Nisi Prius, on a notice of set-off, in a cause where the attorney was defendant, which shewed that it had been delivered a month, and they held that it was then too late to dispute the amount of the items. This case seems to prove only that, after judgment, where a set-off on an attorney's bill has been given in evidence, it is presumed that the bill was delivered a month previous to the commencement of the action.

(3*e*) The words of the statute are, one debt *may* be set against the other, and such matter *may* be given in evidence, &c.

(3*f*) Pitt v. Carpenter, B. R. 1 Wilson's Rep. 19. A. D. 1743. Action upon the case; defendant pleaded a set-off, and upon the trial the plaintiff proved there was due to him from the defendant 4*l.* 15*s.* 3*d.* and the defendant proved the plaintiff owed him 3*l.* 2*s.* so that the balance due to the plaintiff was only 1*l.* 13*s.* 3*d.* for which he had a verdict.* Per curiam. The demand of the plaintiff remains as it did before the statute for setting-off one debt against another: and if the inferior court should have jurisdiction in this case, it would be very inconvenient; for, suppose there are mutual demands of 10,000*l.* between merchants, and upon the balance there should happen not to be above 40*s.* due, *that* court would have jurisdiction in that case, as well as in the present, if we should allow this; so the rule was discharged, and the plaintiff had judgment. This doctrine is recognised in Fitzpatrick v. Pickering, C. B. 2 Wilson 68. A. D. 1775.

Gross v. Fisher, C. B. 3 Wilson 48. A. D. 1770. Assumpsit for goods sold and delivered. Defendant pleaded a set-off; and upon the trial, the plaintiff proved there was due to him from the defendant 43 shillings, and the defendant proved that the plaintiff owed him 4 shillings; so that the balance due to the plaintiff was thereby reduced to 39 shillings, for which sum he had a verdict. Curia. There is a difference between the case of mutual debts subsisting where the plaintiff's demand is more than 40 shillings, the defendant's demand at the time of the commencement of the action reducing it to a less sum; and the case where the plaintiff's original demand was more than 40 shillings, and the defendant, before the commencement of the action, hath, by *payment* in part, reduced it to less than 40 shillings. In the first case the plaintiff must sue here, or lose part of his demand, because he doth not know whether the defendant can or will set-off any demand against him; but in the latter case, the plaintiff, well knowing that he hath been paid such part of his original demand as reduces it to less than 40 shillings, hath no right to come to this court and demand more than 40 shillings, but must

* On an application to the Court, that this was within the jurisdiction of the Court of Conscience.

The commencement of an action or a verdict is no waiver of the right to set-off the debt.(3g)

---

go to the county court. In the first case, mutual debts are subsisting at the commencement of the action; in the latter case, not; for payment of part by the defendant to the plaintiff himself is not a debt owing by the plaintiff to the defendant, but a discharge of the plaintiff's demand pro tanto. No set-off is used or necessary in such cases; but payment of part is proved under non-assumpsit. We cannot allow the suggestion to be entered; so the rule must be discharged.

(3g) Baskerville v. Brown, et e contra, 2 Burr. Rep. 1229. A. D. 1761. (App. 42.) Brown brought an action against Baskerville upon two promissory notes, amounting (both together) to the sum of 30*l.* The cause was entered and tried before Lord Mansfield at the Sittings; and the plaintiff took a verdict for the *whole* of his demand. Baskerville has also brought an action against Brown for 11*l.* 18*s.* for taylor's work done by him for Brown: and this cause was likewise entered and tried at the very same Sittings; but it happened that the former cause (wherein Brown was plaintiff) was first entered and first tried. In the latter cause (wherein Baskerville was plaintiff) the therein defendant (Brown) had given notice of *a set-off of so much* of the before-mentioned two promissory notes as would suffice to answer Baskerville's demand against him; and he was ready at the trial to have done so, notwithstanding his having taken a verdict for the whole 30*l.* in the cause wherein he was plaintiff. But Baskerville's counsel opposed this, and insisted that Brown had estopped himself from making this set-off, by having taken a verdict for the *whole* of his demand; whereas he ought (as they insisted) to have *left out* so much, in taking his verdict, as was equal to Baskerville's demand upon him. Lord Mansfield, at the trial, inclined against allowing the set-off; but he thought it a matter that deserved consideration. It was accordingly brought before the court, for their consideration, in the form of a motion made on the part of the defendant Brown, for a rule upon Baskerville, the plaintiff, to shew cause why the verdict (which had been found for Baskerville) should not be set aside; and why the defendant, Brown, should not have the costs of a nonsuit. Lord Mansfield now delivered the resolution of the Court. Per curiam, unanimously. Verdict set aside, and the defendant to have the costs of a nonsuit; and Brown to remit so much of his damages recovered in the other action, as exceeds the balance of the mutual debts.

Knibbs v. Hall, one, &c. Peake's Cases, N. P. 210. A. D. 1794. This was an action brought for the use and occupation of certain rooms: the defendant pleaded the general issue, and gave notice of set-off for business as an attorney, &c. The defendant had brought a cross action for his bill of costs, which was made the subject of a set-off: That debt had accrued, and the action on it was commenced *before* the debt for which the present action was brought had become due. Garrow, for the plaintiff, objected that these were not such *mutual* debts, at the time of the commencement of the plaintiff's action, as would entitle the defendant to sue the plaintiff; and also to set-off his debt. To enable him to do so, he contended that the debt for which the present action was brought should have been due at the time the

It is said to have been ruled at Nisi Prius that, in an action of indebitatus assumpsit, the defendant may plead a set-off, though he expressly promised to pay the debt for which the action is brought, without availing himself of his right to set-off.(3*h*)

SECTION III.

Of the pleadings and of the mode of setting-off debts.(3*i*)

When there are mutual debts subsisting between a testator

---

defendant commenced his action against the plaintiff. Lord Kenyon overruled this objection; being clearly of opinion that these were *mutual* debts within the meaning of the statute. This and the other cause were referred to arbitration.

(3*h*) Lechmere, Esq. v. Hawkins, Gent. 2 Esp. Cases, N. P. 626. H. 38 Geo. III. Assumpsit on a promissory note for 30*l*. made by the defendant and payable to the plaintiff. Plea non assumpsit, with a notice of set-off. In the summer of the preceding year, the defendant having been in Scotland upon business, where the plaintiff then resided, and being in want of money, applied to the plaintiff for the loan of the sum he wanted. Prior to this period the defendant had been concerned for the plaintiff as his attorney; and the plaintiff was then considerably in his debt. It was stated for the plaintiff, that the defendant had promised to pay this money so lent, notwithstanding the defendant was then his debtor; and letters were produced in evidence from the defendant to the plaintiff, wherein he promises to pay the money the plaintiff had so lent him, and for which the note had been given, without taking any notice of the debt the plaintiff then owed, or affecting to set one demand against the other. Upon this evidence, Erskine, for the plaintiff, contended that the defendant could have no benefit of his set-off. In that case, where a creditor borrows money of his debtor, under an express promise to pay it, it bound him under every circumstance to the absolute payment; nor could his undertaking be satisfied by setting-off the debt against his own demand. Lord Kenyon said he knew no such law, nor did he think there was any such legal obligation on the creditor: it might be an honorary obligation, and such as a man who gave it ought to observe; but if he thought fit not to consider such an obligation as binding, he could not compel him. There were mutual subsisting demands at the time of the action brought, and such as the statutes of set-off gave the party-defendant power to set against the plaintiff's demand: Besides this, if he was to refuse the set-off here, it would drive the defendant into a court of equity, where the judgment obtained here would be set-off against the debt admitted to be due by the plaintiff to the defendant. He therefore overruled the objection, and admitted the defendant to go into evidence of his set-off. The cause was referred. Vide ante, note (*z*) and Atkinson v. Elliot, 7 Term Rep. 378. (Appendix.)

(3*i*) The following is the substance of the two statutes relating to this point, ante, page 16:

The debts may be set-off by being given in evidence upon the general issue, or by being pleaded in bar: except where either of the debts accrues and another person, the executor will be indemnified in setting-off these debts without bringing an action. (3*k*)

When it is intended to give a set-off in evidence, there are two subjects of consideration:

I. Whether it is optional either to plead or to give notice; and, when optional, which mode of proceeding is preferable. II. Of the nature of the notice and of the pleadings.

I. Of the defendant's option either to plead or to give notice, and of the preferable mode of proceeding.

When either of the debts accrues by reason of a penalty contained in a specialty, the debt intended to be set-off must be pleaded in bar: but, in all other cases, the defendant may plead or give notice of set-off at his election. (3*l*) If the defendant's demand be equal to, or greater than, the plaintiff's, the action being barred, it is proper to plead the set-off: but where the defendant's demand is less than the plaintiff's a notice of set-off should be given, and a set-off is usually pleaded in country causes to save the trouble and expense of proving the service of a notice.(3*l*)

When the defendant's demand is less than the plaintiff's the defendant should move the court wherein the action is commenced for leave to pay so much money into court as will satisfy the plaintiff's demand.(3*l*)

It seems not to be settled whether a defendant may plead a set-off after he has been ruled to abide by his plea: but in all cases, except where either of the debts accrues by reason of a penalty contained in a specialty, the same end may be attained by pleading the general issue and giving notice of set-off. (3*m*)

---

by reason of a penalty contained in a specialty; when the debt intended to be set-off must be pleaded in bar, and the plea must state how much is truly and justly due on either side: but, in all cases where the general issue is pleaded, notice must be given, at the time of pleading, of the particular sum or debt intended to be set-off, and upon what account it became due.

(3*k*) Brown v. Holyoak, Bull. Ni. Pr. 179.

(3*l*) Tyd. K. B. 406.

(3*m*) Cochran v. Robertson, M. T. 20 Geo. III. B. R. Cowper moved to set aside a rule to plead several matters, and the plea of set-off pleaded in consequence thereof, upon this objection, that the defendant, having pleaded a judgment recovered in a former action, the plaintiff obtained a rule for the defendant to abide by his plea, or plead such other as he would abide by: the defendant had pleaded a set-off which Cowper insisted he could not do, but could only plead the general issue after waving his special plea. Buller,

II. Of the nature of the notice and of the pleadings.
As to the notice.

The notice of set-off may be given under any general issue to an action where a set-off may be given in evidence.(3*n*)

The notice of set-off must be so framed as to prevent the plaintiff's being surprised at the trial by the nature of the evidence.(3*o*) &(3*p*)

The notice should be nearly as certain as a declaration.(3*o*)

If there are any special circumstances they must be specially stated in the notice.(3*p*)

J. said the practice was so; but that the defendant might have pleaded the general issue, and given notice of set-off; and that this was a fair plea.—Cowper admitted the fairness of the plea, and said that, if the defendant would take short notice of trial, he had no objection to it.

(3*n*) Gower v. Hunt, 1 B. 104. Bull. Ni. Pri. 181. In covenant upon an indenture for non-payment of rent, the defendant pleaded "non est factum," and gave a notice of set-off. Mr. J. Denton, at the assizes, was of opinion he could not, upon this issue: but, upon a motion for a new trial, the court held the evidence ought to have been received, for the general issue mentioned in the act must be understood to be any general issue; and accordingly ordered a new trial.

(3*o*) The notice of set-off was as follows: "Take notice, that you are indebted to me for the use and occupation of a house for a long time held and enjoyed and now lately elapsed." The debt intended to be set-off was rent reserved on a lease by indenture, which, not being mentioned in the notice, could not be given in evidence: for if it had been shown, the plaintiff might probably have proved an eviction, or some other matter to avoid the demand. These notices should be almost as certain as declarations. Bull. Ni. Pri. 179. But note, this was before the statute 11 Geo. II. ch. 19, which gives the action for use and occupation.

(3*p*) Ord, Esq. v. Ruspini, 2 Esp. Cases, N. P. 569. T. T. 37 Geo. III. (App. 16.) Assumpsit on a bill of exchange accepted by the defendant, which was due some time in the year 1784. Pleas—Non-assumpsit—Statute of limitation and a set-off. The set-off consisted of bills of exchange and promissory notes of the plaintiff's, which the defendant had taken up or paid on his account: they were all dated in the year 1784. It was objected that, in order to entitle the defendant to go into evidence respecting those bills and notes, they ought to have been made the special objects of a set-off. Lord Kenyon overruled the objection, and held that they were good evidence under the count for money paid to the plaintiff's use.

Hampton v. Jarrat, 2 Esp. Cases, Ni. Pri. 560. E. T. 37 Geo. III. This was an action for goods sold and delivered. The defendant pleaded the general issue, with notice of set-off. The set-off was in the common form, "that the plaintiff was indebted to him in a larger sum of money than that claimed by the plaintiff, to wit, in 100*l.* for money had and received, 100*l.* for goods sold and delivered," going through the common counts of the decla-

The notice of set-off should regularly be given at the time of pleading the general issue; though, if it be not then given, the court will permit the defendant to withdraw the general issue, and plead it again with a notice of set-off :(3*q*) and such notice may be given after the defendant has been ruled to abide by his plea.(3*r*)

As to the pleadings.

The plea.

A plea of set-off insisting upon a debt equal to a greater than the plaintiff's need not make an offer to set-off the debts, but may conclude as a common plea in bar, with a verification and prayer of judgment, Si actio, &c.(3*s*)

A plea insisting upon a debt which the plea acknowledges to be less than the plaintiff's should conclude with a prayer that the debt from the plaintiff may be deducted from that owing by the defendant.(3*s*)

---

ration. That part of the defendant's case upon which he meant to rely in support of his set-off, his counsel proposed to make out in the following manner. The defendant had for a considerable time before dealt with the plaintiff; and had paid him several bills for articles furnished by the plaintiff, in the course of his trade to the defendant : these bills the defendant now pretended to have been overcharged, and liable to very considerable deduction, and these overpayments he proposed to prove and to set-off against the demand claimed by the plaintiff in the present action. This was opposed by the plaintiff's counsel on the ground that, the accounts upon which these payments had been made having been settled, the accounts could not now be opened ; but that if they could, it should have been made the object of a special set-off, and could not be claimed under the general notice. It was answered by the defendant's counsel, that this money was paid by mistake, and would have been recoverable under the general money counts, and so, under a similar clause in the notice of set-off, could be given in evidence as money had and received to the party's use. Eyre, Ch. J. said, he was of opinion that it could not be given in evidence under the common notice of set-off. It was taking the plaintiff by surprise, and if the defendant meant to have availed himself of it, it should have been the object of a particular notice.— His Lordship therefore rejected it, and the plaintiff recovered.

(3*q*) Blackbourn v. Matthias, 2 Str. 1267. E. T. 20 Geo. II. The defendant pleaded the general issue, but forgot to give notice, at the same time, of a set-off. And upon motion in time, the Court gave leave to withdraw the plea, in order to deliver the same plea again with a proper notice to set-off, and said it had been done so before. Strange, pro defendant.

(3*r*) Cochran, v. Robertson, M. T. 20 Geo. III. B. R. ante, page 40.

(3*s*) Bull. Ni. Pri. 179. Where the plea is of an equal sum, there the action is barred; but if it be for a less sum than for what the action is brought, the defendant must pray to have it set-off.

When either of the debts accrues by reason of a penalty contained in a specialty, the plea must aver what is really due, which averment is traversable. (3t)

(3t) The words of the statute are, "in which plea shall be shown how "much is justly and truly due on either side:"—Symmons v. Knox, 3 Term Rep. 65. A. D. 1789. (App. 44.) Debt on bond in 11,619*l.* The defendant pleaded, "that there was due to the plaintiff the sum of 5809*l.* 11*s.* 8*d.* and no more; and that the plaintiff was indebted to the defendant in more money than is remaining due to the said plaintiff by virtue of the said writing obligatory; and concluded with a set-off in the common form." The plaintiff replied, that there was *and yet is justly and truly owing to the said plaintiff from the said defendant*, by virtue of the said writing obligatory, *a larger sum of money* than the said sum of 5809*l.* 11*s.* 8*d.* in the said plea mentioned, to wit, the sum of 6930*l.* 3*s.* 9*d.* and concluding to the country. To this replication the defendant demurred; and showed for cause, that the plaintiff attempted to put in issue a matter immaterial, and therein traversed a fact, whereon no certain or material issue could be taken. Lord Kenyon, Ch. J. I own I form an opinion on this subject with great diffidence. This is an action brought on a bond, in which case the statute says that, if the defendant wishes to set-off a cross demand against the plaintiff he must first state in his plea what is really due on the bond: the defendant then, in this case, being furnished with the means of ascertaining the extent of the demand upon the bond, states that such a sum only is due; and having thus complied with the requisition of the statute, sets-off a cross demand. And the question is, whether the plaintiff is bound to admit that *that* is the extent of his demand. Now, if he does not deny it in his replication, he admits it: it therefore became necessary for the plaintiff to traverse it; for if the plaintiff were to go to trial, only on the issue, whether his demand did or did not exceed the defendant's, great injustice might be done. And it seems to me that there is reason in requiring that the exact sum should be pleaded, because the purpose of pleading is, to reduce the matter to a point. Here too the sum is not pleaded under a *videlicet*; and it has been long settled that where any thing is laid under a *videlicet*, the party is not concluded by it; but he is where there is no *videlicet*. It would therefore be very hard on this plaintiff if he were bound by the sum, which the defendant has stated not under a *videlicet*, without having an opportunity of traversing it. Ashhurst, J. Here the defendant pleaded that a certain sum was due to the plaintiff on the bond, and no more, which would have concluded the plaintiff, if he had not traversed it in his replication. Grose, J. Under this act the defendant cannot give a notice of set-off with the general issue; but he is required to plead it in bar, in which plea he must state what is really due on the bond. And as far as my experience goes, the plea in this case is warranted by the usual form of pleading: it has not been usual to plead that a large sum, to wit, so much is due, *but that a specific sum is due and no more*. And this mode is certainly consonant to the 8 Geo. II. ch. 24. There, as the defendant set forth what was really due without a *videlicet*, the plaintiff would be taken to have admitted it, if he had not traversed it in his replication. Demurrer overruled.

The different parts of a plea of set-off are as different counts in the same declaration.(3*v*)

If part of a plea of set-off be good, and the rest bad; the plaintiff cannot demur generally to the whole, but must single out the exceptionable part.(3*v*)

The replication.

The general replication now is "not indebted in manner and form," which at once puts the parties on the country; and the onus probandi lies on the defendant.

Grimwood v. Barrit, 6 Term Rep. 460. A. D. 1795. (App. 54.) Debt on bond for 1400*l.* conditioned for 700*l.* The defendant pleaded first, that that there was due from the defendant to the plaintiff on the bond "a much less sum than the 1400*l.* to wit, the sum of 735*l.* and no more," and that the plaintiff, at the time of exhibiting his bill, was indebted to him, (the defendant) in a much larger sum of money, to wit, 1200*l.* for goods sold and delivered, &c. which he is ready to set-off. The plaintiff replied, that there was due on the bond more than 735*l.* namely, 835*l.* 0*s.* 7*d.* concluding to the country. The defendant demurred specially; for causes of demurrer to the replication, (he said) that the plaintiff had not by his replication given any answer to the plea, nor admitted or denied that the plaintiff was indebted to the defendant in manner and form as in the plea alleged. Lord Kenyon, Ch. J. Where an averment is material, the addition of a *videlicet* does not render it immaterial. Grose, J. This plea being founded on the 8 Geo. II. ch. 24. s. 5. it was necessary for the defendant to show how much was due on the bond: he accordingly pleaded that the sum of 735*l.* and no more, was due, and this was traversable according to the case of Symmons v. Knox, supra. But it is said that the averment of the sum here is laid under a *videlicet*, which was not the case in Symmons v. Knox; but the rule is, that where any thing in pleading is material, it is not rendered less material by its being pleaded with a *videlicet*: it is still traversable; and therefore this case must be governed by that of Symmons v. Knox. Lawrence, J. It was *necessary for the defendant to shew the real sum due on the bond* to entitle him to his set-off: and it was decided in Symmons v. Knox, that the averment of that sum, was traversable; the question therefore here is, whether the introduction of the *videlicet* in this case makes any difference: but it certainly does not.

(3*v*) Dowsland v. Thompson, 2 Blackst. 910. C. P. T. T. 13. Geo. III. This was a plea of set-off that certain goods were spoiled on board a ship by the negligence of the plaintiff, whereby he became indebted to the defendant in 10,000*l.* and also of a set-off of 10,000*l.* for work and labour, money had and received, &c. To this plea the plaintiff demurs, and assigns for cause, that the matters of damage above supposed in spoiling the goods could not be set-off. Joinder in demurrer. The Court (without entering into the first question whether the matter of damage could or could not be set-off,) held that the demurrer to the whole plea was wrong; for that the latter part was certainly good: and the different parts are to be considered as different counts in the same declaration.

The plaintiff may reply the statute of limitations. (3*x*)

When either of the debts accrues by reason of a penalty contained in a specialty, the averment in the plea, as to the sum due, must, if necessary, be traversed. (3*y*)

SECTION IV.

The judgment.

If the plaintiff recover, judgment must be entered for no more than appears to be truly and justly due to him after one debt is set against the other. (3*z*)

When the condition of a specialty to which a set-off is pleaded, is for the payment of an annuity or growing sum; the judgment is to be entered for what is due, and the penalty to remain as a security against future breaches. (4*a*)

If the defendant, after recovering in a cross action, bar the plaintiff by means of a set-off; a remittitur must be entered on the first record for the sum proved under the set-off. (4*b*)

(3*x*) The plaintiff to a plea of set-off may reply the statute of limitations. Remington v. Stevens, Str. 1271. Vide ante, note (2*c*).

(3*y*) Vide ante, note (3*t*).

(3*z*) This is by the express words of the act, ante, note (*v*) page 16.

(4*a*) Collins v. Collins, 2 Burr. 820. A. D. 1759. (App. 33.) This was an action of debt on bond conditioned, inter alia, to pay the plaintiff an annuity. To an objection of counsel, that if the plaintiff should take his judgment upon this act of parliament, it would *not* be a *judgment* for the *penalty*, but a judgment *only* for the *sum due*, and *no more;* and that after the matter has once passed in rem judicatum, the plaintiff *cannot afterwards recover any more* upon this bond, whatever may become due by future non-payments; for that here is *no provision* " that the judgment *shall stand as a security for future payments*," as there was in the act of 8 and 9 W. III. ch. 11. made for the better preventing frivolous and vexatious suits. Lord Mansfield, in delivering the judgment, said, that the judgment is indeed by the act of 8 Geo. II. directed to be entered " for no more than shall appear to be justly and truly due to the plaintiff; but it is clearly *within the words and meaning* of the act, that the *penalty* is to *remain* as a security against future breaches, in this case of a *set-off* pleaded, as much as it would have done upon the 8 and 9 W. III. ch. 11. if *payment* had been made agreeably to the directions therein contained.

(4*b*) Bull. Ni. Pri. 180. Baskerville v. Brown, Burr. 1229. (App. 42.) Mutual demands may be set-off in this case, and justice may be done by entering a remittitur on the first record as to so much.

CHAPTER II.

OF SET-OFF IN THE CASES OF BANKRUPTS AND INSOLVENT DEBTORS.

The right to set-off under a commission of bankruptcy arises either upon the particular statute of Set-off in the case of bankruptcy; or upon the general statute of Set-off. The right to set-off in the case of insolvent debtors arises upon a clause in the insolvent debtors' act.

PART I.

OF SET-OFF BY THE PARTICULAR STATUTE IN THE CASE OF BANKRUPTCY.

WHEN there are mutual debts or mutual credits between the bankrupt and any other person, before the baukruptcy, the commissioners or the assignees must set one demand against the other; and the residue, upon the balance of accounts, is the only sum to be claimed or paid on either side.(4*c*)

(4*c*) 4 Anne, ch. 17. s. 11. And be it further enacted by the authority aforesaid, that where there shall appear to the commissioners, or the major part of them, that there hath been mutual credit given between such person or persons against whom such commission shall issue forth, and any person or persons who shall be debtor or debtors to any such person or persons, and, due proof thereof made, and that the accounts are open and unbalanced that then it shall be lawful for the said commissioners, in the said commission named, or the major part of them, or the assignee or assignees of such commission, to adjust the said accounts, and to take the balance due in full discharge thereof, and the person debtor to such bankrupt shall not be compelled or obliged to pay more than shall appear to be due on such balance.†

5 Geo. II. ch. 30. s. 28. And be it further enacted by the authority aforesaid, that where it shall appear to the said commissioners, or the major part of them, that there hath been mutual credit given by the bankrupt and any

† This was a temporary act, and is now expired: there is a like provision in 5 Geo. I c. 24. which is also expired.

This subject is divisible into two parts.

I. The cases in which accounts may be balanced.

II. The modes of balancing them.

SECTION I.

The cases in which accounts may be balanced.

Accounts may be balanced in the case of bankruptcy, when

I. There are mutual debts or credits, which

II. Existed between the parties before the bankruptcy.

I. There must be mutual debts or credits, that is,

1. *The demand of the assignees and of the creditor must be a debt or a credit*; and

2. *The sum claimed must have been due to the bankrupt, and be due to the creditor in their own rights respectively.*

1. *The demand must be a debt or a credit.*

The legal acceptation of the word *debt* has been already explained.(4*d*)

The word *credit* is more comprehensive than the word debt.(4*e*)

---

other person, or mutual debts between the bankrupt and any other person, at any time before such person became bankrupt, the said commissioners, or the major part of them, or the assignees of such bankrupt's estate, shall state the account between them, and one debt may be set against another: and what shall appear to be due on either side, on the balance of such account, and on setting such debts against one another, and no more, shall be claimed or paid on either side respectively.

(4*d*) Page 18, 19, &c.

(4*e*) Lord Hardwicke, in Ex parte Deeze, 1 Atk. 228. said, notwithstanding the rules of law as to bankrupts reduce all creditors to an equality, yet it is hard where a man has a debt due from a bankrupt, and has at the same time goods of a bankrupt in his hands, which cannot be got from him without the assistance of law or equity, that the assignees should take them from him without satisfying the whole debt. And therefore the clause in the act of parliament of the 5 Geo. II. relating to mutual credit has received a very liberal construction, and there have been many cases which that clause has been extended to where an action of account would not lie, nor could this Court upon a bill decree an account. In French v. Fenn, T. T. 1783, (App. 19.) Lord Mansfield said, the act of parliment is accurately drawn to avoid the injustice that would be done if the words were only mutual debts, and it therefore provides for mutual credit.

In Lanesborough v. Jones. 1 P. W. 325. A. D. 1716. the Lord Chancellor, speaking of 4 Ann. ch. 17. s. 11. says, " This clause in the statute was not to be construed of dealings in trade only, or in case of mutual running accounts: but that it was natural justice and equity, that, in all cases of mutual credit, only the balance should be paid."

It seems that any equitable demand is a credit.(4e)

It has been decided that a legacy due from a testator who admits assets may be set-off.(4f)

It has been decided that a party to a contract on which he has taken usurious interest, may set-off the sum really advanced on the contract.(4g)

In Atkinson v. Elliot, 7 T. R. 378. A. D. 1797. (App. 52.) Lord Kenyon says, "The statute 5 Geo. II. ch. 20. s. 28. enacts that, where there are mutual credits or mutual debts between the bankrupt and any other persons, one debt may be set-off against another, and only the balance claimed. Now, in using these words, the Legislature must have intended something more than would have been expressed by mutual debts only, and the decisions referred to, show that this construction has been put upon this act.

I collect this from the two following notes, and from the case of Jeffs v. Wood, which, though in some respects it may, possibly, be doubted, has a tendency to establish this point; which, I am aware, is, perhaps too general.

(4f) Jeffs v. Wood, 2 P. W. 128. A. D. 1723. The defendant was indebted to the father of the plaintiff; and, after the death of the father, became indebted to the plaintiff, the son. The father, by his will, gave 500*l.* to the defendant, and appointed the plaintiff his executor. The defendant sued the plaintiff in the Spiritual Court for the 500*l.* The plaintiff brought his bill against the defendant, and, he becoming a bankrupt, against the assignees under the commission, for an allowance to be made him out of the legacy, for the money which the bankrupt, the legatee, owed to the testator, and likewise to the plaintiff:—there was a cross-bill by the assignees for the legacy. The Master of the Rolls observing that the assignees could not stand in a better situation than the bankrupt stood previous to his bankruptcy, who would not have been able to recover the legacy without deducting what was due to the executor, said—It was objected that this demand of the defendant Wood, or of the assignees, was not a *debt*, but a legacy; and a matter demandable in the Spiritual Court where it was sued for, till such suit was stopped by injunction: and that the statutes of bankrupts mention only *debts* due from, and to, the bankrupt; but to this it was answered and resolved, that a legacy due from an executor who admits assetts (as in the present case,) is in equity a debt due from such executor, and an equitable demand is a debt within the statutes of bankrupts; but vide Farish v. Wilson, 31 Geo. III. Peake 73. Decks v. Strutt, A. D. 1794. 5 T. R. 690.

(4g) Ryall, assignee of Harvest, v. Rowls, executor of Stevens, 1 Vez. sen. 375. A. D. 1750. A sum was reported to be due to Rowls as executor from Ryall as assignee; the assignees attempted to set-off 2000*l.* due from Stevens upon a contract in which he had taken exorbitant and usurious interest. The question was, whether the assignees should have the 2000*l.* as a distinct independent demand, or whether Rowls should be permitted to set-off. Lord Chancellor. The defendants insist on a reasonable rule; the bankrupt and his assignees were certainly entitled to have the benefit of this 2000*l.* with interest from the time it ought to be paid. But, as to the general question whether this case is within the act for mutual credit, I am of opinion it

The holder of a bill of exchange who obtains possession of it, after acceptance, in the course of its negociation, credits the acceptor, and may set-off the demand arising upon it against any debt or credit claimed from him by the assignees of the acceptor.(4*h*)

In an action by the assignees of a bankrupt for damages for the breach of a special agreement; the defendant cannot avail himself of a notice of set-off, unless the assignees are obliged to have recourse to the common counts.(4*i*)

It has been decided that if any person have goods of the bankrupt's entrusted to him in the course of his trade or occupation; he cannot, solely on account of such trust, set-off against a demand for these goods any sum beyond that for which he has a lien.(4*k*)

---

is: and that there is no distinction taken, on what consideration it is that the debt ought to be set-off, has arisen. There are several cases, where demands have been set-off against one another, that could not have been brought into the general account, if there had not been a bankruptcy; but wherever the Court has found a demand on one side or the other, the Court has always endeavoured, that one should be set against the other, which is founded on the act, "that where there are mutual debts, &c."—This is a debt due from Stevens to Harvest: a debt in equity, though possibly no remedy at law, because the law admits not the party to an usurious contract to have a remedy.

(4*h*) Hankey and others, assignees, v. Smith, 3 T. R. 507. A. D. 1789. (App. 46.) Assumpsit for goods sold and delivered. Set-off. Verdict for the plaintiffs subject to the opinion of the Court on a case which stated that the defendant, before the bankruptcy, discounted for one Towgood a bill accepted by the bankrupt, which bill became due a few days before the bankruptcy; and that, at the time when the bill was discounted for Towgood, he did not indorse the same, but, by a memorandum in writing, agreed to indorse when he should be thereunto required: that he did indorse it after the bankrupt had stopped payment; and that the reason why the bill was not indorsed, was, that, if the bankrupts had stood their ground, it might be presented for payment without the indorsement of Towgood and Co. as he, Towgood, wished that their names should not appear. The question was, whether the defendant could set-off this bill against a demand upon him for goods sold, &c. Lord Kenyon said, that taking this bill constituted a credit. And per Buller, J. in order to constitute mutual credit, it is not necessary that the parties mean to trust each other in that transaction; for, if a bill of exchange, which is accepted, be sent out into the world, credit is given to the acceptor by every person who takes the bill.

(4*i*) Colson and others, assignees of Hunter, v. Welsh, 1 Esp. Cas. 378. A. D. 1793. ante, page 19.

(4*k*) Ex parte Deeze, 1 Atk. 228. A. D. 1748. A merchant borrowed of

A creditor, who has bills of exchange entrusted to him by a trader, for the purpose of appropriating them to the payment of particular debts and then to return the residue to the trader, may, upon the bankruptcy of the trader, set-off any debt or

---

the petitioner, who was a packer, the sum of 500*l.* on note: to whom the merchant afterwards sent six bales of cloth to pack and press. At the time of the bankruptcy of the merchant part of the 500*l.* had been paid; and there was 19*l.* due to the petitioner for the packing and pressing these bales; and there was due from the petitioner to the merchant near 19*l.* for wine: but there were no goods in the hands of the petitioner when first he lent the money, nor had there been dealings between them for many years. It appeared in evidence that it was usual for packers to lend money to clothiers, and the cloths to be a pledge, not only for the work done in packing, but for the loan of money likewise. (Vide Ex parte Ockenden, A. D. 1754. 1 Atk. 235.)—upon a question, (inter al.) whether there was mutual credit, and how far it extended.

The Lord Chancellor. It is very hard to say mutual credit should be confined to pecuniary demands; and that, if a man has goods in his hands belonging to a debtor of his, which cannot be got from him without an action or bill in equity, that it should not be considered as mutual credit: and Lord Cowper's opinion (in 2 Vern. 691.) plainly favours that construction.

And here, though, if there had been no bankruptcy, in an action for these goods, the debt could not have been set-off; yet, as the clause of mutual credit has been extended, I think it may come within that rule, especially as here is an account between them, on the one side 19*l.* due for packing &c. on the other side, much about the same sum due to the bankrupt's estate for wine.

Ex parte Ockenden, 1 Atk. 235. A. D. 1754. A flour-factor entrusted some corn with a miller to grind. The flour-factor became a bankrupt; being indebted to the miller for the price of grinding the corn; and, on a general balance, for other corn which he had ground. The miller was in possession of the corn at the time of the bankruptcy, and had trusted the flour-factor on the general balance upon the supposition that he had always a lien for his whole debt. Upon a question whether the corn was a security for the general balance,

Lord Chancellor. In Ex parte Deeze before me, there was evidence that it is usual for packers to lend money to clothiers, and the cloths to be a pledge not only for the work done in packing, but for the loan of money likewise. Then it must come to the question upon the clause in the act relating to mutual credit, and I own I am extremely doubtful as to that. Here is a quantity of corn delivered from time to time by a mealman to a miller. The law gives a lien *pro tanto* as is due to the miller for grinding the corn, and no contract appears, in this case, to extend it further; and I must presume therefore it was not intended to be carried further. The clause in the act of 5 Geo. II. relating to mutual credit has been carried, to be sure, further, and rightfully, than a mere matter of account; but I do not know that a court of equity has gone further than courts of law in the cases of a set-off.

credit due to him from the bankrupt against a demand upon him by the assignees, for the residue.(4*l*)

II. To constitute mutuality of debts or of credits, it is also necessary, *that the sum claimed was due to the bankrupt and is due to the creditor in their own rights respectively.*(4*m*)

These cases go further indeed than cases of accounts, but can any case be put where, in the present instance, there could have been a set-off. The case stood over till the 20th of August, (Vide Green v. Farmer, 1 Blackst. 653.) when his Lordship determined that the corn was not a security for the general balance.

Wilkins v. Carmicheal, Doug. 101. A. D. 1779. In an action of trover brought by the assignees of a bankrupt for a ship of the bankrupt's against the captain who claimed a lien upon it for wages, stores and provisions, for which he was liable before the bankruptcy of the owner, and had paid after the bankruptcy. Lord Mansfield. If there is no lien, can there be a set-off? This is no item of any sort in account between the bankrupt and the defendant; the ship remained in specie till after the bankruptcy: and the conversion arises from an act done in the specific property of the assignees, not of the bankrupt.

(4*l*) Atkinson v. Elliot, 7 T. R. 378. A. D. 1797. (App. 52.) In an action of assumpsit a case was reserved, from which it appeared that the defendant, on the 3d of May, 1796, drew at six months date on Hodges, the bankrupt for 430*l*. and on the 6th of November, at six months date, for 230*l*. The bills were accepted, and were for value received. On the 6th of November, when the first bill became due, the bankrupt was not able to pay it; but on the 9th of the same month he gave the defendants a bill of Walpole and Co. for 100*l*. due on the 11th of December following, and on the 10th of November gave the defendants a bill accepted by Bullock and Son for 500*l*. due also on the 11th of December. At the time of giving this last bill the defendants gave the bankrupt the following memorandum: "Memorandum. I promise to pay to Mr. H. Hodges 170*l*. when his bill on Messrs. Bullock and Son is paid." It was not in the contemplation of either party to do more than take up the first bill for 430*l*. The bills for 100*l*. and for 500*l*. were duly paid on the 11th of December. On the 13th of December, the commission of bankruptcy issued against Hodges.

The Court was clearly of opinion that the defendant was entitled to set-off the 170*l*. against the second bill for 270*l*. drawn by them on the bankrupt, and not due till the 9th of March. Postea, to defendants. Vide note (*z*) page 19.

(4*m*) Vide page 23, where many of the cases respecting the nature of debts due in *the rights of the respective parties* will appear to have originated in bankruptcy. They are arranged in the former part of the work, because their operation is not confined to *Set-off in the case of bankruptcy*, but extends to "*Set-off in general.*" But see the decisions in the case of Set-off in Equity (postea) where this doctrine, in the case of partners, seems to be a little shaken; unless those cases stand on equitable principles, without any relation to the statute of Set-off. N. B. Meliorucchi v. Exchange Assurance, ante 28, and all the cases to pages 31 and 32. are cases in bankruptcy.

2. The next requisite to enable the parties to balance accounts in the case of bankruptcy is, "*that the debt or credit exist between the parties before the bankruptcy*.(4n)

The cases on this head are divisible into two classes.

1st. Whether the debt or credit existed *before the bankruptcy*; 2dly. Whether the debt or credit existed *between the parties* before the bankruptcy.

As to the existence of the debt or credit before the bankruptcy.

A demand arising upon an instrument payable after the bankruptcy, cannot be set-off; unless it is payable at all events, on a day certain.(4o)

(4n) The words of the statute are: "When there hath been mutual, &c. between the bankrupt and any other person at any time *before* such person became bankrupt," &c. Vide note (4c) page 46.

(4o) The cases on this head are of two classes.

1st. *Where the instrument is payable, at all events, on a day certain after the bankruptcy.*

2dly. *Where the payment after the bankruptcy is uncertain, either as to the time or as to the event.*

1st. *Where the instrument is payable, at all events, on a day certain after the bankruptcy.*

Ex parte Prescott, 1 Atk. 231. A. D. 1753. A creditor for 110*l.* and a debtor upon bond given to the bankrupt for 340*l.* payable on the 4th of March, 1756, with interest, petitioned that the 110*l.* might be set-off against the debt of 340*l.* Lord Chancellor ordered that, upon the petitioner's agreeing to pay the balance forthwith to the assignees, which the act of parliament (alluding to 7 Geo. I. relating to creditors where debts are payable at a future day,) requires, the balance only should be paid.

Smith v. Hodson, 4 Term Rep. 211. A. D. 1791. (Appen. 49.) The defendant accepted a bill for 442*l.* drawn by the bankrupt on the 4th of March, 1788, and payable on the 7th of May, 1788. The bill was for 42*l.* for a valuable consideration, and 400*l.* for the accommodation of the bankrupt. The bankruptcy happened on the 29th of April, 1788. The Court, upon a verdict for the plaintiff, on a special case, were of opinion that the defendant was entitled to set-off his demand upon this bill, and ordered a nonsuit to be entered.

Atkinson v. Elliot, 7 T. R. 371. A. D. 1797. (App. 52.) Assumpsit and case reserved. On the 6th of September, 1796, the bankrupts accepted a bill of the defendant's at six months date, for 230*l.* for goods sold to the bankrupts by the defendant. On the 13th of December, 1796, the bankruptcy happened. In an action commenced on the 12th of February, 1797, by the plaintiffs against the defendant, the defendant insisted upon his right to set-off the above bill for 230*l.* though it was not due till the 9th of March 1797.

Lord Kenyon. In my opinion, the case Ex parte Prescott was properly decided, and that has since been followed by a series of determinations.

If the demand depend upon a contingency, but is secured by

Lawrence, J. This is directly within the authority of the case, Ex parte Prescott. Postea to the defendant.

2dly. *Where the payment after the bankruptcy is uncertain, either as to the time, or as to the event.*

Ex parte Groome, 1 Atk. 115. A. D. 1744. On articles previous to the marriage of the petitioner, the husband covenants to leave his wife 600*l.* on the contingency of surviving him: a commission of bankruptcy is taken out against the husband, who dies before any dividend is made. The petitioner applied to be admitted a creditor for the 600*l*; but the petition was dismissed, the Chancellor observing that there was no such thing as drawing a line between the contingency not happening before the bankruptcy, and yet happening before the time of the distribution.

Hancock v. Entwissle, 3 Term Rep. 435. A. D. 1789. (App. 47.) In an action on a bill of exchange, the plaintiffs having proved their case, the only question was, whether the defendants were entitled to a set-off, arising from an agreement made in March 1788, between the defendants of one part, and the bankrupt of the other, by which, (after reciting that a loss had been sustained by the defendants, in consequence of the purchase of some cotton, by the bankrupt as their broker, for reimbursing which they made a claim on him,) in order to put an end to all controversy, it was agreed that the loss, though exceeding 1900*l.* should be fixed at that sum and no more; and that, in payment or satisfaction of that sum, the bankrupt should, from time to time, within the space of four years, recommend parcels of cotton, not exceeding 130 bags at one time, to the defendants for their purchase, and that the defendants should purchase them, paying for them in notes at three months date. *And the bankrupt undertook that the clear profits on such sales should, in the course of four years, be sufficient to discharge the* 1900*l. but if the same should not be paid within that time, then the bankrupt agreed, immediately after the expiration of four years, in case he should then be living, to pay them the difference.* And if the purchases should occasion a loss to the defendants, the bankrupt undertook to make good such loss. Lord Kenyon, before whom the cause was tried, being of opinion that the defendants were not entitled to set-off, the plaintiff obtained a verdict. And upon a motion for a new trial, Lord Kenyon, Ch. J. said, if this deed had never been entered into, the claim which the defendants had on the bankrupt could not have been set-off in this action, because it rested merely in damages; it arose from the misconduct of the bankrupt, and might have been settled in an action. But by this deed the damages are liquidated, and the parties agreed on certain things to be done in the course of four years, as the means of making a recompense to the defendants, to the amount of that sum. If a certain sum of money had been payable at all events by instalments, and one of the payments had become due before the bankruptcy, the whole might have been proved under the commission. But it is clear that the bankrupt was not discharged by his bankruptcy, from the operation of this deed; for when he obtains his certificate, he may be enabled to perform the stipulations contained in it. Then, if he were not discharged from his covenants by his certificate, this debt could not be proved under the commission, nor can it be a penalty which is forfeited at law before the bankruptcy, it may be set-off.(4p)

If the payment depend upon the survivorship of two persons who are alive at the bankruptcy, it cannot be set off.(4q)

It seems that an instrument of indemnity given by a principal to a surety, and payable after the bankruptcy of the princi-

---

set-off, for it had no existence as a debt at the time of the bankruptcy. The distinction has been well settled in a variety of cases, as in those of Ex parte Groome, and Ex parte Winchester, that if the demand be payable at all events, though at a future day, it may be proved under the commission; but where it depends on a contingency, whether it will be paid or not, it cannot be proved unless it be secured by a penalty which is forfeited at law, in which case the Court will take hold of the legal right to give the party a remedy under the commission. But in this case there was no legal demand at the time of the bankruptcy. And the rule was discharged.

Dobson, assignees, v. Lockhart, 5 Term Rep. 133. A.D. 1793. (App. 1.) Assumpsit for goods sold. Set-off, of a bond on the following facts.

On the 11th of October, 1788, the bankrupt and the defendant became bound to A. and B. in 900*l.* conditioned to pay 450*l.* and interest on demand.

On the 16th of May, 1789, the bankrupt, one Foster, and the defendant, became bound to C. D. and E. in 1000*l.* conditioned to pay 500*l.* and interest, on the 1st of June, 1789. These two bonds were executed by the defendant, as a surety for the bankrupt and for his debt only.

On the 21st of May, 1789, to indemnify the defendant against these bonds, the bankrupt became bound to the defendant and G. Lockhart (who was only trustee for the defendant) in 1400*l.* conditioned to pay 700*l.* on the 13th of February, 1790.

Afterwards, and after the bankruptcy of the principal, viz. on the 14th of December, 1789, the defendant was obliged to pay 470*l.* to A. and B. on the first bond, and 236*l.* 17*s.* to C. D. and E. on the second bond. Plaintiffs nonsuited, with liberty to apply to the Court to enter up a verdict, if the Court should be of opinion that they were entitled to recover. The judgment of nonsuit was affirmed on the general issue, but part of the judgment of Buller, J. may be applicable to this plea. He says, I agree with the plaintiff's counsel that there is no case in which it has been held that, where it depends on some future event which does not take place until after the bankruptcy, whether or not there will be any debt against the bankrupt, the debt can either be proved under the commission, or set-off against a demand made by the assignees.—N. B. It does not appear in this case, at what time the bankruptcy happened; but it seems to have been between the 21st May, 1789, and the 14th December, 1789. Vide Drinkwater v. Goodwin, Cowp. 251. and Cowper v. Birch, 6 T. R. 28.—Where a liability to pay before the bankruptcy, though no payment be made till after the bankruptcy, is sufficient to entitle a person to a lien.

(4p) D. Lord Kenyon in Hancock v. Entwissle, 3 T. R. 435. in the last note.

(4q) Ex parte Groome, 1 Atk. 115. note (4o).

pal, may be set-off: if the surety be liable to pay, before the bankruptcy, though no payment is made by him till after the bankruptcy.(4r)

The debt cannot be set-off, though the event be determined after the bankruptcy, and before the dividend is made.(4s)

If a loss happen upon a policy of insurance before the bankruptcy of a principal who has entrusted the broker with the policy; the broker may set-off any debt or credit due to him, to a demand upon him by the assignees for the amount of the losses which he receives from the underwriters after the bankruptcy.(4t)

If a purchase be made on speculation by three persons before the time when one of them becomes a bankrupt; and if, after such bankruptcy, the speculation be carried into effect by those who continue solvent, and it turn out beneficial, the amount of the produce may be set-off to any demand due from either of the solvents to the bankrupt before the bankruptcy.(4v)

As to the existence of the debt or credit between the parties before the bankruptcy.

A bill of exchange taken up and paid, after the bankruptcy

(4r) Dobson v. Lockhart, 5 T. R. 133. note (4o). Vide 2 T. R. 100, and Ex parte Cockshott, Cooke's Bank. Laws. 149.

(4s) Ex parte Groome, note (4o).

(4t) Whitehead v. Vaughan, T. T. 25 Geo. III. B. R. Cooke's Bank. Laws, 579. Mitford put a policy of insurance into the hands of Vaughan his broker, that he might get it underwritten, which was done on the 3d May, 1781, by different persons, Vaughan being himself one. In May, 1784, a loss happened; but, being an average loss, the actual sum due from the underwriters on the policy was not liquidated and ascertained till a time subsequent to the bankruptcy of Mitford, which was in July, 1784. The assignees demanded the average loss received by the defendant, but, by setting-off what he had received in the general account with the bankrupt, the balance was 108*l*. 5*s*. 6*d*. which the defendant paid into Court. Upon a question whether the defendant was entitled to insist upon this set-off, it was argued for the plaintiff, that the debt became due from the defendant upon the receipt of the average loss, which was after the bankruptcy, and therefore could not be set-off. Mr. J. Buller said, the plaintiff was wrong every way: 1st. The bankrupt had a good cause of action before the bankruptcy, for this debt was due before the bankruptcy, though not ascertained; 2dly. The statute 5 Geo. II. c. 30. is decisive; for, by that statute, the balance only is the debt. The assignees are to take the account, and nothing is received to their use but the balance.

(4v) Ante, page 25, and Appendix 19.

of the acceptor, by an indorser, cannot be set-off by him under a commission against the acceptor.(4*x*)

A note indorsed to the claimant after the bankruptcy cannot be set off.(4*y*)

It is incumbent upon an indorsee to show that the indorsement was made before the bankruptcy: but the possession by the payee of a note made before the bankruptcy seems to be reasonable evidence that it came into his possession at the time it bears date.(4*y*)

SECTION II.

The mode of balancing the accounts.

The aceounts may be balanced either upon an action at law or before the commissioners or the assignees.(4*z*)

(4*x*) Ex parte Hale, 3 Vez. jun. 304. A. D. 1796. The acceptor of a bill of exchange for 200*l.* indorsed by the petitioner, becoming a bankrupt, the petitioner was obliged to take it up; and, being indebted to the bankrupt's estate to the amount of 90*l.* he prayed that he might be at liberty to set-off the 90*l.* The Lord Chancellor dismissed the petition so far as it sought to set-off the 90*l.* and there was not any objection to the proof of the 200*l.* But vide Hankey v. Smith, 3 T. R. 509. (App. 46.)

(4*y*). March, assignee of May, v. Chambers, T. T. 18 Geo. II. Bull. N. P. 180. 2 Str. 1234. The assignee of of a bankrupt brought an action for work and labour; the defendant gave notice of set-off; and, at the trial, produced a negotiable note given by the bankrupt antecedent to his bankruptcy, to Scott; and Scott's hand was proved to the indorsement to the defendant, but no proof was given when it was indorsed; upon which the plaintiff called two witnesses, who gave strong evidence to show it was after the bankruptcy; however, the defendant had a verdict; but a new trial was granted, because such indorsee ought not be in a better condition than the drawer, who would only have come in as a creditor under the commission.

Dickson v. Evans, 6 T. R. 59. A. D. 1794. The Court granted a new trial, Mr. J. Rooke having nonsuited the plaintiff, by allowing the defendants to give in evidence, upon a set-off, notes made, but without any proof that they were indorsed to the defendant before the bankruptcy. Lawrance, J. observed, that if the notes had been made payable to the defendant himself, he should have thought it reasonable evidence of their having come to his hands at the time they bore date.

(4*z*). The words of the statute are: "The said commissioners, or the major part of them, or the assignees of such bankrupt's estate, shall state the account between them, and one debt may be set against another: and what shall appear to be due on either side, on the balance of such accounts, and on setting such debts against one another, and no more, shall be claimed or paid on either side respectively.

Lock v. Bennet, 2 Atk. 49. A. D. 1740. Where there are mutual demands between a creditor and a bankrupt under the clause in 5 Geo. II. ch. 30. s. 29. in which are these words, "no more shall be claimed and paid

Upon an action at law in the case of bankruptcy, it seems that a set-off may be given in evidence without special pleading or notice.(5a)

When an account is balanced before the commissioners or the assignees, it cannot be litigated but by an application to the Great Seal.(5b)

---

than appears to be due on either side, upon a balance of accounts stated."—The master of the rolls was of opinion, that upon an action at law the defendant might set-off his demand against the plaintiff, as is done in other cases by virtue of the statute of 2 Geo. II. ch 22. s. 13. and 8 Geo. II. ch. 24. s. 6. and that there is no occasion to come into a court of equity to pray an injunction to a suit at law, and that the plaintiff at law may account.

(5a) Grove v. Dubois, 1 Term Rep. 112. A. D. 1786. (App. 25.) In the case of bankruptcy the defendant gave a notice of set-off for money had and received by the assignees for his use. It appeared in evidence that the assignees had not received any money, but that the defendant had paid and laid out money on account of the bankrupt. Buller, J. I agree that the notice of set-off is bad ; but this loss may be proved and set-off under the general issue by the 28th section of 5 Geo. II. ch. 30. The words of the section are : "That where it shall appear to the commissioners, or the major part of them, that there hath been mutual credit given by the bankrupt and any other person, at any time before such person became bankrupt, the said commissioners, &c. shall state the account between them, and one debt may be set-off against another, and what shall appear to be due on either side, on the balance of such account, and no more, shall be claimed and paid, on either side respectively." Therefore we see, by this section of the statute, that the assignees could legally claim no more than the balance upon the account between the parties. In Dickson v. Smith, 6 Term Rep. 57. A. D. 1794. Lord Kenyon. "It is said that the rule by which we are to proceed in a court of law under the statutes of set-off, is a different rule from that by which the commissioners proceed under the statute of 5 Geo. II. ch. 30. but it must be remembered that that act proceeds on the law of the case, and applied the same rule to the commissioners of bankrupts—N. B. the practice is to plead or give notice of set-off upon an action at law in the case of bankruptcy, in the same manner as under the general statutes relating to set-off: and this practice seems to be just, and to be attended with many advantages.

(5b) Brown, executor, v. Bullen, assignee. Doug. 407. A. D. 1780. This was an action for money had and received for the amount of a dividend declared by the commissioners to be due to the testator. The defendants alleged that there was a balance due from the testator to the bankrupt. The defendants pleaded the general issue, with notice of set-off. At the trial, Lord Mansfield would not permit the defendants to avail themselves of the notice of set-off, saying, that as the commissioners have a power of setting-off mutual debts, the sum proved must be taken to be the balance due ; but if it should happen that only one side of the account appeared before the commissioners, or that any article was omitted, on either side, on application to

PART II.

OF SET-OFF IN BANKRUPTCY BY THE GENERAL STATUTES OF SET-OFF.

THE general statutes of set-off extend to the case of bankruptcy.(5c)

If the assignees of a bankrupt proceed at law on a contract made by the bankrupt after the bankruptcy, it seems that the defendant may set-off any debt on a contract made on his part after the bankruptcy.(5d)

---

the Great Seal, the account would be again opened, and referred to the commissioners, or, in cases of difficulty, to the Master. Verdict for the plaintiffs, with leave to move for a nonsuit: the Court unanimously agreed that Lord Mansfield's direction was right.

(5c) Ryal v. Larkin, B. R. M. 20 Geo. II. 1 Wils. 155. B. N. P. 181. (App. 48.) To an action of indebitatus assumpsit by the assignees of a bankrupt, the defendant pleaded a set-off of a greater sum due to him from the bankrupt before the bankruptcy; and upon demurrer, it was holden that the statute for setting off mutual debts does not extend to assignees of bankrupts; that these can never be considered as mutual debts, for where there are mutual debts, there must be mutual remedies. (Ante page 23, where it is expressly required that the debt of each party should be due *in his own right.*)

Ridout, assignees, v. Brough, Cowp. 133. T. T. 14 Geo. III. A. D. 1774. Assumpsit for money had and received for the use of the assignees since the bankruptcy, and the same for the use of the bankrupt before the bankruptcy. Set-off of money due from the bankrupt *before* the bankruptcy, and also of money due from the assignees since the bankruptcy. Demurrer. The Court were clearly of opinion that the defendant might set-off a debt due to him from the bankrupt, for the assignees are the bankrupt; and seemed to impeach the decision in 1 Wils. 155. That the statutes of set off do not extend to assignees under a commission of bankruptcy, as against the general principles of law, justice and good sense. But, on the other grounds, judgment was for the plaintiff.

(5d) I class these under the *general statutes of set-off*, because the particular statute in the case of bankruptcy expressly requires that the debts should be due *before* the bankruptcy.

Billon v. Hyde, 1 Vez. 326. A. D. 1749. There were dealings between the plaintiff and a bankrupt before the bankruptcy; which continued after a secret act of bankruptcy had been committed. The assignees brought assumpsit against the plaintiff, and recovered all sums which had been paid to him by the bankrupt after the bankruptcy.

PART III.

OF SET-OFF IN THE CASE OF INSOLVENT DEBTORS.

WHEN there is mutual credit between an insolvent debtor whose property is assigned under the Lords' act, and any other

---

The plaintiff in equity insisted that, notwithstanding that recovery by the strict rule of law, still an allowance ought to be made him for all that was paid by him to the bankrupt within the same period of time; which was not allowed at the trial, or by the commissioners.

The Chancellor, on the ground that the assignees ought not to have the power of affirming the contracts on one side and disaffirming them on the other, ordered the cause to stand over, and recommended it to the assignees to compound in some manner: to which recommendation they afterwards attended.

Smith, assignees, v. Hodson, 4 T. R. 211. A. D. 1791. (App. 49.) The defendant had accepted a bill for 400*l*. for the accommodation of the bankrupts, which was not due at the time of the bankruptcy. On the eve of the bankruptcy, the bankrupt sold to the defendant goods to the amount of 500*l*. at six months credit. In an action by the assignees for the price of these goods, the defendant pleaded a set-off of the bill which he had accepted; and on a case reserved, Lord Kenyon, in delivering the opinion of the Court, said: "This is an action on the contract for the goods sold by the bankrupt; and, although the assignees may either affirm or disaffirm the contract of the bankrupt, yet, if they do affirm it, they must act consistently throughout; they cannot, as has often been observed in cases of this kind, blow hot and cold: and, as the assignees in this case treated this transaction as a contract of sale, it must be pursued through all its consequences, one of which is that the party buying may set up the same defence to an action brought by the assignees, which he might have used against the bankrupt himself, and consequently may set-off another debt which was owing from the bankrupt to him. Therefore, on the distinction between trover and assumpsit, we are all of opinion judgment of nonsuit must be entered.

N. B. Though, in the foregoing case, the decision may be founded upon the 5 Geo. II. ch. 30. as both the debts were due before the bankruptcy, so as to be set-off under that statute, yet the principle seems to be the same as that laid down in Billon v. Hyde.

person, the assignee must balance the accounts; and the residue alone passes by the assignment.(5e)

(5e) 32 Geo. II. ch. 28. s. 23. And be it further enacted, that in all and every case and cases where mutual credit shall have been given between any prisoner or prisoners who shall be discharged under this act, and any other person or persons, bodies politic or corporate, before the delivery of any schedule or inventory of the estate and effects of such prisoner or prisoners upon oath, as by this act is herein before directed: then, and in every such case, the respective assignee or assignees of such prisoner or prisoners shall have power, and is and are hereby required, on his or their part or parts, to state and allow an account between them, and nothing more shall be deemed to be vested by any assignment which shall be made in pursuance of this act, as the estate or effects of such prisoner or prisoners, than what shall appear to have been due to him, her, or them respectively, and to be justly coming to him, her, or them, on or before the balance of such account when truly stated.

BOOK II.

OF SET-OFF IN EQUITY.(5f)

A Court of Equity will grant relief in any case where there is an equitable, without a legal, right to set-off. (5g)

If, upon the dissolution of a partnership, there is a surplus after payment of partnership debts: a debtor to the partnership, who is a separate creditor of either of the firm against whom a commission of bankruptcy has issued, may set-off the joint debt against the surplus to which the bankrupt is entitled.(5h)

(5f) I class the cases in notes (5h) and (5i) under *Set-off in Equity*, because they appear to be decided solely on equitable principles: for the words *mutual credit* in the 5 Geo. II. extends to questions at law as well as to questions arising on petition to the Chancellor: and it seems to be clear that in these cases there could not be any set-off at law. In Ex parte Ockenden, 1 Atk. 235. ante, page 50, the Lord Chancellor says; "The clause in the act of 5 Geo. II. relating to mutual credit has been carried, to be sure, further, and rightfully, than a mere matter of account: but I do not know that a court of equity has gone further than courts of law in the cases of a set-off."

It is, perhaps, scarcely necessary for me to say that I consider this Book as incomplete.

(5g) Vide James v. Kynnier, 5 Vez. jun. 108. A. D. 1792. ante p. 3, (App. 5.) and the following notes.

(5h) Lanesborough v. Jones, 1 P. W. 325. It seems if A. and B. are joint traders, and T. S. owes A. and B. on their joint account 100*l*. and A. owes the said T. S. 100*l*. on his separate account: T. S. cannot deduct so much as A's proportion of the 100*l*. comes to, out of the joint debt; for that the copartnership debts of A. and B. are to be first paid, before any of the separate debts: but if there be a surplus, beyond what will pay the partnership debts, then, out of A's share of the surplus, T. S. may deduct the separate debt of A.

Ex Parte Quintin, 3 Vez. jun. 248. A. D. 1796. The partnership between Shepherd and Williams, attornies and solicitors, was dissolved in November 1794. In January, 1795, a commission of bankruptcy issued against Shepherd. Williams paid all the partnership debts. The petitioners were indebted to the partnership for business done, &c. and were separate creditors of Shepherd to a greater amount, for money received by him as their agent. The prayer of the petition was to be permitted to set-off the bankrupt's share of the debts due to the partnership, against the debts due separately from the bankrupt to the petitioners, and to prove the residue of such separate debts

If there are two commissions of bankruptcy against the same person, the one a joint, the other a separate commission, and there are the same assignees under both commissions, it is said that a debtor under the joint commission may set-off a debt due to him under the separate commission.(5*i*)

---

under the commission. Williams was contented to receive one fourth of the debt due to the partnership; which was the proportion of the interest. Solicitor General and Mr. Cooke for the petition cited what is added by the reporter to Lanesborough v. Jones, 1 P. W. 326. and Mitchell v. Oldfield, 4 Term Rep. 123. Attorney General, contra, cited Ex parte Edwards, 1 Atk. 100, and said the petitioners had no such right to set-off at the time of the bankruptcy; and the intermediate act of the other partner paying the partnership debts could not put them in a different situation. Lord Chancellor. As at law there can be no doubt; for the action must be brought in the name of the two, and you cannot set-off the separate debt of one; I agree the right is not to be varied by any thing that has been done since the commission; but the right is manifest, the account being clear. In equity it would be very hard where it appears that all joint debts are paid and that the other partner is satisfied, and there is a surplus in which he is interested in one moiety, and the indebted partner in the other—it would be very hard if, to the extent of that moiety, the creditor of that partner cannot set-off? I make the arrangement. The assignees are to stand in the place of Shepherd; Williams, being contented to receive his fourth, is only nominal: then shall I allow the assignees to take the rest, and not permit the debtor to set-off? I think the equity is a clear and and a strong one. In Ex parte Edwards, there could be no purpose in directing the account, but with a view to allow it. Ordered according to the prayer of the petition.

(5*i*) Ex parte Edwards, 1 Atk. 100. A. D. 1745. The petitioner, being a creditor under a separate commission against A. and a debtor to a joint commission against A. and B. petitioned that the action brought by the assignees for the debt he owed to the joint commission might be stayed, and that his demand upon the separate estate might be allowed, as a set-off against the debt he owed the joint estate, especially as the same persons are assignees under both commissions. Lord Chancellor. I doubt whether the debt could be set-off under the statute relating to mutual debts; because different persons are concerned in one debt and in the other, and in distinct rights: but, as the petitioner's case appears to be a hard one, I will refer it to the commissioners of the bankrupts to see how much the petitioner owed to the joint estate, and how much was owing to him from the separate estate, and to certify the same to me, and let the action brought by the assignees be stayed, and, in the mean time, all further considerations reserved till the commissioners have certified. In Ex parte Quintin, 3 Vez. jun. 248. A. D. 1796, the Lord Chancellor says: In Ex parte Edwards, there could be no purpose in directing the account, but with a view to allow it.

PRACTICE.

In Practice, when an application is made to set-off judgments against each other by the party to whom the larger sum is due, the rule is for a stay of proceedings on acknowledging satisfaction for the lesser sum; but when the lesser sum is due to the party applying, the rule is to have it deducted, and for a stay of proceedings on payment of the balance.(5*k*)

The notice of set-off is usually written underneath the plea, and delivered therewith to the plaintiff's attorney; and a copy of the notice should be kept by the defendant's attorney, it being necessary to prove the delivery of it at the trial.(5*l*)

The plaintiff may demand a particular of the sum which the defendant intends to set-off.

(5*k*) Bull. N. P. 336. Say costs, 24. Tyd. K.B. 679. Tyd's costs, 66. Mitchell v. Oldfield, 4 T. R. 124. (App. 13.)
(5*l*) 1 Cromp. 160. Tyd K. B. 408.

APPENDIX.

Dobson and Another, Assignees of Patrick, against *E. Lockhart, K. B. H. T* *33 Geo. III. A. D.* 1793. 5 *Ter. Rep.* 133.

THIS was an action of *assumpsit* for goods sold and delivered by the bankrupt against the defendant as a surviving partner; to which the defendant pleaded, 1st. The general issue; 2dly. A set-off on a bond given by the bankrupt to the defendant, and *G. Lockhart*, his late partner; 3dly. (Another plea, not supported in fact;) 4thly. That on the 11th of October 1788 the bankrupt and the defendant became bound to *S. Nicholson*, and two other persons, in 900*l.* conditioned to pay 450*l.* with lawful interest on demand; that on the 16th May 1789, the bankrupt, one *Foster*, and the defendant, became bound to *J. Wakefield* and two other persons in 1000*l.* conditioned to pay 500*l.* and interest on the 1st of June 1789; that those two bonds were executed by the defendant as a surety for the bankrupt, and for his debt only; that before the bankruptcy, *ss.* on the 21st of May 1789, the bankrupt became bound to *G. Lockhart* and the defendant in 1400*l.* conditioned to pay 700*l.* on the 13th of February 1790; that the last bond was given for the purpose of indemnifying the defendant against the two former, and that the name of *G. Lockhart* was used merely as a trustee for the defendant; that afterwards, and after *Patrick* became a bankrupt, on the 14th of December 1789, the defendant was obliged to pay *Nicholson* and Co. 470*l.* on the first bond, and *Wakefield* and Co. 236*l.* 17*s.* on the second bond; that those two sums are still due to the defendant, and exceed the money due to the plaintiffs on the promises mentioned in the declaration, and that the defendant would set them off against the demand of the plaintiffs, &c. 5thly. (after stating the two first bonds as in the last plea, and that the defendant was merely a surety, *&c.*) that before the bankruptcy of *Patrick*, to wit, on the 21st of May 1789, it was agreed between the defendant and the bankrupt that, in order to indemnify the defendant against these two bonds, the latter should become bound to the former in 1400*l* conditioned to pay 700*l.* with interest on the 13th of February 1790, and as a further indemnity, that the defendant should retain and keep such money, not exceeding the money to be secured by the last bond, as should at any time be due from *G. L.* and the defendant to the bankrupt, in respect of any dealings between them in trade, until the two first bonds should be satisfied, and that the defendant should, out of the money which should be due from *G. L.* and himself to the bankrupt, retain and set-off so much money, not exceeding the last bond, as he should at any time pay on the two first bonds; that the bankrupt accordingly executed such bond for 1400*l.* &c. that after the bankruptcy, in December 1789, the defendant was obliged to pay to *Nicholson* and Co. and to *Wakefield* and Co. &c. (as in the last plea;) that the money due from the defendant to the bankrupt on the promises in the declaration was so due and owing to him for and on account of certain dealings between him and *G. L.* and the defendant in trade; and that the sums paid by the defendant on the two first bonds exceed the money due to the bankrupt &c. and that the defendant would set-off, &c. Replication to second plea, that at the time of bringing the action there was nothing due to the defendant on the bond, &c. to the 4th and 5th pleas, that the bankrupt was not indebted to the defendant in manner and form, &c,

On the trial at Appleby before Lord *Kenyon*, the facts contained in the last plea being proved, it was agreed that the plaintiff should be non-suited, he having liberty to move to enter up a verdict for him if this court should be of opinion that he was entitled to recover under these circumstances. A rule having been obtained in the last term, calling on the defendant to shew cause why the verdict should not be entered for the plaintiff, cause was now shewn against it by

Chambre, and *Lambe*, who contended that the defendant was entitled to a verdict, either on the general issue, or on the fourth or fifth pleas. First. On the general issue: though the assignees of a bankrupt are entitled to the benefit of all contracts made by the bankrupt, and may therefore recover the value of goods sold by him, they cannot vary those contracts, but, as representing the bankrupt, they are bound by every part of them. Now here the contract was that the price of these goods should remain in the defendant's hands until it was determined what would be the consequence of the surety-bonds given by him for the bankrupt; if those bonds were discharged by the bankrupt, then the defendant was to pay for these goods, but if the defendant were compelled to pay the bonds, then the money so paid was to be considered as a payment for the goods. This therefore was not a general sale of goods, but a special contract, by which time was given to the defendant, and until the happening of a particular event he was not to be called upon to pay for them. In the event that has happened the defendant must be considered as having paid for the goods according to the agreement, and of course the plaintiffs have no demand against him. Secondly. Considered on the special pleas, the defendant is entitled to a verdict on the ground of mutual credit between the bankrupt and the defendant. By "mutual credit" is meant "mutual trust and confidence." Here the bankrupt gave credit by selling the goods, and the defendant by becoming surety for the bankrupt. It is not necessary that the demand, which is to be set-off under the clause in the stat. 5 *Geo.* II. *c.* 30. respecting mutual credit, should arise before the bankruptcy, if the debt be paid afterwards in consequence of a liability before. *Grove* v. *Dubois*, *ante* 1 *vol.* 122; *Hankey* v. *Smith*, *ante* 3 *vol.* 507; *Smith* v. *Hodson*, *a.* 4 *vol.* 211; *French* v. *Fenn*, there cited; *Toussaint* v. *Martinnant*, *a.* 2 *vol.* 100; and *Martin* v. *Court*, *ib.* 640.

Law, *Holroyd*, and *Bell*, *contra*. This is distinguishable from the cases cited, because at the time of the bankruptcy it was uncertain whether or not there would be any debt from the defendant to the bankrupt; for if the bond were paid by the bankrupt, the defendant, who was a mere surety, would of course have been discharged. And it never has been held that a debt, which rested in contingency at the time of the bankruptcy, could be set-off. In *French* v. *Fenn*, and *Hankey* v. *Smith*, there was mutual credit; in the former, money had been advanced by the defendant in order to purchase goods, the profits arising from which were afterwards to be divided; and in the latter, the bankrupt had sold goods, and the defendant was in possession of a bill of exchange given by the bankrupt; that bill created a certain debt, not a contingent one like the present. The case of *Toussaint* v. *Martinnant* only decided that *assumpsit* would not lie, not that an action on the bond might have been supported. *Martin* v. *Court* was an action on an absolute bond which was proveable under the commission: there the counter-bond was made payable before the principal bond; and *Buller*, J. observed on it that it was the intention of the parties that the surety should have the money in his hands before he should be called upon. But here the defendant is not entitled to set-off, because the debt was not only uncertain at the time of the bankruptcy, but there was a time when, if the action had been brought by the assignees, the counter-demand by the defendant did not exist; and the set-off ought not to arise by matter *ex post facto*. But even if the debt from the bankrupt to the defendant were certain, still there was no mutual credit between them. This action is brought against the defendant, as a surviving partner, for goods sold to him and *G. Lockhart*: the defendant therefore cannot set-off a debt due to himself alone to a debt due from him and another person. Only those debts, which exist between the same parties and in the same right, can be set-off. Here credit was only given, on the one side, to the bankrupt by the defendant alone, and on the other by the bankrupt to the defendant and another person. As to the special pleas; there is one objection applicable to them both. It is stated that the two bonds were given by the defendant as a surety, and that the counter-bond was given by the bankrupt to the defendant to indemnify him: but that agreement cannot be considered as incorporated in the bond, because that would be to defeat the bond by an agreement of less solemnity than the bond itself; and if not, the agreement is void for want of a consideration; it was *nudum pactum*. And even if it could be considered as part of the bond, it is objectionable on another ground, that it was given as a security not for any balance then due, but for a floating balance to arise on an account not then in existence.

Lord KENYON, Ch. J. Some of the arguments urged at the bar go beyond the question now for decision; there being one short ground, on which we cannot be mistaken, in saying that the case is in favour of the defendant. This is an action for goods sold and delivered by the bankrupt to the defendant; and the question is whether the plaintiffs, who are the assignees of the bankrupt, have a right, under all the circumstances of the case, to exact payment for the goods. The defendant had various transactions with the bankrupt; among others, he became security for him in two several sums of money; and at the time of becoming such security the latter engaged that the defendant should not be called upon to pay for the goods until he was indemnified against those bonds. That agreement having been proved, I see no objection to it in point of law; I think it is a good defence to this action under the general issue, and that the defendant need not have pleaded it specially. The consequence is that the plaintiffs have brought this action to enforce payment of a sum of money, which the defendant is not bound either in law or conscience to pay under these circumstances.

ASHHURST, J. This case falls within the statue 5 *Geo.* II. *c.* 30. *s.* 28, which enacts that, where there have been either mutual credits or mutual debts between the bankrupt and any other person, before the bankruptcy, the commissioners shall state the account between them, and one debt may be set-off against another; and what shall appear to be due on either side on the balance of such account, and no more, shall be claimed. But it has been contended that the agreement in this case must be so restrained in its construction that the defendant is not entitled to retain any money that he should pay, under the surety-bonds, after the bankruptcy. The intention of the parties, however, in making this contract was that the defendant should not pay for the goods until he was indemnified against any payment he should make upon either of the bonds; he had a security deposited in his hands; and though, in fact, he was not damnified until after the bankruptcy, yet the payment under this agreement has a retrospect to, and must be considered as if made before, the bankruptcy. It is true that, generally speaking, a creditor of the bankrupt cannot prove any debt under the commission that does not become due before the bankruptcy; but this agreement and bond take this case out of the general rule; and though the defendant was not called upon to pay either of the bonds, which he had executed as surety for the bankrupt, until after the bankruptcy, yet he may have recourse to a security which has a retrospect to a time antecedent to the bankruptcy.

BULLER, J. I agree with the plaintiffs' counsel that there is no case in which it has been held that, where it depends on some future event which does not take place until after the bankruptcy whether or not there will be any debt against the bankrupt, the debt can either be proved under the commission, or set-off against a demand made by the assignees. But that is not like the present case. The question here arises not on the set-off, but on the plaintiffs' demand; and it must be considered in the same light as an action brought by the assignees to recover goods sold by the bankrupt, he having given a day of payment; if goods be sold, and twelve months' credit be given by the seller, he cannot maintain an action until that time be expired. Now in this case the goods were sold on the express condition that the defendant should not pay for them till the bonds were discharged by the bankrupt; those bonds were not discharged by him, but the defendant was obliged to satisfy them, and therefore the plaintiffs cannot maintain their action; for according to the terms of the original contract they have no cause of action. It has been argued however that the defendant could not, by virtue of this agreement, have a lien on a floating balance; whatever may be the general rule respecting such a lien where there is no agreement, there is no reason why the parties may not by express agreement make a lien on a floating balance; and here they have done so.

GROSE, J. I am sorry to see such an action as this brought by the assignees of a bankrupt in a case where it is impossible to doubt about the justice of the case, even though there were any doubt about the law respecting it. But I think that the plaintiffs' demand is as clearly against law as it is against conscience. This question does not depend on the statutes of set-off, but on the original agreement between the parties, which (I think) entitles the defendant to a verdict under the general issue. To an action for goods sold by the bankrupt the defendant answers that he is not liable to pay because before the sale he had become a surety in two bonds for the bankrupt who, in order to indemnify the defendant, engaged that he should retain any money that should be due from him to the bankrupt, in respect of any dealings between them in trade, until those bonds should be satisfied, and that he should retain out of such money whatever he should pay on those bonds; it appears that in fact he has paid as co-obligee of these bonds more than the value of the goods in question, and yet the assignees now insist that he shall pay for the goods themselves. But on this state of the case no money is due under the agreement; and consequently the plaintiffs are not entitled to recover.

Per Curiam. Judgment of nonsuit.

Sturdy and Another, Assignees of Blakiston a Bankrupt, against *Arnaud, K. B. E. T.* 30 *Geo. III. A. D.* 1790. 3 *Ter. Rep.* 599.

DEBT on a bond from the defendant to the bankrupt before his bankruptcy, dated 27th September 1788, conditioned for the payment of an annuity of 100*l.* by quarterly payments by the defendant to the bankrupt. The defendant pleaded that at the time of commencing this action only four quarterly payments were due; that on the 29th September 1788, and before this action was brought, and also before the bankruptcy, the defendant had lent 200*l.* bearing interest, to the bankrupt and another on their promissory note, payable on demand; that the bankrupt, before his bankruptcy, agreed, and, *by a writing under his hand* of the same date, *authorised and empowered the defendant to retain out of the annuity*, as the same should become due, the 200*l.* and interest; which 200*l.* and the interest still remain due in arrear and unpaid, otherwise than by retaining the same out of the annuity so due; and that the arrears of that annuity are still insufficient to satisfy the same. The plaintiffs replied the bankruptcy of *Blakiston* after the above authority given, and the assignment of his effects to the plaintiffs before either of the quarterly payments of the annuity became due. To this replication there was a demurrer and joinder in demurrer.

Holroyd was to have argued in support of the demurrer; but the Court desired *Shepherd*, on the other side, to begin; who contended, First. That the defendant had no right to retain the arrears of this annuity against the debt due by him to the bankrupt, on the ground that the agreement operates as a defeasance, because there can be no defeasance to a deed by a mere writing not under seal. *Blemerhasset* v. *Pierson*, 3 *Lev.* 234. Secondly. Neither could the defendant retain on the ground of a lien; for in all the cases where that defence has been allowed, something existed which was put into the hands of the creditor, as a bill of lading, a policy of insurance, a bond, or the like; but here nothing existed, which could be deposited with the defendant. Thirdly. Still less can this retainer be supported on the ground of a set-off. The agreement was a mere authority to retain the payments of an annuity *if* they became due: but none of those payments were due at the time of the bankruptcy, and it was contingent whether or not any would become due, it depending on the defendant's life. This therefore was nothing more than a contingency which could not have been proved under the commission of bankrupt; and consequently cannot be set-off.

Lord KENYON, Ch. J. The doctrine of lien and of set-off bears no relation to the question now before us; and indeed I should be sorry for the plaintiffs themselves if the law were with them, since their conduct is so unconscientious that if the defendant were to apply to a court of equity for relief, that court would not only give such relief, but would also decree the plaintiffs to pay the costs both in law and equity; on the same principle on which Sir *Thomas Moore*, when Lord Chancellor, proceeded when he first gave relief against the penalty of the bond, the obligee in that case having paid the sum mentioned in the condition after, though not on, the day. This is an action brought on a bond, which was made for securing the payment of an annuity at certain times in the year; and before the time of the first instalment the obligor lent to the obligee 200*l.* in order to secure the repayment of which he entered into this agreement, stated in the plea, by which he was authorised to retain the payments of the annuity from time to time till the 200*l.* and interest should be paid. But in answer to this it is said that these payments did not become due till after the bankruptcy of the obligee, and that therefore they cannot be retained against his assignees. Now in justice and conscience it is impossible to raise any doubt; neither is there any doubt in point of law; for the condition of the bond has not been broken, and consequently no action can be maintained upon it. It cannot be said that the condition has been broken, when it appears that payment has been made according to the terms of it. For though this is not a formal plea of *solvit ad diem*, yet it is equivalent to it. But it is said that this cannot be so considered, because the assignees had a right to those payments which became due after the bankruptcy: but they have only that property to which the bankrupt is entitled, and they must take it subject to his equity; and here those payments were anticipated.

ASHHURST, J. The defence stated in the plea does not contradict the annuity bond; on the contrary, it is perfectly consistent with it, and proceeds on the supposition of there being such a bond. The plea affirms the bond, and specifies the mode by which the money lent to the obligee was to be repaid, namely, by retaining the payments secured by the annuity bond. And it was competent to the bankrupt to enter into such an agreement before his bankruptcy.

BULLER, J. This case does not want the assistance of an act of parliament, or of a court of equity. There is indeed an old case which said that payment *before* the day would not discharge the bond. But, in the first place, that case has been frequently over-ruled; and if it were still law, it would not govern this case; because it has been held that the obligor may plead it as payment *at* the day, and this would be evidence of such payment.

GROSE, J. declared himself of the same opinion.

Judgment for the defendant.

James v. *Kynnier*, *In Chan. A.D.* 1799. 5 *Ves. Jun.* 108.

IN 1789 *Rice James* and *Richard Beckford* carrying on business in partnership in London as merchants, borrowed 19,000*l.* on their joint and several bonds; and for further security assigned a mortgage upon an estate in Jamaica for 45,000*l.*— Of the money borrowed 2,500*l.* was advanced by the house of *Hutchinson*, *Robert* and *William Mure*.

In May 1793, an agreement was entered into for the sale of *James*' interest in the partnership to *James English Keighley*, for 30,500*l.* payable by instalments. This agreement, though consented to at a meeting of the creditors, was not completed till 1797; when the deeds were executed, and the bonds of *Beckford* and *Keighley* were exchanged for those of *James* and *Beckford*, except the bond for the debt of 2,500*l.* to the *Mures*; but the money was deposited by *Keighley* at a banker's. In October 1793, the *Mures* applying for payment of their bond, *Beckford* said, it was not then convenient; upon which they requested that they might be accommodated with such sum of 2,500*l.* as a loan, to be repaid at a future period.— *Keighley* offered to lend part of the money deposited by him in pursuance of the agreement for the purchase of *James*' share in the partnership, if *James* would consent. *Robert Mure* accordingly upon the 21st of October wrote to *James*; stating their want of money, the application to *Beckford* to relieve them "by an application to Mr. *Keighley* to take up your debt to us secured upon *William Beckford's* estate either wholly, or to accommodate us with the amount upon our engaging to repay it at a future period: this latter mode *Beckford* told me would be most agreeable to him; and that he would mention it to *Keighley*."

This letter proceeded to state that *Keighley* had no other money disengaged but what is lying at the banker's to be paid to *James* upon the signature of the deeds; but professes himself ready to accommodate them, provided *James* will give his consent to his appropriating so much of the money to that purpose.

Upon this letter *James* came to London, and received from *Keighley* 2,500*l* which he immediately, upon the 24th of October 1793, delivered to the *Mures*; and he received from them a promissory note for that amount, payable to him three months after date. Upon the 31st of December 1793, the *Mures* became bankrupt.

Since 1793, the interest upon the debt to the *Mures* was paid up to 1797, by *Beckford* and *Keighley*, or by *Keighley* after the death of *Beckford*.

The bill was filed by *James*; praying, that it may be declared that the sum of 2,500*l.* paid by the plaintiff to the *Mures*, was a payment or part payment of the debt then owing to them from the plaintiff and *Beckford*; or that the plaintiff is entitled to have such payment set-off against such debt; that an account may be taken of what remains due after allowing such payment or set-off; and that upon payment of the balance by the plaintiff, the assignees of the *Mures* may be decreed to deliver up the bond, and to assign their interest in the mortgage to the plaintiff.

The bill stated, that as there remained an unsettled account respecting the interest of the said debt of 2,500*l.* no final discharge was given to the plaintiff upon his paying over the money to the *Mures*; and therefore by way of acknowledgment for the receipt of that sum he received their promissory note; by means whereof the principal debt was paid off; and nothing remained owing in respect of the said debt except some small sum for interest at that time owing.

The defendants, the assignees, by their answer stated, that they believe, the *Mures* at the time of the application to *Beckford* intended, that the money, which should be advanced in consequence, should be in discharge of the debt due to them; but that the plaintiff advanced the same as a distinct loan from himself to them, and took a note accordingly; and for that reason, not for that in the bill mentioned, no final discharge was given upon that occasion for the debt of 2,500*l.* due from *Beckford* and *James*; and that ever since May 1793, *Keighley* has not only been understood to be the debtor instead of the plaintiff to all the creditors of the house, but has actually been in possession jointly with *Beckford* of the effects of the partnership.

The defendants therefore insisted that the plaintiff ought not to be considered as interested in the said debt of 2,500*l.* as surviving partner of *Beckford*; and as assignees of the *Mures* they claim the whole debt; contending, that the advancement of that money to the bankrupts was no payment or part payment of the debt; and the plaintiff is entitled only to prove that sum under the commission.

The book-keeper of the partnership by his depositions stated, that the bond to the *Mures* had not been exchanged, because *Keighley* did not know who had a right to it. He also stated, that the instalments of the purchase-money for the sale of the plaintiff's share were paid by *Beckford* and *Keighley* out of the funds arising from the property of the late house of *Beckford* and *James* and monies provided by *Keighley*.

The Attorney General, Mr. Mansfield, and Mr. Steele for the plaintiff, after mentioning *Ex parte Quintin* (*a*), *French* v. *Fenn* (*b*), *Ex parte Prescot* (*c*), and Lord *Kenyon's* opinion in *Smith* v. *Hodson* (*d*) in support of the conclusion, that to sustain a set-off in equity there need not be strictly mutual debts, where there is clear mutual credit, (*e*) were stopped by the Court.

Lord CHANCELLOR. Is there any doubt, that, where there are upon account mutual credits between two parties, though they cannot set-off at law, yet it is the common ground of a bill? If *James* had brought an action against *Mure* upon the note supposing no bankruptcy had taken place, I should have stopped that action, while he was debtor upon the bond. When there comes a case of bankruptcy, it is much stronger. Between solvent persons, there might be a ground to say, Indulgence was given, the credit extended; and therefore that credit ought to be continued. But the moment a bankruptcy comes the account is to be settled. They might sue *Beckford's* executors at law: but I should stop the action. Therefore there is a clear mutual credit.

The Solicitor General, Mr. Cox, and Mr. Mure for the defendants.—It is unnecessary to controvert, that your Lordship would allow an equitable set-off, if there were either mutual debts or mutual credits: but this is a case neither of mutual debts nor mutual credits in equity. This debt was one of those, which by the agreement in 1793 *Keighley*, took upon himself. The plaintiff was from that moment completely released; though his name remained upon the bond. The debt was wholly transferred. Though the bond was not exchanged, the agreement

(*a*) *Ante*, vol. 3. 248. (*b*) 1 *Cook's Bank. Law*, 569 (*c*) 1 *Atk.* 231.
(*d*) 4 *Term Rep. B. R.* 211. (*e*) See more authorities collected 1 *Cook's Bank. Law*, 568.

extended to this debt as well as the rest; and after that agreement your Lordship would not have permitted *James* to be sued. He was therefore a mere stranger as to that bond at the time of the transaction of the note. Then the *Mures* apply for payment, not to *James*, but to *Beckford* and *Keighley*. The case first attempted by the bill was, that the money was paid in the discharge of the bond. That is now given up; and it is admitted that another arrangement took place. The proposition was, that *Keighley*, not *James*, should advance the money; and the question was, whether *Keighley* should be authorised for that accommodation to use the sum which he had deposited for the purchase of *James'* share. If that transaction had taken place, and *Keighley* had, instead of making the payment, taken a note, all this equity would have arisen between him and the *Mures*; upon this ground, that upon the consideration that he was bound to pay the bond, he agreed to pay the money. But what was done was not in pursuance of that; for the plaintiff thought fit to take up part of that sum from *Keighley's* banker. That became his money; and he chose to lend it to the *Mures* for their accommodation. In what sense is the plaintiff indebted to the *Mures?* Whatever was the consideration, that did not make a mutual credit. In *French* v. *Fenn* there were direct mutual credits between two persons themselves. In *Ex parte Quintin* all your Lordship did was to get over the point of form. There could not have been a set-off at law; but the partner, who would have been entitled to a moiety of the clear surplus, was himself debtor individually to the petitioners. There were clear mutual debts; and the only difficulty was as to the form of the action at law. But it is not upon any difficulty of that kind that we rest, but that after the purchase of *James'* interest there was no mutual debt or credit between *James* and *Mure*, but only between *Keighley* and *Mure;* and what *James* did was only for the accommodation of his former partnership, himself not being liable, or even asked for payment. They only desired him to permit *Keighley* to lend so much of that money; but he says, he will himself do it.

Lord CHANCELLOR. I have not a particle of doubt upon this case; which is the clearest I ever heard. It might have been matter of consideration, whether the bill should be filed by *Keighley* or *James;* and I rather think the equity of the former the more pregnant and obvious, for with the knowledge of the *Mures* he has paid part of the consideration, for which, he was to make himself liable to the debts, through the medium of *James*. Giving up the bond will put an end to the suit completely; and I may as well make the declaration upon this bill as any other.

At the time of this transaction the *Mures* had not accepted *Keighley*, nor given up that particular bond. The transaction of the change of the partnership was not then a completed transaction. Under these circumstances *Keighley* going on with the purchase had money applicable to the settlement of that transaction, when the business could be finished. The application was made to *James*, that he would agree, that money should go to the relief of the *Mures*, creditors of the partnership. The mode, in which he does it, is by taking this note. The transaction going on between *Keighley* and him, I never would let him proceed upon that note. The fact is beyond a doubt, that the partnership effects of *Beckford* and *James* have paid this debt to the *Mures*. The decree must be according to the prayer of the bill, without costs; I cannot make the assignees pay costs. The plaintiff must pay the defendant *Keighley* his costs. If any thing is due to the plaintiff, he must come in as a creditor. The note must be delivered up.

Thrustout on the Demise of Barnes v. *Crafter*. *C. P. T. T.* 12 *Geo. III.* 2 *Blacks. Rep.* 826.

BARNES, the lessor of the plaintiff, had a judgment last Michaelmas term, for 40*l.* 5*s.* against the defendant, for his debt and costs, on an action, for the use and occupation of the premises; but was non-suited in the present cause, the *Hilary* term afterwards; the costs of which are taxed at 12*l.* 5*s.* for non-payment of which, an attachment is taken out against the plaintiff.

Now *Sayer* for the plaintiff moved, that the 12*l.* 5*s.* might be deducted out of the 40*l.* 5*s.* and proceedings, on the attachment, be stayed.

Walker shewed for cause, that it was a new attempt, to set-off mutual debts due on judgment. That the statute relates only to mutual debts at the time of trial, upon an action of debt, or in such a case, wherein action of debt would lie. But this is an application to stop the execution of the law. There is also a difference in the nature of the executions themselves. One for debt as well as costs, for which an action would lie on the judgment; the other for costs only, to be recovered by process of contempt.

Sayer, in support of the rule, cited *Tulo* and *Lowe*, 16 *Geo.* II. 1 *Barn.* 102.—*Scoffin* and *Robinson*, 26 *Geo.* II. 2 *Barn.* 128, a rule, for deducting costs of one verdict, from those of another. And, if the court will set-off costs at common law; *a fortiori*, they will do it under a rule for judgment as in case of non-suit.—Also *Roberts* and *Figgs*, 28 *Geo.* II. 2 *Barn. Suppl.* 12. And *Roberts* and *Macoul*, *Trin* 9 *Geo.* III. a rule to shew cause, why thirteen guineas costs, taxed against the plaintiff in a former cause, should not be set-off against sixteen guineas costs, recovered against the defendant in this cause. It was shewn for cause, that the plaintiff was insolvent; and, that his attorney had a lien upon these costs for his bill. But it was held, by *Wilmot* chief justice *et Cur.* that the attorney's lien was, only upon what the plaintiff was entitled to have, *viz.* the difference.

And, by *De Grey* chief justice, *Gould*, *Blackstone*, and *Nares*, justices, the cases cited have settled the point; and on the justest ground.—Rule absolute.

Barker adminstratrix v. *Braham*, *C. P. H. T.* 13 *Geo.* III. 2 *Blacks.* 869. *S. C.* 3 *Wils.* 396.

THERE being due to the defendant *Braham* 102*l.* 18*s.* 1*d.* from the plantiff as administratrix of her husband, on the judgment recovered in the *King's Bench* in *Hil.* 1769, (as stated in the preceding case) the plaintiff, in the same right as administratrix, brought this action against *Braham* in this court for a debt due to the intestate, and had a verdict for 106*l.* 9*s.* 6*d.* last Trinity term, and judgment thereupon. Now in last Michaelmas term, *Sayer* for the defendant moved, that the said 102*l.* 18*s.* 1*d.* might be deducted out of the 106*l.* 9*s.* 6*d.* and on payment of the balance to the plaintiff with costs, execution might be stayed.

Davy and *Burland* were prepared to shew cause; but having informed the court, that there was a writ of error then pending in the *Exchequer Chamber*, on the suit *Braham* and *Barker* administratrix in the *King's Bench* (which was sworn not to be brought for delay, but upon real error) the court enlarged the rule till the second Monday in this term.

In the mean time the defendant *Braham* (having discovered the error in the record of the court of *King's Bench*) had leave to amend, whereupon that judgment was affirmed.

And now it was shewn for cause against the present rule, that it was a new attempt, and went beyond the statute, which only allows a set-off to be pleaded or given in evidence on the *trial*; but does not allow one judgment to be set-off against another. And that in the present case, it might possibly entangle the plaintiff in a *devastavit*, as there may be debts of a higher nature than this judgment. Besides, the former judgment being given in the court of *King's Bench*, this court can take no cognizance of it; for a question may arise in that court, whether *Braham's* whole debt was not satisfied, by the *ca. sa.* (though illegal) which she there sued out against *Barker*.

Sayer and *Glyn* in support of the rule, insisted, that this would have been allowed had the intestate been living; and the same rule will hold for the administratrix.—That there is no reason to preclude this motion now, because the debt was not pleaded or set-off at the trial. In *Thrustout on the demise of Barnes* and *Crafter* in this court last *Trinity* term, the costs of one judgment of non-suit in this court were ordered to be deducted out of the debt and costs of another judgment—and this court will also take notice of judgments in other courts, as by staying proceedings in ejectment here, till costs of nonsuit in ejectment in the *King's Bench*, are paid. Nor can there be any *devastavit*; for this money, if stopped by the court will never come to *Barker's* hands. And it is impossible to suppose, that any court can determine, that a taking on a *void ca. sa.* is satisfaction of the debt.

De Grey, chief justice. This case is singularly circumstanced. Each party is entitled to an execution against the other. The question is, whether this court will narrow the plaintiff's execution here, because she is liable to the defendant's execution for a less sum in another court.

The common law was very narrow in its principles with respect to stoppage or set-offs: very different from the *Roman* law of compensation, which proceeded on a more liberal plan. This our courts of equity adopted, made just allowances to each side, and struck the balance. *Jeffs* and *Wood* 2 *Wms.* 128. But there was not any legal interposition of this kind, till the bankrupt laws, 4 & 5 *Ann.* 5 *Geo.* 1. and 5 *Geo.* 2.

The statute 2 *Geo.* 2. allowed set-off to be pleaded or given in evidence at the trial. In the construction of this statute, Lord *Hardwicke*, Chief Justice, differed from *Eyre*, Chief Justice, with regard to setting-off debts of superior nature against inferior, and *vice versa*. This occasioned the stat. 8 *Geo.* 2.

The courts have gone a little further than the letter of the statutes, by the rule of analogy, in cases within their power. Costs have been long set-off against costs; ——and in *Barnes* and *Crafter* the court allowed *costs* to be set-off against *debt* and *costs*. The present case goes a step farther; it is an application to us to *restrain* and *narrow* our own process of execution, by the same equitable rule. Doubtless this judgment in the *King's Bench* might have been pleaded or given in evidence. But that is no reason why we should not allow it now; and no mischief can follow from allowing it. No *devastavit* can happen, unless the plaintiff *Barker* knows of any superior debt; and, if she knows it, she might disclose it and shew it for cause. The same answer may be given to the strange supposition of the debt's being satisfied, by executing a void *ca. sa.* for which *Barker* has been amply repaid in damages. If it has been so determined, she might have shewn that for cause. I am therefore for allowing the present motion; but desire it may be remembered that this is a case of one judgment against another, both in the same right; and must be distinguished from setting-off private debts, not in suit, and upon which no judgment has been obtained.

Gould, Justice of the same opinion.

Blackstone, Justice concurred. The courts have been gradually extending this equitable remedy. In the out-set of a suit they compel the plaintiff to make a set-off in the affidavit to hold to bail, and will not suffer him to swear to one side only of the account. So in costs at the close of the suit, the same reason and the same analogy extend to set-off mutual judgments, and thereby narrow the greater execution, in whatever court it happens to be.

Nares, Justice of the same opinion. There can be no clashing of jurisdictions in this case, for we do not meddle with the process of any court but our own.

Rule absolute.

Glaister v. *Hewer, and two Others. M. T.* 39 *Geo. III.* 8 *Ter. Rep.* 69.

THE plaintiff brought an action of trover against the defendants, who suffered judgment to go by default, and on executing a writ of enquiry the jury gave 40*l.* damages. Afterwards the defendants sued the plaintiff, and recovered 36*l.* 13*s.* 6*d.* Whereupon the defendants obtained a rule, calling on the plaintiff to shew cause why the proceedings in the former action should not be stayed on the defendant's undertaking to deduct and allow to the plaintiff 40*l.* the amount of the damages recovered by him, and the costs when they should be ascertained by the Master, by entering a remittitur for the amount of such damages on the record in the action brought by the defendants, on an affidavit that the sum of 36*l.* 13*s.* 6*d.* (the damages recovered by the defendants) together with the costs of the latter action which had not yet been taxed would, when taxed, considerably exceed the damages and costs recovered by the plaintiff against them.

Gibbs and *Park* now shewed cause against that rule. 1st. At all events the rule is too general, because the plaintiff's attorney has a lien on the judgment recovered by him for his costs, which ought not to be disturbed in a dispute between the parties. (*Law*, who was on the other side, admitted that this rule must be subject to the attorney's lien.) 2dly. The defendants are not entitled to set-off their judgment against that which the plaintiff recovered against them, because the plaintiff has another demand against *Hewer* one of the defendants.(*a*) In the case of *Mitchel* v. *Oldfield*,(*b*) where the plaintiff had recovered a judgment against the defendant, the court permitted the latter to set-off a judgment which he had recovered against the plaintiff *and another person* against the judgment obtained against him. Then by a parity of reason, as the plaintiff has a separate demand against one of the defendants in this case, it will be unjust that the defendants should set-off their judgment against that recovered by the plaintiff without also taking this second demand into the account. This is an application to the equitable jurisdiction of the court, who will therefore be guided by the rule that is adopted in a court of equity, that he who asks equity must do equity. But

The court thought that this would be carrying the rule too far; for that the effect of discharging this rule would be to subject the two other defendants to the payment of a separate debt of *Hewer*.

Rule absolute.(*c*)

O'Connor v. *Murphy*, *T. T.* 31 *Geo. III. A. D.* 1791. 1 *Hen. Blacks.* 657.

A RULE was obtained by ADAIR, Serj. to shew cause why the costs of a nonsuit in an action of trover, brought by *Murphy*, the present defendant, against one *O'Loughlin*, should not be set-off against the costs of a nonsuit in this cause; it appeared that the action of trover had been brought for a ship claimed by *Murphy*, but which proved to be the joint property of *O'Connor* the present plaintiff, and one *O'Sullivan*, (who were partners in trade) and of which *O'Loughlin* was the master. The present action was brought by *O'Connor* as indorsee of a promissory note against *Murphy* as drawer, in which *O'Connor* was nonsuited: and he now made this application, upon the ground, that the action against *O'Loughlin* was defended at the joint expense of *O'Connor* and *O'Sullivan*, and that *O'Sullivan* was interested together with *O'Connor* in the promissory note, on which the present action was brought, MARSHALL, Serj. shewed cause; he said the courts had in several instances (*d*) after the statute of set-off, refused to allow the costs of one action to be set-off against those of another; and the reason then given was, that it required the assistance of an act of parliament to enable the defendant in action to set-off a mutual debt, and that act did not extend to the case of costs. Afterwards, however, by a sort of equitable interpretation of the statute, the court allowed the costs of cross actions to be set agaist each other. But they had never allowed this to be done, where the costs were not mutual debts, and for the recovery of which there were not mutual remedies: for, had they gone beyond that, they would have extended this equitable construction of the statute further in a case for which it was evidently not intended than in those cases for which it was expressly made. As *O'Sullivan* did not join in the action on the promissory note, he ought not now to be permitted to say that he was interested in it merely to entitle himself to the benefit of a set-off; and as *Murphy* had a remedy only against *O'Connor* for the costs of the present nonsuit, those costs were a debt due from *O'Connor* alone, and not jointly from *O'Connor* and *O'Sullivan*. Therefore, supposing the costs of the action of trover could be taken as a debt due from *Murphy* to *O'Connor* and *O'Sullivan* jointly, yet even then the costs of the two nonsuits could not be deemed mutual debts. This he said distinguished this case from *Nunez* v. *Modigliani*, ante 217, and *Schoole* v. *Noble*, ante 23. Besides, *Murphy* could not bring an action against *O'Connor* and *O'Sullivan* jointly for the costs of the present nonsuit, neither could any person but *O'Loughlin* sue *Murphy* for the costs of the former one. The costs therefore of the two nonsuits could not by any means be taken to be mutual debts. The cases of *Paynter* v. *Walken*, *C. B. East* 4. *Geo.* III *Bull. N. P.* 179. *Ryal* v. *Larkin*, 1 *Wils.* 155, and *Ridout* v. *Brough*, *Cowp.* 133, shew that under the statutes of set-off, where the defendant has an equitable claim on the plaintiff, however

(*a*) It appeared in an affidavit produced on shewing cause that *Hewer*, one of the defendants, was indebted to the plaintiff in 67*l.* on two promissory notes drawn by *Hewer*, one payable to the plaintiff, and the other to *Smith* and Co. or order, and by them indorsed to the plaintiff.

(*b*) *Ante*, 4 vol. 123.

(*c*) Subject to the lien of the plaintiff's attorney; and it was referred to the Master to see what was the extent of that lien.

(*d*) 2 St. 1203.

clear and just; yet if an action will not lie for it, at the suit of the defendant *alone*, and *in his own right*, it cannot be deemed a mutual debt, and therefore cannot be set-off.(a)

Lord LOUGHBOROUGH stopped *Adair*, who was going to reply, and said, that without any regard to *O'Sullivan's* interest in the promissory note, *O'Connor* was equitably entitled to the costs of the nonsuit in the action of trover against *O'Loughlin*, and therefore he ought to be permitted to set them off, as far as they would go, against the costs in the present action.

Rule absolute.

Schoole v. *Noble, Lett, and Byrne. T. T.* 28 *Geo. III. A. D.* 1788. 1 *Hen. Blacks.* 23.

THE plaintiff brought trespass against the defendants for breaking and entering his house, &c. Defendants *Lett* and *Byrne* had suffered judgment to go by default. *Noble* went on to trial, and obtained a verdict. *Damages* were assessed against *Lett* and *Byrne* at one halfpenny each. On which, RUNNINGTON, Serj. obtained a rule to shew cause why the costs which might be taxed against *Lett* and *Byrne* on the judgment by default, and the damages assessed, should not be deducted out of the costs taxed to *Noble* on the postea, and allowed to the plaintiffs, and in the mean time execution against them stayed.

This was moved on an affidavit, stating that the defendants *Lett* and *Byrne* had acted under the authority of *Noble*, who had undertaken to pay the damages and costs.

BOND, Serj. against the rule, said that this was a new application, and against justice, in as much as it tended to deprive the attorney of that lien on the costs, to which he was legally intitled. But

The court held that the attorney could only have such a lien on the costs as was subject to the equitable claims of the parties in the cause, and therefore made the

Rule absolute.

Vaughan v. *Davies.* 2 *Hen. Blacks.* 440. *H. T.* 35 *Geo. III. A. D.* 1795.

THE plaintiff recovered a verdict for 200*l.* against the defendant in an action of trespass for taking his goods, and the defendant had previously obtained judgment against the plaintiff, on a bond for 2000*l.* who was surrendered in execution of that judgment. And now on the motion of BOND, Serj. a rule was granted to shew cause, why it should not be referred to the prothonotary to take an account of the damages recovered on the verdict obtained by the plaintiff, and tax his costs thereon, and why the defendant should not be discharged from the payment of such damages and costs, when so ascertained and taxed, upon his entering satisfaction for the amount thereof on the judgment recovered by him, in part discharge of that judgment. 2 *Blacks.* 826. *Thrustout* v. *Crafter, ante vol.* 1. 23. *Schoole* v. *Noble*, 217. *Nunez* v. *Modigliani*, 657. *O'Connor* v. *Murphy.*

ADAIR Serj. shewed cause, on the part of the attorney for the plaintiff, on affidavits, stating that he had no fund to resort to but the sum recovered by the plaintiff for the payment of his bill, the plaintiff himself being insolvent, the set-off therefore ought not to be allowed, till the attorney's bill was satisfied. He said that the court would protect an attorney who was their officer, who would otherwise be without remedy, and that in the court of *King's Bench* the equitable right of setting off the sum recovered in one action against that recovered in another, was always subject to the attorney's lien for his bill, for which he cited *Mitchell* v. *Oldfield*, 4 *Term Rep. B. R.* 123. and *Moreland* v. *Lashley, B. R. Trin.* 34 *Geo.* III. But

On this day, after consideration, the court said that the attorney's lien did not extend to prevent the parties in the cause from having the benefit of the set-off which was applied for in this case, and therefore made the

Rule absolute.

BULLER, J. mentioned that a similar decision had taken place this term in the court of *Chancery*, in a case of *Barton* v. *Etherington.*

(a) But see those cases, and qu. whether they support this proposition in its fu extent.

Morland and Hammersley v. *Lashley*. *Same* v. *Lashley and Ux*. *T. T.* 34 *Geo. III.* 2 *Hen. Blacks*. 441.

BOTH these causes were tried at the sittings *Tr.* 34 *Geo.* III. The first was an action upon the separate bond of the defendant; the second upon the joint bond of the defendant and his wife. In the first, the plaintiff obtained a verdict, and in the second was nonsuited. In the same term, *Henderson*, on the part of the plaintiff, obtained a rule to shew cause why the costs of the nonsuit should not be deducted from the sum given by the verdict in the first cause.

Palmer shewed cause, contending on the authority of *Mitchell* v. *Oldfield*, 4 *Term Rep. B. R.* 123, that the attorney for the defendants had a lien on the judgment for his costs. In support of the rule *Henderson* cited *Barker* v. *Braham*, 3 *Wils*. 396, and attempted to distinguish the present case from *Mitchell* v. *Oldfield*, because there were different attornies in the different causes in that case, but here the attorney was the same in both. But

Lord KENYON said that circumstance made no difference between the cases, and as to the case in *Wilson*, it did not there appear that any application was made on the part of the attorney. That an attorney had a lien on the judgment for his costs, which it would be unjust in the court to take from him. The rule therefore was made absolute, with a reservation of the attorney's lien. But as his costs were equal to the costs of the nonsuit, the rule was afterwards abandoned.(*a*)

Dennie v. *Elliott*, *Hill*, *and another*. *M. T.* 36 *Geo. III.* 2 *Hen. Blacks*. 587. *A. D.* 1795.

IN this case a rule was granted to shew cause why execution for the damages and costs recovered by the plaintiff in this cause, amounting to the sum of 52*l*. should not be stayed, the defendant *Hill* undertaking to stay all proceedings on the judgment by him obtained in another action brought by the plaintiff, wherein *Hill* had his costs taxed at the sum of 43*l*. 19*s*. 3*d*. and also undertaking to pay to the plaintiff or his attorney the sum of 8*l*. 9*d*. being the balance due to the plaintiff, after setting-off the costs so due to the defendant *Hill* from the plaintiff, on an affidavit by *Hill*, that the plaintiff appeared to be insolvent, that his goods were all distrained for rent, and that he himself was not to be met with.

In opposition to the rule, *Le Blanc*, Serjeant, produced an affidavit of the plaintiff, stating that *Hill* had told him that *Elliot*, one of the other defendants, was to indemnify *Hill*, as having acted under his orders, and that the plaintiff had offered not to take out execution against *Hill*. The attorney for the plaintiff also made an affidavit that he had no security for his costs, which the plaintiff was unable to pay, and which he verily believed he should lose, if the set-off were allowed, as he had no chance of recovering them, but out of the damages and costs to be received under the judgment for the plaintiff.

Le Blanc also relied on the practice of the court of *King's Bench*, and cited *Mitchell* v. *Oldfield*, 4 Term Rep. B. R. 123, and *Randle* v. *Fuller*, 6 Term Rep. B. R. 456.

In support of the rule, *Bond*, serjeant, insisted on the known practice in this court, that the attorney's lien for his costs was subject to the equitable claims of the parties in the cause, which he said was settled in the cases of *Schoole* v. *Noble*, ante vol. 1. 23; *Nunez* v. *Modigliani*, 217; *O'Connor* v. *Murphy*, 657; and *Vaughan* v. *Davies*, vol. 2. 440.

The court held the practice here to be clearly established by those cases, whatever might be the rule in the *King's Bench*, and therefore that it was not now to be disputed.

Rule absolute.

Hall v. *Ody*, 2 *Pull. and Bos.* 29. *M. T.* 40 *Geo. III. A. D.* 1799.

COCKELL, Serjeant, this day shewed cause against a rule nisi, for setting-off the costs of an action of ejectment recovered by the present defendant, against the present plaintiff in the *King's Bench*, against the costs of an action of trespass in

(*a*) See also 6 *Term Rep. B. R.* 456. *Randle* v. *Fuller*.

this court, in which the plaintiff had recovered a verdict; and insisted that in all the cases where a set-off of this kind had been allowed, both actions had been in the same court; as in *Thrustout* d. *Barnes* v. *Crafter*. 2 *Blacks*. 526. *Schoole* v. *Noble* and others, 1 *Hen. Blacks*. 23. *Nunez* v. *Modigliani*, 1 *Hen. Blacks*. 217. *Vaughan* v. *Davies*, 2 *Hen. Blacks*. 440, and *Dennie* v. *Elliot*, 2 *Hen. Blacks*. 537. But the court overruled the objection, saying that a set-off had even been allowed between costs in a court of equity, and costs in a court of law; and *Heath*, J. observed that he remembered a case, where an ejectment having been brought in the *King's Bench*, and afterwards a formedon in this court, proceedings were stayed in the latter until the costs of the former were paid.

Cockell, serjeant, then stated that he opposed the rule on the part of the plaintiff's attorney, who had not been paid his costs, and represented that the plaintiff himself was now in prison. He cited *Mitchell* v. *Oldfield*, 4 Term. Rep. 123, to shew that the attorney had a lien on the judgment for the amount of his costs.

Shepherd, serjeant, contra, relied on *Dennie* v. *Elliot*; where it was held, that whatever might be the rule in the *King's Bench*, yet according to the practice of this court, the lien of the attorney was subject to the equitable claims of the parties.

Lord Eldon, Chief Justice, finding it to be the practice of this court that an attorney shall not take his costs out of the fund, which by his diligence he has recovered for his client, where the opposite party is entitled to set-off, it does not become me to say more that I find it to be the settled practice with much surprise, since it stands in direct contradiction to the practice of every other court, as well as to the principles of justice. In the court of *Chancery* the same parties are often concerned in many suits; and I never knew the idea entertained of arranging the funds, till the respective attornies were paid their costs. However, as the attorney in this case has acted with a knowledge of the settled practice of the court, he can have a right to claim the advantage of a more just principle; and it will only remain for the court to consider, whether the practice of the court of *King's Bench* should not be adopted here for the future.

Heath, J. I have no objection to have the practice reconsidered.

Rooke, J. There can be no objection to reconsidering the practice; but it does not appear to me to be unfair as it stands at present. The attorney looks in the first instance to the personal security of his client, and if beyond that he can get any further security into his hands, it is a mere casual advantage.

Rule absolute.

Mitchell v. *Oldfield*. *H. T.* 31 *Geo.* III. *A. D.* 1791. 4 *Term. Rep.* 123.

In this action the plaintiff recovered a judgment against the defendant for 18*l*. 10*s*. But the defendant, having also recovered in another action against this plaintiff and another, obtained a rule to shew cause why the debt and costs in the latter should not be set-off against the judgment in the former action; suggesting (among other reasons) that *Mitchell* had absconded.

Bearcroft now shewed, on behalf of *Mitchell's* attorney in the first action; contending that, as he was not concerned as attorney in the other action, he had a lien for his costs on the judgment obtained by his client. He also hinted that perhaps the court would not interfere at all in this case; inasmuch as one debt was due to the plaintiff alone, whereas the other was the joint debt of the plaintiff and another to the defendant; and he observed that this was not such a debt as could be set-off under the statute. But,

Lord Kenyon, Ch. J. said, that this did not depend on the statutes of set-off, but on the general jurisdiction of the court over the suitors in it; that it was an equitable part of their jurisdiction, and had been frequently exercised. But, as to the other point, he observed, that the attornies and solicitors of the different courts have a lien on all papers in their hands, and judgments recovered, for their costs; that in the court of Chancery they were permitted to retain title deeds for that purpose(*a*); and he thought it right that the attorney in this case should be satisfied for his costs before the defendant was allowed to make the set-off.

Buller, J.—Though this court have said that they will not interfere on the

(*a*) *Vide ante*, 3 *vol*. 275.

behalf of the attorney, and prevent the plaintiff settling his own cause without first paying the attorney's bill(*b*) yet when the adverse party, against whom a judgment has been obtained, applies to get rid of that judgment, the court will take care that the attorney's bill is satisfied.

The court made the rule absolute, on the defendant's undertaking to pay the attorney's bill, and on his entering a remittitur in the cause in which this defendant was plaintiff.(*c*)

Randle v. *Fuller*, *M. T.* 36 *G.* III. *A. D.* 1795. 6 *T. R.* 456.

A RULE was obtained to shew cause why the master should not, upon taxation of the costs in this cause, set off the sum of 37*l.* 3*s.* 6*d.* against such costs as should upon taxation be found due from the defendant to the plaintiff, and if more should be found due to the plaintiff than that sum then why upon payment of the balance execution should not be stayed. This was founded upon an affidavit stating that the above-mentioned sum was due from the plaintiff to the defendant upon a judgment in a former action; and that the plaintiff had already received part of his debt under an execution.

Shepherd shewed cause upon an affidavit of the plaintiff's attorney, claiming a lien upon the costs and damages recovered in the present action, and requiring to have such lien, which amounted to more than the sum demanded by the defendant, to be set-off, satisfied in the first instance; and stating further that the plaintiff had absconded, and that the attorney had no other security for his bill than the costs and damages recovered. He contended that the practice of the court permitting a set-off in such cases as the present was never enforced adversely to the attorney's lien if insisted upon by him; and that in justice it ought not to be extended further, as the attorney who had been at the trouble and expense of prosecuting a suit ought not to be in a worse situation because his client was liable to other demands on other accounts than those included in the suit prosecuted by such attorney. And he referred to *Mitchell* v. *Oldfield*(*a*)

Vaughan in support of the rule said that the principle had been laid down in the court of Common Pleas to be that the attorney had only a lien subject to the equitable claim against his client; if therefore the plaintiff here could only conscientiously recover the balance as between him and the defendant who had a cross claim upon him, the attorney ought not to stand in a better situation than his principal, and still less ought he to prejudice the rights of the defendant as against the plaintiff in the cause. And he cited *Thrustout* d. *Barnes* v. *Crafter*(*b*) *Schoole* v. *Noble*(*c*) and *Nunez* v. *Modigliani*(*d*) as shewing the practice in the Common Pleas; and *Welch* v. *Hole*(*e*) where this court refused to oblige the defendant to pay the attorney's demand, the defendant having compromised his debt with the plaintiff without the attorney's knowledge.(*f*)

The court desired the matter to stand over for further inquiry; and on this day,

Lord KENYON, Ch. J. said—It had been expressly determined in *Mitchell* v. *Oldfield* that the attorney had a general lien on the costs and damages recovered, without any such restriction as was now attempted to be put upon it; and that upon the reason and justice of the case he could find no ground to impose such a restriction. That whatever might be the practice in the court of Common Pleas, he was glad to find that his opinion was warranted by the settled practice of this court.(*g*)

Rule discharged.

Sapsford v. *Fletcher*, *H. T.* 32 *Geo.* III. *A. D.* 1792, 4 *T. R.* 511.

REPLEVIN for taking goods in the plaintiff's dwelling house. Avowry for 50*l.* rent due at Christmas 1790 from *Brookes* to *Fletcher's* testators for this house; another avowry for the same rent due at the same time from the plaintiff to the defendant's testator. Pleas in bar, first, as to 20*l.* (parcel of the 50*l.*) nothing

(*b*) *Vid. Welch* v. *Hole*, *Dougl.* 226, and *Griffin* v. *Eyles*, *Hen. Blacks. Rep. C. B.* 122.
(*c*) See *Read* v. *Dupper*, *post*, 6 *vol.* 361, and *Randle* v. *Fuller*, *post*, 6 *vol.* 456.

(*a*) *Ante*, 4 vol. 123.
(*b*) 2 *Black. Rep.* 826.
(*c*) 1 *Hen. Black. Rep.* 23.
(*d*) *Ib.* 217.
(*e*) *Dougl.* 238. 3d. edition.
(*f*) Vide *Read* v. *Dupper*, *ante*, 361.
(*g*) *Morland* v. *Rashleigh*, *Tr.* 35 *G.* 3. *B. R. S. P.*

in arrear; 2dly. As to 30*l.* the residue, a tender and no subsequent demand; 3dly. "That *William Fletcher* (deceased) in his life-time and at the time of his death, "and the said *William Fletcher* (the defendant) from the time of his death until "and at the same time when, &c. held the said dwelling house in which, &c. "with the appurtenances as tenants thereof to the Duke of *Portland*, at and under "the yearly rent of 5*l.* of lawful money of *Great Britain* to be paid at the four most "usual feasts or days of payment of rent in the year, that is to say, &c. by even "and equal portions. And that before the said time when, &c. 20*l.* of the said "last mentioned rent for four years, ending at the feast of the Nativity of our Lord "*Christ* 1790, became due and in arrear from the said *William Fletcher* (the de-"fendant) to the said Duke. And thereupon the said Duke, at the said feast of, "&c. demanded payment of the arrears of the said rent from the said *W. Fletcher*, "(the defendant) but the said *W. Fletcher* then and there refused to pay the same; "whereupon the said Duke afterwards, and before the said time when, &c. de-"manded the payment of the said arrears of rent from the said *W. Brookes*, as the "occupier of the said dwelling house, and threatened to distrain upon the goods "and chattels in and upon the said dwelling house and premises; whereupon the "said *W. Brookes*, in order to prevent the said goods and chattels in and upon the "said dwelling house and premises from being distrained, long before the said time "when, &c. to wit, on the 25th day December 1790, paid to the said Duke the "said 20*l.* the rent aforesaid, so being in arrear and unpaid as aforesaid; and so "the plaintiff says that nothing of the said 20*l.* of the rent aforesaid was in arrear "to the said *W. Fletcher* (the defendant) in manner and form as the said *W. "Fletcher* (the defendant) hath above in his said avowry alleged; and this the "plaintiff, &c. wherefore," &c. A similar plea to the last avowry.

To both these there was a general demurrer.

Chambre, in support of the demurrer, urged, that the plea in bar was no answer to the avowry, for though it was not pleaded in form as a set-off, it was so in effect; and it has been held that the statutes of set-off do not extend to a replevin. *Absolom* v. *Knight*.(a) Neither can the payment of a debt of the avowant be considered as payment of rent, so as to prove the plea that nothing is in arrear. The plaintiff, having stated the special grounds from which he draws the conclusion that nothing is in arrear, cannot be permitted to resort to other grounds to support it. Now the circumstances here pleaded at the most only amount to this, that the avowant has contracted a debt with him; for the relation in which he stands to the plaintiff cannot vary the case. It does not appear that the avowant had any notice that the plaintiff had paid the ground-rent; and no person can be allowed to charge another with a debt against his consent, or without his knowledge. This therefore cannot be considered as a payment for the avowant, because the plaintiff was not authorised to make it. But even if it had been paid with the avowant's consent, and he had afterwards repaid the plaintiff, the former might have avowed for the whole rent in arrear; and yet if it could have been considered as part payment of the rent by the tenant at first, the defendant could not afterwards have avowed for that part of the rent; and it is not alleged in the plea that the defendant has not repaid him. In all the land-tax acts a special provision is made to enable the tenant to deduct the land-tax which is a charge upon the land, out of the rent to be paid to the landlord: this furnishes a strong argument to shew that in the contemplation of the legislature paying the land-tax by the tenant would not have been considered as part payment of the rent to the lessor, otherwise it would have been nugatory to have inserted this clause in those acts.

Lord KENYON, Ch. J.—It is incumbent on a party, who wishes to establish a point contrary to all justice and equity, to produce some direct authority, shewing that there is an inflexible rule of law established in opposition to justice: but no such authority has been produced by the defendant to support his claim. The general principles that have been relied on in the argument, that a set-off cannot be pleaded to an avowry for rent, and that no person can make another his debtor by voluntarily paying the debt of that other person against his consent, are not questioned. With regard to the first, it is much to be lamented that it should have been so decided; however, for the sake of certainty in the law, we must submit to

(a) *Barnes* 450. 4to edition, and *Bull. N. P.* 181. *Graham* v. *Fraine*, *H.* 24 *G.* 2 *B. R.* and *Laycock* v. *Tuffnel*, *E.* 27 *G.* 3. *B. R. S. P.*

those decisions, till the legislature alter the law. But this is not a cross demand: the ground-rent paid by the plaintiff was in discharge of a demand superior to the improved rent; it was the first charge from which the defendant was to exonerate himself before he put any of the rent due from the plaintiff into his own pocket. This was a payment in respect of the occupation. And to the other position I perfectly subscribe; but it cannot govern this case. Here the plaintiff was sub-tenant to an estate of the defendant's held under the Duke of *Portland;* the ground-rent being in arrear, the Duke of *Portland's* agents applied to the plaintiff for payment, which they had it in their power to enforce by distress; and they even threatened to do so; it was therefore *by compulsion* that the plaintiff paid this money, which was due in repect of the very property which he held as tenant to the defendant, and of the same property for which this distress was made. This then is clearly distinguishable from the case of a *voluntary payment* made to charge another person with a debt against his consent. And now the defendant insists that, though all this property was liable to the ground-rent, and though this was the first charge on the land, he is to receive the whole of the reserved rent from the plaintiff, without making any deduction from the ground-rent. But a more unconscientious proposition was never stated in a court of justice.

BULLER, J. (*a*)—There is a great difference between a payment and a set-off; the former may be pleaded to an avowry, though the latter cannot. That is a good payment which is paid as part of the rent itself in respect of the land: but a set-off supposes a different demand, arising in a different right. A case put at the bar admits of a decisive answer: it was said that if the tenant had paid the ground-rent, and the defendant had afterwards repaid him, the latter could not avow for the whole rent; but, whether the payment of a sum of money is to be considered as a payment by one person for the debt of another must depend on the will and consent of both parties; and if it be once considered by both as payment, the debt cannot afterwards be revived. And my answer to the case supposed is this, that the payment there never was considered by both as a payment; and, if not, the whole rent remains due. I consider this case as a lease by the defendant to the plaintiff at the annual rent of 50*l.* out of which 5*l. per annum* was to be paid to the ground-landlord; and therefore a payment of that ground-rent is a payment of so much rent to the defendant, and may be pleaded in answer to the avowry for rent. Neither can we suppose upon this record that the defendant ever repaid the plaintiff this ground-rent; for, if he had, he might have replied that fact.

GROSE, J.—The principles relied on by the defendant's counsel are not disputed, but they are not applicable to this case. It must be admitted that a plaintiff cannot plead a set-off to an avowry for rent, and that one person cannot make another his debtor by a voluntary payment. But this is neither the one nor the other. It is a compulsory payment made by the plaintiff to protect him from a distress for the ground-rent due to the original landlord.

Judgment for the plaintiff.

Ord v. *Ruspini*, *T. T.* 37 *Geo. III.* 2 *Esp. Cas.* 569.

ASSUMPSIT on a bill of exchange accepted by the defendant, which was due some time in the year 1784.

Pleas. *Non-assumpsit*, Statute of Limitations, and a Set-off.

The set-off consisted of bills of exchange and promissory notes of the plaintiff's, which the defendant had taken up or paid on his account; they were all dated in the year 1784.

Two objections were made to the set-off.—First. That in order to entitle the defendant to go into evidence respecting those bills and notes, they ought to have been made the special objects of a set-off.

Lord KENYON overruled the objection, and held, that they were good evidence under the count for money paid to the plaintiff's use.

The second objection was, that though the plaintiff's demand against the defendant had accrued so far back as the year 1784, yet in fact he had kept it alive by having sued out process within the six years, and continued it; but that as the defendant had not done so, his demand against the plaintiff must be held to be barred by the statute; and so not such as could demand a set-off.

(*a*) Abs. *Ashhurst*, J.

Lord KENYON said, that as the transactions between the plaintiff and the defendant were all of the same date, and as the bills seemed to have been given in the course of those transactions, and for their mutual accommodation, it would be the highest injustice to allow one to have an operation by law and not the other, and that he would therefore hold the latter to be good as well as the former, and suffer them to be set-off.

The defendant proved the payment of the bills and notes as a set-off, and had a verdict.

Dunmore v. *Taylor*, *H. T.* 31 *Geo. III. Peake* 41.

ASSUMPSIT for goods sold and delivered. Set-off for goods sold and delivered, and also for goods *bargained* and *sold.*

On the cross examination of the plaintiff's witness it appeared that the defendant had made a waggon for the plaintiff, but had refused to deliver it unless the plaintiff would get some person to join him in giving a security for the balance which the delivery of the waggon would make in his favour. The plaintiff was then insolvent.

It was objected that this contract, being only executory, could not be made the subject of a set-off.

BULLER, J. thought it could be set-off as goods bargained and sold. When the cause had proceeded further, it appeared that it was afterwards agreed that the plaintiff should not have the waggon, but that the defendant should keep it. Upon which the plaintiff had a verdict.

Note. After the cause was over Mr. J. *Buller* said that he thought an *indebitatus assumpsit* would lie in this case, but that there was some nicety in the question.

Freeman v. *Hyatt*, *M. T. Geo. III. K. B.* 1 *Blacks.* 394.

ACTION for money due for a parcel of cloth. *Dunning* moved to stay the trial of the cause, in order to send a commission into Portugal, to establish a fact by way of set-off; viz. That in a former parcel of cloths, sent to Portugal, and bought of the same plaintiff, it appeared on opening the bale, that they were burnt in the pressing, which had greatly lowered their value.

Norton, Solicitor-General, objected, that the set-off was not maintainable.——You might as well set-off the damages which you are entitled to recover for a battery. You should bring your special action on the case:

And of that opinion was the court, and denied the motion.

Howlet and *Another* v. *Strickland*, *E. T.* 14 *Geo. III. A. D.* 1774. *B. R. Cowp.* 56.

THIS was an action of covenant. The defendant pleaded that he had sustained greater damages by reason of the breaches committed on the part of the plaintiff, than the value of the damages sustained by the plaintiff on account of the breaches alleged in the declaration: all the breaches assigned in the plea were for non-delivery of alum in due time. The plaintiff demurred, and for special cause assigned, that it was not competent to the defendant to plead these damages by way of set-off.

Mr. *Chambre* for the plaintiff. The covenant is not for money, therefore the damages cannot be set-off, either by *stat.* 2 *C.* 2. *c.* 22. or 8 *G.* 2. *c.* 24. For they are not debts, nor recoverable as such. A tender is only pleadable to an action of contract for money.

In no part of the plea is it alleged, that these are mutual debts. But further in this case, the damages to be recovered upon the covenant are totally uncertain; the measure of them depending upon the discretion of the jury. It is impossible therefore for the parties to affix any precise balance; consequently the act of parliament cannot extend to them. If the construction which is contended for on the other side, is to prevail, damages upon a breach of marriage contract might be insisted upon as debts: and the same reasoning might extend to the setting-off damages in an action of trover.

Mr. Serjeant *Walker* for the defendant. By stat. 2 *G.* 2. *c.* 22. a defendant is at liberty to set-off any demand that he may have against the plaintiff; or to plead it in bar as the nature of the case may require, and by stat. 8 *G.* 2. *c.* 24. this power is extended to debts of a different nature.

The present action is an action for damages, and the set-off is of the same nature as the demand; viz. unliquidated damages: the verdict therefore will decide the balance. The uncertainty of the damages cannot be a foundation for the distinction insisted on: for the words of the stat. are general, "mutual debts:" and in almost all the cases where a set-off is allowed, the balance is uncertain. In an action upon a *quantum meruit*, the very expression shows that the damages are unliquidated: so in an action for work or labour done, for goods sold and delivered, the damages are unliquidated. No inconvenience can arise in the present case, because these damages arise upon the same instrument, and make but one transaction: the jury therefore can decide with equal ease upon both.

Lord MANSFIELD. I take this plea to be merely for the purpose of delay. The act of parliament, and the reason of the thing, relate to mutual debts only. These damages are no debts. An *indebitatus assumpsit* could not be brought for them.

Mr Justice ASHHURST. Debts to be set-off must be such as an *indebitatus assumpsit* will lie for.

Mr. Justice ASTON. Clearly an unliquidated demand or uncertain damages cannot be set-off. Mr. Justice WILLES concurred.

Judgment for the plaintiff.

Weigall v. *Waters*, *M. T.* 36 *Geo.* 3. *A. D.* 1795. 6 *T. R.* 488.

TO an action of covenant for half a year's rent, 27*l.* 10*s.* due at *Christmas* 1794, for a house demised by the plaintiff to the defendant for 21 years from *Christmas* 1788, the latter pleaded that by the said indenture (on which the action was brought) he the defendant covenanted to repair and to surrender to the plaintiff at the end of the term the same premises well and sufficiently repaired, "casualties by fire and tempest excepted;" that before the 24th of June 1794, a violent tempest arose and threw down with great force and violence a stack of chimneys belonging to the house on the roof of the house, &c. and damaged the house so much that it would soon have become uninhabitable, if he (the defendant) had not immediately repaired it; that he was obliged to lay out in the repairs 30*l.* which the plaintiff became liable to repay to him; that that sum is still due to the defendant, and exceeds the damages sustained by the plaintiff by reason of the breach of covenant assigned; and that he is ready to set-off that 30*l.* &c. according to the statute.

To this plea there was a special demurrer, assigning these causes; that it is not alleged in the plea that the plaintiff had any notice of the tempest or of the damage thereby done to the house, nor that he was requested to repair the same before the defendant made the repairs stated in the plea, &c.

Holroyd was to have argued in support of the demurrer, and

Toller against it. But

The court said that the plea could not possibly be supported, and that it did not admit of any argument.

Lord KENYON, Ch. J. One objection to the plea is, that it does not set-off any certain debt, but uncertain damages. I do not indeed see by what covenant the landlord is bound to repair damages occasioned by fire or tempest; the exception was introduced in the lessee's covenant for his benefit, and to exempt him from particular repairs. But if the defendant can maintain any action against the plaintiff, (his landlord) the sum to be recovered is uncertain; it must be assessed by a jury; and there is no pretence to say that those uncertain damages may be set-off to the present action. If the plaintiff has fairly laid out money in repairing what he was not bound to repair, perhaps a court of equity will give him relief.

Judgment for the plaintiff.(*a*)

(*a*) Vid. *Paradine* v. *Jane*, *All.* 26. *Monk* v. *Cooper*, 2 *Str.* 763. *Belfour* v. *Weston*, *ante* 1 *vol.* 310. *Doe* v. *Sandham*, *ib.* 705. and *Brown* v. *Quilter*, *Amb.* 619.

French, Assignee, v. *Fenn*, *T. T.* 1783. *Cooke*, 634.

IN an action brought against the defendant for money had and received to the use of the plaintiffs as assignees of *Cox*.

The defendant pleaded the general issue, a verdict was found for the plaintiffs, subject to the opinion of the court on the following case:

That on the 24th of January 1778, *Cox*, *Holford* and *Fenn*, agreed to purchase a row of pearls for an adventure in trade, and that *Fenn* should advance the money. The agreement was as follows: "London, 24th January 1778, *J. Cox*, *J. Holford*, "and *J. Fenn*, purchased a row of pearls of *James Le Jeune*, for 2050*l.* including "the commission. The said sum was advanced by *J. Fenn*, upon an agreement "that profit and loss thereon should be equally divided between them in thirds; "in consequence of which we the undersigned do hereby agree to pay two-thirds "of the interest thereon, from the said 24th of January 1778, till the said row of "pearls are sold. Signed by *Holford*, and *Cox*."

In November 1778, *Cox* became a bankrupt, after which the defendant sent the row of pearls to *China*, where it was sold for 6000*l.* and the nett produce thereon being 5000*l.* was remitted to the defendant.

Cox, at the time of his bankruptcy, was indebted to the defendant in a much larger sum than a third of the profits of this adventure.

The defendant in this action had pleaded *non assumpsit*, and given notice of set-off: the question for the consideration of the court therefore was, whether he was entitled to set-off the sums owing to him from the bankrupt in bar of the action brought by the bankrupt's assignees for a third of the profits arising from the sale of the pearls.

It was argued by *Davenport* and *Lee*, at different times, for the plaintiff, and by *Baldwin* and *Wilson*, for the defendant.

For the plaintiff it was insisted, that if these partners were part owners in a ship, and one of them became bankrupt, the third share of the ship vests in the assignees, and afterwards when the ship is sold the assignees must be paid a third, and if he was privately indebted to the other partners it could not be set-off.

Suppose these pearls had consisted of three of equal value, had not the assignees a right to one if they had been divided? Then sending them abroad afterwards and changing them into money can make no difference.

There is not any usage which peculiarly decides this point.

In *Prescot's* case, 1 *Atk.* 230 the petitioner was a creditor of the bankrupt for 100*l.* and 10*l.* and a debtor to him on bond for 340*l.* payable on the 4th of March 1756, with lawful interest, and applied to set-off his demand of 100*l.* against the principal and interest due on the bond, and not be obliged to prove his debt under the commission, and take a dividend upon it only. The Lord Chancellor said, though this is not in strictness a mutual debt, yet it is a mutual credit, for the bankrupt gives credit to the party in consideration of the bond though payable at a future day, and he gives the bankrupt credit for the debt upon simple contract, and therefore it is a case within the equity of the 5 *Geo.* 2.

In the case *ex parte Deeze*, 1 *Atk.* 228. it was determined that the purchaser may retain goods till he is paid the price of packing; and if he has another debt due to him from the same person, the goods shall not be taken from him till he has paid the whole, notwithstanding the debtor is become a bankrupt.

None of the cases that have been determined ruled this. *Cox* at the time of his bankruptcy was indebted to the defendant in a much larger sum; there was at that time no mutual credit at all; at the time he broke there was no mutual debt; no mutual credit; *Fenn* was the only creditor.

It is stated that the nett produce was remitted to the defendant without any consent of *Cox* as far as it appears, and even without his knowledge.

There was no remittance till some years after the bankruptcy, so that the case excludes the possibility of *Cox*, or any person standing in his place, having at that time any demand upon *Fenn*.

The 5 *G.* 2. *c.* 30. *s.* 28. enacts, that where there hath been mutual credit given by the bankrupt or any other person, or mutual debts between the bankrupt and any other person at any time before such person became bankrupt, one debt may be set against another, and what shall appear to be due on either side on balance of such account, and on setting such debts one against another, and no more, shall be claimed or paid on either side respectively.

The accounts by this statute must be before the bankruptcy. This is the essential difference between this case and those decided.

Fenn owed *Cox* nothing at the time of the bankruptcy. The very pearl was in England at that time.

The moment he became a bankrupt there was an entire stop put to all his affairs.

Could *Fenn* have gone before the commissioners and said, I don't choose to prove this, because there is an adventure between us: when the proceeds are remitted home I will retain my debts.

There was no credit, nor no idea of credit till long after the bankruptcy.

The statute seems to make that event a stop and a rest in the affairs, beyond which nothing should go on.

There is no case decided circumstanced like this.

Had *Cox* any demand upon *Fenn*, at the time of buying the row of pearls?

Fenn could not have brought an action against any of them till the goods were sold.

To allow this set-off would be contrary to the words of the act.

The court on the second argument stopped Mr. *Wilson* for the defendant, and Lord *Mansfield* said, The act of parliament is accurately drawn to avoid the injustice that would be done if the words were only mutual debts, and it therefore provides for mutual credit.

In this case credit is given to the defendant for a row of pearls, which is to belong in thirds to three persons. As *Fenn* advanced the whole money, the other two were to pay him interest for their shares till the pearls were sold; there is no doubt but there was a mutual credit. *Cox* had trusted him with the pearls, and he had trusted *Cox* with other goods, which in all probability he would not have otherwise done.—This is the real justice of the case if there had been no bankruptcy, and the bankruptcy ought not to alter the real justice of the case.

Mr. Justice Buller.—Where there is a trust between two men on each side, that makes a mutual credit.

The whole of the Solicitor's (*Lee*) argument goes to shew there are no words in the act but mutual debts, which is directly contrary to the fact.

On principle and justice there is no difference between this case and those of *Prescot* and *Decze*.

The set-off being allowed, the postea was ordered to the defendant.

Slipper and Others, Assignees of Lane v. *Stidstone. H. T.* 34 *Geo. III. A. D.*...1794. 5 *T. R.* 493.

TO this action for work and labour done by the bankrupt, goods sold and delivered, and money lent by him, the defendant pleaded the general issue, and gave a notice of set-off for work and labour of the defendant and one *P. Abbot*, since deceased, whom the defendant survived, by them performed for the bankrupt, &c. At the trial before Lord *Kenyon*, the sum set-off exceeded the plaintiff's demand, upon which the plaintiff was nonsuited, though it was contended on his behalf that the set-off was in *auter droit*, and ought not to be allowed in this action.

Law on a former day in this term moved to set aside the nonsuit, contending that the set-off should not have been allowed, for that there was no mutuality of debt; that the fund out of which the satisfaction was to be made by the plaintiff to the defendant as surviving partner was not the same as that from which satisfaction was to be made to the plaintiff by the defendant; that the only mutuality here consisted in the persons of the plaintiff and defendant; that before the death of *Abbot* it could not be pretended that the debt due from the plaintiff to him and the defendant could be set-off in an action against the defendant; and that on principle, the death of *Abbot* could not vary this question. That this set-off could not be permitted any more than a debt due from the plaintiff to any person to whom the defendant happened to be executor; and that if this set-off were allowed, it would create confusion in the arrangement of the costs of the different suits.

The court then granted a rule *nisi*: but on this day they recommended it to the plaintiff not to draw up the rule, as it would only enhance the expense of the suit, the question being perfectly clear with the defendant. They said that the defendant might have declared against the plaintiff for this demand and also for any sum due to him separately(a) if any such had been due; and that therefore there was no reason why the set-off should not be allowed. Rule refused.

French v. *Andrade*, *H. T.* 36 *Geo. III. A. D.* 1796. 6 *T. R.* 582.

THIS was an action upon promises; to which the defendant pleaded that the plaintiff and one *J. Newton* who died before the commencement of the action were indebted to the defendant in divers sums of money, &c. for work and labour, money paid &c. that those sums remained unpaid at the death of *J. Newton*, and at the time of commencing this action were and still are due from the plaintiff to the defendant; and that they exceed the sum due from the defendant to the plaintiff, against which sum the defendant is willing to set-off, &c.

To this plea there was a general demurrer.

Marryat, in support of the plea, mentioned the case of *Slipper* v. *Stidstone*(b) as decisive of the present; which

Wood, contra, admitted.

Per Curiam. It is perfectly clear that the debt due from the plaintiff as surviving partner may be set-off against the demand he has in his own right on the defendant. Judgment for the defendant.

Fletcher v. *Dyche*, *T. T.* 27 *Geo. III. A. D.* 1787. 2 *T. R.* 33.

ASSUMPSIT for work and labour, for goods sold and delivered, money paid, &c. Pleas, *non assumpsit*; 2dly. Set-off for money paid, and had and received; 3dly. A plea of set-off as follows: That heretofore, to wit, on the 27th day of June 1785, to wit, at, &c. the plaintiff by a certain writing obligatory sealed, &c. became held and firmly bound to the defendant in the sum of 236*l.* to be paid to the defendant, when he the plaintiff should be thereto afterwards requested, with and under a certain condition thereto subscribed and underwritten, reciting that the defendant had contracted and agreed with the committee chosen for the ordering, appointing, and directing of the repairs of the parish church of St. Mary-le-Bow, London, for repairing of the said parish church, according to a certain particular or plan thereof given; and reciting, that one *John Dowley*, therein called the above bounden *John Dowley*, but who never executed the said writing obligatory, and the plaintiff, had contracted and agreed with the defendant, that they would do, perform, and execute, all the smith's and ironmonger's work, to be done and performed in and about the repairs of the said parish church, and which were mentioned and expressed in the said particular plan, or estimate, and in the manner therein directed to be done, and find and provide all the materials for the doing thereof within the time or space of six weeks from the day of the date of the said writing obligatory, at and for the price or sum of 118*l.* 18*s.* which was agreed to be paid in three months after the said parish church should be completely repaired; and had agreed that if they should not have done and performed the said smith's and ironmonger's work within the time therein before mentioned to have been agreed upon and limited for the doing thereof, they would forfeit and pay to the defendant the sum of 10*l.* for every week after the expiration of the time agreed upon and limited for the doing thereof, until the said smith's and ironmonger's work should be completely finished; the condition therefore of the said writing obligatory was, that they the said *John Dowley* and the plaintiff should within the time or space of six weeks perform in a good and workmanlike manner, according to the said plan, all the smith's and ironmonger's work, &c. and should find and provide the materials, &c. and should keep indemnified the defendant, his executors, &c. and that if they the said *John Dowley* and the plaintiff should make default, or should neglect to do the said smith's and ironmonger's work within the time limited, they should well and truly pay to the defendant, his executors, &c. the sum of 10*l* for every week from the time the said smith's and ironmonger's work ought to be done, being six weeks from the day of the date of the said writing obligatory, as therein above mentioned, until the same should be completely finished. And the

(a) Vide *Hancock* v. *Haywood*, ante, [illegible] vol. 1[illegible]. (b) Ante, 5 vol. 19.

defendant in fact saith, that the said *John Dowley* and the plaintiff did not, nor did either of them, within the said time or space of six weeks from the day of the date of the said writing obligatory, do, perform, or execute, or cause, &c. all the smith's and ironmonger's work, &c. but neglected and omitted so to do, and therein failed and made default, and on the contrary thereof suffered and permitted the said smith's and ironmonger's work to be and remain unfinished for the space of four weeks next after the expiration of the time agreed upon and limited for the doing thereof as aforesaid; whereby, and by force of the said writing obligatory, and condition, the plaintiff became liable to pay to the defendant the sum of 40*l.* being at and after the rate of 10*l.* for each and every week of the said four weeks, after the expiration of the time so agreed upon and limited for the doing of the said smith's and ironmonger's work, during which the same so remained unfinished as aforesaid; and the said sum of 40*l.* and every part thereof at the time of the commencement of this suit was and still is really and justly due and owing from the plaintiff to the defendant upon and by virtue of the said writing obligatory, and the condition thereof; and which said sum of 40*l.* so due and owing from the plaintiff to the defendant exceeds the damages sustained by the plaintiff, by reason of the not performing of the said several promises and undertakings in the said declaration mentioned, and out of which said sum of 40*l.* he the defendant is ready and willing and hereby offers to set-off and allow the amount of the damages sustained by the plaintiff, according to the form of the statute, &c. and this the defendant is ready to verify, wherefore, &c.

To this third plea there was a general demurrer, and joinder in demurrer.

Law, in support of the demurrer, contended that the third plea setting off the four penalties, at the rate of 10*l.* for four weeks after the expiration of the time limited for doing the smith's and ironmongers's work, could not be supported, First, because it attempts to set-off a penalty instead of the money justly due. If this set-off can be allowed at all, it must be under the 8 *Geo.* 2. *c.* 24. *s.* 5. But that statute does not extend to this case; for that only allows the debt really and justly due to be set-off. So that a penalty cannot be set-off at all; now this is strictly a penalty; the words creating the penalty are "that the plaintiff shall *forfeit and pay* 10*l.* weekly, &c. And it cannot be considered as a mere compensation to the defendant for non-performance of the work within the time limited; for it does not appear that the defendant was himself under any limitation in point of time as to the performance of his contract with the commissioners. It is likewise excessive, because it bears no proportion to the whole sum to be paid for the work done. And there are no other limits to the penalty than the penalty of the bond itself. If it be contended by the defendant's counsel, that this is in the nature of a liquidated satisfaction, it is to be observed that this is not like any of those cases which have been determined on that ground. In the case of *Rolfe* v. *Peterson*(a) where the lessee covenanted to pay an increased rent for ploughing up meadow ground, it was considered not as a penalty, but as a liquidated satisfaction: for it was only an agreement to pay a larger sum for using the land in a particular way. But the present case is that of a strict penalty, in consequence of not performing an agreement, for which there does not appear to be any equivalent to the party. There are several cases where penalties have been considered in the nature of liquidated damages, but those are cases where the penalties have barely exceeded the sums really due, and they have been allowed to save the parties expense. Such was the case of *Tall* v. *Ryland*, 1 *Ch. Cas.* 183. In *Nedriffe* v. *Hogan*,(b) it was determined that a penalty cannot be set-off. If an action had been brought on this bond, it would have been competent to the jury to have given less damages than the amount of these penalties. 2 *Rol. Abr.* 703. *pl.* 9.(c) Before the statute 8 and 9 W. 3. the jury *might* have given less damages than the penalty. 1 *Lev.* 111. And since the statute they *ought* to give the damages *really* sustained by the non-performance of the work. Here the party might be put in as good a plight as if the condition of the bond had been performed: this rule was laid down by Lord *Somers*,(d) that in such case a court of equity would relieve; therefore the defendant should have averred that the damages really incurred by the non-performance of the agreement amounted to the sum which he intended to set-off. This is not

(a) 6 *Bro. Parl. Cas.* 470.
(b) 2 *Burr.* 1024.
(c) *Vide* 4 *Burr.* 2229. 2231.
(d) *Prec. in Chan.* 487.

like the case of demurrage, which is a stipulated rate of hire, and not a forfeiture; for there the owner of the ship loses the use of her during the whole time she is detained, and the other party has the use of her the whole time.

But secondly. This cannot be set-off, because there is no strict mutuality. It sets off money, which, by the condition of the bond, was to become due from the plaintiff and another, and not from the plaintiff alone, by virtue of an antecedent agreement between the three. And though this bond was only executed by the plaintiff yet the defendant is estopped from saying that this debt is not due from the plaintiff and another; he cannot dispute their joint liability. Besides, the breach assigned is not warranted by the condition. The bond is conditioned for the performance of certain work in a limited time by two, or payment by two of 10*l.* *per* week. The breach should have been assigned, that the two had neither done the work, nor paid the money, whereby the penalty became forfeited. Whereas it is assigned, that the two had not done the work, &c. whereby the one became liable to pay the 10*l.* *per* week: but no such liability was created by the bond itself.

The other side was stopped by the court.

Ashhurst, J. The sums set-off are in the nature of liquidated damages, and are such a kind of penalty, if they may be called by that name, as a court of equity would not relieve against. The object of the parties in naming this weekly sum was to prevent any altercation with respect to the *quantum* of damages which the defendant might sustain by reason of the non-performance of the contract. It would have been difficult for the jury to have ascertained what damages the defendant had really suffered by the breach of the agreement; and therefore it was proper for the contracting parties to ascertain it by their agreement. So that this is a case of stipulated damages, and it is not to be considered as a penalty. If so, and the parties have entered into a joint and several bond, it becomes the separate debt of both, and therefore may be set-off against either. Then it has been objected, that there is no mutuality in the debts; because, first, it is a joint debt; and secondly that the plaintiff should have a compensation from the other party. As to the first, it is sufficient to say, that this is a *separate* as well as a *joint* debt, and therefore may be set-off. And as to the other ground of objection, it is not necessary to determine that question in this case; but if it were, I think he might have compensation in another form, by bringing an action for money paid, laid out, and expended to his use. But that is not material as between these parties.

Buller, J. The principal question to be considered is, whether this is in the nature of liquidated damages or a penalty. When there is a penalty in the bond, it is strange that the sum mentioned in the condition could be called a penalty. I do not know how there can be an equitable and a legal penalty. But this is as strongly a case of liquidated damages as can possibly exist, and is like the case of demurrage. In either case it is impossible to ascertain precisely what damages the party has really sustained; and therefore the contracting parties agree to pay a stipulated sum. Then it was contended that the defendant might have recovered less damages than the amount of this stipulated sum before a jury; but that is not so. In the case of *Lowe* v. *Peers*,(*a*) where a stipulated sum was claimed for breach of a marriage contract, Lord *Mansfield* said, "where the precise sum is "fixed and agreed upon between the parties, that very sum is the ascertained da-"mage, and the jury are confined to it." As to the case in 1 *Lev.* that was determined on the ground of its being a catching bargain. The plaintiff's counsel then objected to this set-off because there was no mutuality; but that depends on the question, whether the debt is due from the plaintiff and another person, or from the plaintiff alone. If the former, the debt cannot be set-off: but it appears that the bond was executed by the plaintiff alone. No debt can arise upon the bond from the other party who did not execute. The plaintiff therefore alone can be sued upon the bond; so that there is a mutuality.

Grose, J. was of the same opinion.

But the court afterwards gave the plaintiff leave to amend on payment of costs.

(*a*) 4 *Burr.* 2225.

Puller and Others, Assignees, &c. of Forbes and Gregory, Bankrupts, v. *Roe and Others, M. T.* 34 *Geo. III. Peake* 197.

ASSUMPSIT on a promissory note for 9800*l.* dated March 8, 1793, payable to *Charles Caldwell*, Esq. *and Company*, or order, and by them indorsed to the bankrupts under the firm of "Messrs. *B. Burton, Forbes* and *Gregory*."

The defendants pleaded the general issue, and gave notice of set-off.

Bartholomew Burton, and the bankrupt *Forbes*, carried on the business of general merchants in London, from the year 1762 to 1769, and on the 31st of January 1769 the bankrupt *Gregory* was admitted a partner in the house. *Burton* died on the 27th of April 1770, but the business was still carried on under the old firm of "*Burton, Forbes* and *Gregory*."

On the 21st of May 1774, *Forbes* and *Gregory* became partners with *Charles Caldwell* and *Thomas Smith*, in a banking-house at Liverpool, under the firm of *Charles Caldwell* & *Co.* and that partnership continued to the time of their respective bankruptcies, which happened in the month of March 1793, viz. that of *Forbes* and *Gregory* on the 16th, and that of *Caldwell* & *Co.* on the 18th of that month.

The two houses of *Forbes* and *Gregory* and *Caldwell* & *Co.* were distinct and separate houses; *Caldwell* and *Smith* having no concern in the business carried on by *Forbes* and *Gregory* in London, though the latter were partners in, and equally concerned with *Caldwell* and *Smith* in the banking business carried on at Liverpool, under the firm of "*Charles Caldwell* & *Co.*"

Caldwell and *Smith* were also in partnership with the defendants under the firm of *Roe* & *Co.* which company kept a banking account with the house of *Caldwell* & *Co.* at Liverpool; and that house being in advance for the defendants, they, on the 8th of March 1793, made and signed the note on which the action was brought; and the house of *Caldwell* & *Co.* at Liverpool, being indebted to *Forbes* and *Gregory* to a large amount, indorsed the note to them.

This note was given for the balance then supposed to be due from the defendants to *Caldwell* & *Co.* but it was afterwards discovered that a sum of 3859*l.* 1*s.* with which the defendants were debited for sundry bills supposed to have been drawn by *Major* (*Caldwell* & *Co.'s* agent at Truro) was improperly charged; such bills never having been in fact drawn.

BOWER, for the defendants, contended that *Forbes* and *Gregory* being partners in the house of *Caldwell* & *Co.* must take this note, charged with every incumbrance which it would be liable to in the hands of *Caldwell* & *Co.* and therefore that the defendants had a right to deduct the abovementioned sum of 3859*l.* 1*s.* and to set-off not only the sum of 680*l.* 8*s.* 10*d.* due to them from *Forbes* and *Gregory* as the *acceptors* of several bills drawn by *Caldwell* & *Co.* on them; but also the sum of 260*l.* 18*s.* 3*d.* due to the defendants from *Caldwell* & *Co.* on several bills drawn by *Caldwell* & *Co.* on *Forbes* and *Gregory*, which were *not accepted* by them. Some of these bills had been drawn by *Caldwell* & *Co.* for checks drawn upon them by the defendants as their bankers; and the bills not being paid when they became due, in consequence of the failure of *Caldwell* & *Co.* and *Forbes* and *Gregory*, the defendants were obliged to take them up, and had paid to the several holders of them the full value thereof. The others were either payable to the defendants, or indorsed to them by the respective payees.

ERSKINE, for the plaintiffs, contended that *Forbes* and *Gregory* being a distinct and separate house, and creditors of *Caldwell* & *Co.* to an amount much beyond that for which this note was given, were not liable to pay the before mentioned sum of 3859*l.* 1*s.* or the bills which they had *not accepted*. For payment of those sums the defendants must look to the estate of *Caldwell* & *Co.* who were their debtors.

Lord KENYON. This note was given to *Caldwell* & *Co.* as a banking house, and constitutes an article in the accounts between the defendants and them. They cannot *as between themselves* raise a distinct account, though they might indorse to a third person. The affairs of the company are in presumption of law known to all the partners, and all are equally liable. The defendants send this bill to *Caldwell* & *Co.* to cancel part of the debt due to them: Can they, by an act between themselves, divert this money to another purpose, and leave the whole of the defendant's debt outstanding?

The plaintiffs, therefore, had a verdict for the balance due to them, after deducting the several before mentioned sums of money, and also the sum of 1024*l.*

which it was admitted that *Forbes* and *Gregory* had received of the defendants previous to their bankruptcy. In the following term a motion was made for a new trial, but the court refused to grant a rule to shew cause.

Grove and Another, Assignees of Liotard, a Bankrupt, v. *Dubois*, *H. T.* 26 *Geo. III. A. D.* 1796. 1 *T. R.* 112.

THIS was an action for money had and received by the defendant to and for the use of the bankrupt, before he became a bankrupt; and for money had and received to and for the use of the plaintiffs, as assignees; to which the defendant pleaded the general issue, *non assumpsit;* whereupon issue was joined. The defendant also gave a notice of set-off for money had and received by the assignees for his use.

The case came on to be tried at the sittings after Michaelmas Term 1785, before Lord *Mansfield*, at Guildhall, when the jury found a verdict for the plaintiffs, damages 375*l.* 16*s.* and costs 1*s.* subject to the opinion of this court on the following case.

"That the bankrupt, *John Liotard*, being an underwriter, subscribed policies "filled up with the defendant's name for his foreign correspondents, who were "unknown to the bankrupt.

"That losses happened on the policies before the bankruptcy of *Liotard;* that "the defendant paid the amount of the losses to his foreign correspondents after "such bankruptcy.

"That the defendant had a commission *del credere* from his correspondents; "was made debtor by the bankrupt for premiums; and always retained the poli- "cies in his hands.

"The question for the opinion of the court is, Whether, under the notice of "set-off, or under any of the statutes respecting bankrupts, the defendant be "entitled to set-off this account with *Liotard?*

"If the Court shall be of opinion that the defendant is entitled to set-off, then a "verdict to be entered for the defendant."

S. Haywood, for the plaintiffs, relied upon the 28th section of the 5 *Geo.* 2. *c.* 30. which requires *mutual credit* to be given, in order to enable the defendant to set-off; which was not the case here; for the credit was not given to the broker, but to the principal; like the common case of insurance brokers, who were nothing more than mere agents, and were always so considered. The case of *Wilson* and others, assignees of *Fletcher* v. *Creighton* and another(*a*) is in point. That was an action for money had and received, &c. to and for the use of the bankrupt, and to and for the use of the assignees, and on an account stated. The defendant pleaded the general issue, *non assumpsit*, and gave notice of set-off; That the plaintiffs were indebted to the defendant in 3000*l* for losses upon several policies of assurance underwritten by the bankrupt, and which losses happened before the bankruptcy. It was tried before Lord *Mansfield* at *Guildhall*, at the sittings after Easter Term, 1782, when the jury found a verdict for the plaintiffs, subject to the opinion of the court on the following case: "That the defendants had considerable dealings with the "bankrupt, as agents or factors to various correspondents. That they paid to him, "or were debited by him for premiums upon insurance on behalf of those corres- "pondents. That they had credit for the losses as they happened, and for the re- "turns of premium. That they had no commission *del credere*. That none of "the correspondents for whom they insured were insolvent; but to all, except one, "they were in advance, more or less, on account of the policies." In that case the court were all clearly of opinion that under those circumstances the defendants were not entitled to set-off any of the subsequent losses to an action brought by the assignees for the recovery of the premiums debited to the defendants by the bankrupt.

The only difference between that case and the present was the circumstance of the defendant's having a commission *del credere* from his correspondents. It is material then to see, whether any, and what, difference such a commission could make, as between these parties.

A commission *del credere* might be considered several ways. It is an undertaking by the broker, for an additional premium to insure his principal against a contin-

(*a*) Trin. 22 Geo. 3. B. R.

gency, which contingency is the failure of the underwriter; and therefore it is only to be considered as a collateral security, which vested no such interest in the policy, as the broker could have proved under the commission at the time of issuing it; much lest did it vest any interest in him at the time of making the policy. *Ex parte Adney. Cowp.*

The broker could not have brought an action in his own name upon such a policy, without averring the interest to be in the principal,(a) by which it would have appeared that no credit had been given to him, and consequently that he did not come within the meaning of the 5 *Geo.* 2. *c.* 30. *s.* 28. If therefore he could not have brought an action in his own right, and had not such an interest in the policy as would have enabled him to have proved his debt under the commission at the time of its issuing, it is absurd to say that he could set it off to a clear demand which accrued before the bankruptcy. *Chilton* v. *Wiffin* and another, 3 *Wils.* 13. *Goddard* v. *Vanderhaven*, 3 *Wils.* 262.(b)

But even supposing an interest vested in the broker, and he could have brought an action in his own right, yet he could not set-off the present demand; for in fact there was no debt existing at the time of the bankruptcy. The payment was made to the principal afterwards; and at any rate the broker's claim could not arise before such payment. This comes directly under the principles uniformly laid down in the cases last cited. No particular event had then happened to fix the broker; no demand had been made on the underwriter, and refusal. It does not appear upon this case but that it was a voluntary payment; and if the defendant paid this sum before the expiration of the time which was allowed to him, he ought not to be permitted to take advantage of his act in prejudice to the rest of the creditors, and set-off this debt.

The broker was in the nature of an assignee of a bond, or indorsee of a promissory note. And it was determined in the case of *Marsh* and another, assignees of *May*, against *Chambers*,(c) that a note, indorsed to the debtor of a bankrupt after the bankruptcy, could not be set-off. So here, whatever interest the broker had in the policy as against the plaintiffs, it accrued after payment of the loss to his principal; but that interest, being transferred subsequent to the bankruptcy, could not be set-off against a debt vested before. At all events, it was setting up a debt in right of another person against a personal demand upon himself.

That upon the whole, whatever difference the commision *del credere* might make between the broker and his employers, it could make none between the present parties. The transaction between them would have been exactly the same, if no such commission had existed; and it was too much to contend that a private agreement between two of the parties, without the knowledge of the third, should vary the nature of the contract, and materially affect and injure the rights of his creditors.

Smith, contra, distinguished this case from that of *Wilson* and another, assignees, against *Creighton*; for here, the broker was the only person who had any dealings with the bankrupt; his name alone was inserted in the policy; no other person was known to the bankrupt, who must therefore have treated with him as principal; and who, it was more natural to suppose, gave the credit to him, than to any other person, to whom, from the nature of the transaction, he must have been an utter stranger.

He observed that this case was very different from that of sureties; for there the obligee relied upon the principal; the whole dealing was with him; and he only looked to the other as a collateral security; but here the broker was liable in the first instance.

He was then stopped by the court.

Lord Mansfield, Ch. J. The whole turns on the nature of a commission *del credere* Then what is it? It is an absolute engagement to the principal from the broker, and makes him liable in the first instance. There is no occasion for the principal to commmicate with the underwriter, though the law allows the principal, for his benefit, to resort to him as a collateral security. But the broker is liable at all events.

Buller, J. I remember many actions brought at *Guildhall* against brokers with commissions *del credere*; and I never heard any inquiry made in such cases,

(a) *Vide* 19 *Geo.* 2. *c.* 37. (b) *Vide Young and another* v. *Hockley*, 3 *Wils.* 346. (c) 2 *Stra.* 1234.

whether there had been a previous demand upon the underwriter and refusal; and I can venture to say, that such is not the practice. It makes no difference at the time of making the policy, whether the underwriter knew the principal or not; he trusted to the broker; the credit was given to him, and not to the other.

I agree that the notice of set-off is bad; but this loss may be proved and set-off under the general issue of the 28th section of the 5 *Geo.* 2. *c.* 30. The words of that section are, "That where it shall appear to the commissioners, or the major "part of them, that there hath been mutual credits given by the bankrupt and any "other person, or mutual debts between the bankrupt and any other person, at any "time before such person become bankrupt, the said commissioners, &c. shall state "the account between them, and one debt may be set against another, and what "shall appear to be due on either side on the balance of such account, *and no more,* "*shall be claimed,* and paid on either side respectively."

Therefore we see by this section of the statute that the assignees could legally *claim* no more than the balance upon the account between the parties.

Judgment for the defendant.(*a*)

Bize v. *Dickason and Another, Assignees of Bartenshlag, T. T.* 26 *Geo.* III. *A. D.* 1786. 1. *T. R.* 285.

THIS was an action for money had and received by the defendants, as assignees of the bankrupt, for the plaintiff's use. Plea, the general issue.

The cause came on to be tried at the sittings after Easter Term, 1787, at *Guildhall, London,* before *Buller,* Justice, when the jury found a verdict for the plaintiff; damages 661*l.* 9*s.* 10*d.* and costs 40*s.* subject to the opinion of the court on the following case:

That the bankrupt, *John Rodolph Bartenshlag,* being an underwriter, subscribed policies filled up with the plaintiff's name for his foreign correspondents, who were unknown to the bankrupt.

That losses happened on such policies to the amount of 655*l.* 9*s.* 7*d.* *before the bankruptcy* of *Bartenshlag,* and were adjusted by him. That a loss on another policy to the amount of 6*l.* 0*s.* 3*d.* happened *before the said bankruptcy, but was not adjusted till after such bankruptcy.*

That the plaintiff paid the amount of the losses to his foreign correspondents after such bankruptcy.

That the plaintiff had a commission *del credere* from his correspondents; was made debtor by the bankrupt for the premiums; and always retained the policies in his hands.

That a dividend of 10*s.* in the pound was declared under the said commission on the 15th of June 1782.

That at the time of the bankruptcy there was due from the plaintiff to the bankrupt the sum of 1356*l.* 0*s.* 3*d.* And there was due from the bankrupt for the above losses 661*l.* 9*s.* 10*d.*

That on the 15th March 1782, the plaintiff paid to the defendants the sum of 750*l.* and on the 17th November 1785, the further sum of 606*l.* 0*s.* 3*d.* amounting to 1356*l.* 0*s.* 3*d.*

And on the 18th November 1785, the plaintiff proved the said sum of 661*l.* 9*s.* 10*d.* under the said commission.

That the plaintiff never received any dividend under the commission for or on account of the said losses.

That a final dividend of the effects of the said bankrupt was declared by the said commissioners on the 24th day of January 1786.

That on the first of February 1786, previous to such dividend being paid, the plaintiff caused a notice to be served on the defendants, purporting that he had *paid* them the said sum of 1356*l.* 0*s.* 3*d.* *under a mistaken idea, without deducting therefrom* the said 661*l.* 9*s.* 10*d.* for the aforesaid losses on the said several policies, sub-

(*a*) *Vid. Bize* v. *Dickason* and another, Assignees of *Bartenshlag,* post.

scribed by the bankrupt, for whom he was *del credere* to the said foreign correspondents, and had paid such losses accordingly; and cautioning them against making any dividend until he was paid the said sum of 661*l.* 9*s.* 10*d.*

That there are now in the hands of the said defendants effects of the bankrupt more than sufficient to satisfy the demand of the plaintiff.

The question for the opinion of the court is, Whether the plaintiff is entitled to recover in this action? If the plaintiff is entitled to recover in this action the verdict to stand. But if the court shall be of opinion that the plaintiff is not entitled to recover, then a verdict to be entered for the defendants.

Smith was to have argued for the plaintiff, but *Mingay* for the defendants declined arguing the case.

The court were of opinion that it came within the principle of the case of *Grove* and *Dubois.*(a) And

Lord MANSFIELD, Ch. J. said, the rule had always been, that if a man has actually paid what the law would not have compelled him to pay, but what in equity and conscience he ought, he cannot recover it back again in an action for money had and received. So where a man has paid a debt, which would otherwise have been barred by the statute of limitations; or a debt contracted during his infancy, which in justice he ought to discharge, though the law would not have compelled the payment, yet the money being paid, it will not oblige the payee to refund it. But where money is paid under a mistake, which there was no ground to claim in conscience, the party may recover it back again by this kind of action.

Judgment for the plaintiff.

Meliorucchi v. *R. Exchange Assurance Company*, *T. T.* 1728. 1 *Eq. Abr.* 8.

THE plaintiffs were assignees under a commission of bankruptcy awarded against Sir *Justus Beck*, and brought this bill against the defendants, to compel them to assign and transfer to the plaintiffs several shares in their stock, to which Sir *Justus Beck* was entitled, and which in the year 1720 cost him between 10 and 1200*l.* The defendants by answer insisted, that Sir *Justus Beck* was one of the directors of their company, and that in the year 1720, after his purchase of the before-mentioned stock, the company lent him about 12,000*l.* and insisted, that they ought not to be obliged to let the plaintiffs transfer or dispose of the interest which Sir *Justus* had in their stock, without payment of the 12,000*l.* borrowed, and that by virtue of the act 5 *Geo.* 1. one account ought to be set-off against the other; and for that purpose they had come in as creditors under the commission of bankruptcy, and had proved their debt; there was no pretence that the money was lent on the security of the stock; but it was insisted, that on the credit of the great parcel of stock, which Sir *Justus* had in their company at that time, that they lent him this money, and therefore would now stop his stock till payment thereof, or as far as the value of the stock would extend, which now by the great fall of the stocks would by no means satisfy their debt; but it was decreed at the Rolls, and that decree, on an appeal, affirmed by the Lord Chancellor, that the defendants ought to permit the plaintiffs, the assignees, to transfer and dispose of the stock for the most they could make of it, and that they could not stop or retain the stock for their satisfaction, either before or by virtue of the statute 5 *Geo.* 1. And it was resembled to the case of the lord of a manor and his copyholders, that the lord could not refuse to admit a person to whom one of the copyholders had sold his estate, on account of any debt due to the lord by that copyholder; that as the lord of the manor in that case, though he had the freehold of all the copyhold estates in him, yet he had no right to any of the copyholders private copyhold; so here, though the company had the whole stock of the company in them in their corporate capacity, yet the stock of each proprietor was distinct, and vested only in himself, wherewith the company had nothing to do further than

(a) *Ante*, 112.

they were invested therewith by the charter, or act of parliament wherewith they were incorporated and impowered, or ordered to transfer each one's stock by transfers to be made in the books of the company; which otherwise every proprietor might by deed, or otherwise, have transferred as he thought fit. And it was held, that this case differed from that of the *Hudson's Bay Company*, decreed *per* Lord Chancellor, assisted by *Raymond*, C. J. and Mr. Justice *Price*, where there was an express bye-law to subject the stock of each member to satisfy the debts they should owe to the company. And it was said, that this was not like the case of *Demanary* and *Metcalf*, where a banker lent 200*l*. on a pledge of jewels, and afterwards lent the same person a further sum of money on his bare note; yet he was not admitted to redeem the jewels without payment of the note likewise; for there it was between two private persons. And it was held not to be within the statute of 5 *Geo*. 1. which speaks only of mutual dealings and accounts, which is not this case, as Sir *Justus* had a fixed permanent interest in the stock, and the money borrowed without regard thereto. And the court held this was not like the case of partnership, where if any of the partners borrowed any of the partnership's money, his own share should be answerable for it, and he should not be permitted to come into a court of equity, and pray an account of his share of the partnership stock, and effects, without making satisfaction for the debt he owed to the partnership; for this was a transaction between them as private persons, and on a mutual credit and trust; but the loan of the 12,000*l*. in the present case to Sir *Justus*, was not in their corporate capacity, wherein only he stood related to them, and held his stock, but was a loan by them as private persons, for which they could not stop his stock, which he held as a member of the company in their corporate capacity.

George v. *Clagget and Another*, *T. T.* 37 *Geo. III. A. D.* 1797. 7 *Term Rep*. 359.

ON the trial of this action, which was assumpsit for goods sold and delivered to the amount of 142*l*. 1*s*. 9*d*. before Lord *Kenyon* at the Guildhall sittings, the case appeared to be this: The plaintiff, a clothier at Frome, employed Messrs. *Rich* and *Heapy* in London, Blackwell-hall factors, as his factors under a commission del credere, who besides acting as factors bought and sold great quantities of woollen cloths on their own account, all their business being carried on at one warehouse. The factors sold at twelve months credit, and were allowed two and a half per cent. On the 30th of September 1795, *Delvalle*, a tobacco broker, and who had been in habits of dealing with the defendants, bought several parcels of tobacco of them and gave them in payment a bill of exchange for 1198*l*. 16*s*. drawn by one *Fisher* on *Rich* and *Heapy* on the 24th of September 1795, payable two months after date to *J. Stafford*, who indorsed to *Delvalle*, who indorsed it over to the defendants, it having been previously accepted by *Rich* and *Heapy*. On the 12th of October 1795, the defendants bought a quantity of woollen cloths for exportation of *Rich* and *Heapy*, amounting to 1237*l*. 18*s*. 3*d*. at twelve months credit; the goods were taken out of one general mass in *Rich* and *Heapy's* warehouse; *Rich* and *Heapy* made out a bill of parcels for the whole in their own names, and the defendants did not know that any part of the goods belonged to the plaintiff. Early in November 1795, *Rich* and *Heapy* became bankrupts; and afterwards on the 20th of the same month the plaintiff gave the defendants notice not to pay *Rich* and *Heapy* for certain cloths specified, part of the above, amounting to 142*l*. 1*s*. 9*d*. they having been his property, and having been sold on his account by *Rich* and *Heapy* on commission. The question was whether the defendants were or were not entitled to set-off their demand against *Rich* and *Heapy* on the bill of exchange, on the ground that the defendants dealt with them as principals. Lord *Kenyon* was of opinion that they were, as well on principle as on the authority of *Rabone* v. *Williams*;(*a*) and a verdict was accordingly found for the defendants.

(*a*) RABONE jun. v. WILLIAMS, Middlesex sittings after Mich. 1785; which was thus stated.—Action for the value of goods sold to the defendant by means of the house of *Rabone* sen. and Co. at Exeter, factors to the plaintiff. The defendant, the vendee of the goods, set-off a debt due to him from *Rabone* and Co. the factors, upon another account, alleging that the plaintiff had not appeared at all in the transaction, and the credit had been given by *Rabone* and Co. the factors, and not by the plaintiff

A rule having been obtained, calling on the defendants to shew cause why the verdict should not be set aside, and a new trial had, on the authority of the case of *Estcott* v. *Milward, Co. Bank. Laws* 236,

Gibbs and *Giles* were now to have shewn cause against that rule: but

Erskine and *Walton* were called upon to support it. They relied on the cases of *Scrimshire* v. *Alderton*,(a) and *Estcott* v. *Milward*, as reported in *Co. Bank. Laws*, to shew that under the circumstances of this case the principal might resort to the buyer at once, he having given notice before actual payment by the defendants to the factors.

But a more accurate note of the case of *Estcott* v. *Milward*(b) having now been obtained from Mr. J. *Buller*, before whom that cause was tried, and read,

The court were clearly of opinion that the directions given by the learned judge on the trial of this cause were right; and that this case was not distinguishable from that of *Rabone* v. *Williams*. Therefore they discharged the rule.(c)

Millisent Shipman v. *A. Thompson*, *T. T.* 11 *and* 12 *Geo. II. C. P. A. D.* 1738. *Willes' Rep.* 103.

THIS came before the court on a case reserved at the trial before Mr. Baron *Fortescue*.

The plaintiff's late husband by his will made the plaintiff and Dr. *Morgan* (since deceased) his executors. In his life-time he had appointed the defendant his steward by letter of attorney, who after the testator's death received of several tenants several sums of money due to the testator in his life-time. The plaintiff brought this action in her own name, not naming herself executrix, for the money so received. The defendant gave notice to set-off several sums due from the testator to him, which the judge would not permit the defendant to set-off.

The questions reserved were; 1st. Whether the plaintiff sould not have declared as executrix;

Lord *Mansfield*, Ch. J.—"Where a factor, dealing for a principal but concealing that principal, delivers goods in his own name, the person contracting with him has a right to consider him to all intents and purposes as the principal; and though the real principal may appear and bring an action upon that contract against the purchaser of the goods, yet that purchaser may set-off any claim he may have against the factor in answer to the demand of the principal. This has been long settled." Upon this opinion, the rest, being a mere matter of account, was referred. In *Bayley* v. *Morley*, London sittings after Mich. 1788, Lord *Kenyon* recognized the law of this case.

(a) 2 *Str.* 1182.

(b) London sittings after Mich. 1783. Action for goods sold. The goods were sold by *Farrar* a corn factor, who gave no account of the sale to the plaintiff, nor made any entry of it in his books. He was insolvent for some time before, had avoided all dealing for a month, had desired that there might be no buying in his name, and had not dealt with the defendant for a year before, but was then in his debt. There was a verdict for the plaintiff on the ground of fraud.

(c) The same point was also ruled by Lord *Kenyon* in *Stracey*, *Ross*, and others, v. *Decy*, London sittings after Mich. 1789. Assumpsit for goods sold; pleas non assumpsit and a set-off. The plaintiffs jointly carried on trade as grocers, but *Ross* was the only ostensible person engaged in the business, and appeared to the world as solely interested therein. By the terms of the partnership *Ross* was to be the apparent trader, and the others were to remain mere sleeping partners. The defendant was a policy broker, and being indebted for grocery (as he conceived) to *Ross*, he effected insurances and paid premiums on account of *Ross* solely, to the amount of his debt, under the idea that one demand might be set-off against the other. *Ross's* affairs being much deranged, payment of the money due from the defendant was demanded by the firm, and was refused by him upon the ground of his having been deceived by the other partners keeping back and holding out *Ross* as the only person concerned in the trade. Lord *Kenyon* Ch. J. was of opinion that as the defendant had a good defence by way of set-off as against *Ross*, and had been by the conduct of the plaintiffs led to believe that *Ross* was the only person he contracted with, they could not now pull off the mask and claim payment of debts supposed to be due to *Ross* alone, without allowing the parties the same advantages and equities in their defence that they would have had in actions brought by *Ross*.

Verdict for the defendant.

2dly. Whether the defendant ought not to have been permitted to set-off the money due to him from the testator.

The Court, after argument, gave judgment for the plaintiff.(a)

(a) The reasons given by the Court of Common Pleas do not appear in Lord Chief Justice *Willes'* papers; but the same case was referred to the opinion of Mr. *B. Fortescue*(1) before whom the cause was tried, and who, in the *Easter* term preceding, after hearing the case argued by Mr. *Makepeace* for the defendant, and Sir *T. Abney* for the plaintiff, gave the following judgment in favour of the plaintiff:

" It is insisted on for the defendant that this money received by him is vested in the executrix in auter droit, that as she hath no right of her own the action must follow the right, and that therefore she should have brought the action as executrix and not in her own right. And the case of *Hutton*, cited in 6 *Mod.* 4. was cited, where it is said if executor bring trover and *declare that he is possessed as executor to J. S.* if on evidence it appear that they were his own goods he shall be nonsuited and pay costs; and it was insisted that by a parity of reasoning where the executor brings an action in his own name and it appears that they were the goods of the testator, he ought to be nonsuited. As to this; there is no doubt but that the plaintiff in this case is entitled to all the effects of the testator in auter droit, and all executors are: but if this were a universal rule that therefore the action must follow the right and be brought as executor, the executor could in no case bring an action in his own name for any goods or effects of the testator, which in some cases it is certain that he may. As where the testator's goods are taken out of the possession of the executor, he may bring trover in his own name,(2) because it is an immediate tort to him, though he is possessed of these goods in auter droit. By this also it appears that it is not a necessary consequence that, because if the action is brought in the plaintiff's name as executor and the goods appear to be his own he must be nonsuited, therefore he must be nonsuited if he bring the action in his own name and the goods appear to be the testator's; for in that case it is manifest that he cannot recover his own goods as executor, and fails in proving his cause of action which was to recover the goods as the goods of the testator.

But the true distinction, I think, is this, that where the thing sued for is assets in the hands of the executor or administrator before the recovery, or where the cause of action arises in the executor's own time and never did arise to the testator, there the executor may bring the action either in his own name or as executor. And this is laid down as law in the case of *Jenkins* and his wife v. *Plombe*, *Salk.* 207. but better and more fully reported in 6 *Mod.* 92, 181. That was an action brought by the husband and wife as executrix upon an indebitatus assumpsit for money had and received by the defendant to their use as executrix: it is true that the judgment of the court was only that upon being nonsuited the plaintiffs ought to pay costs: but the reason of the judgment was because they might have brought the action in their own name and not as executrix; for wherever an executor may have the action in his own name he shall pay costs. And the case of *Eaves* v. *Morato, Salk.* 314. was cited there, and this difference taken, that there were several counts by the plaintiff as executor, one whereof was an insimul computasset, and being nonsuited be

(1) It seems to have been not unusual at this time to refer the case at first to the judge who tried the cause, and afterwards to the court if the parties were dissatisfied with his opinion.

(2) So in an action of assumpsit brought on a foreign judgment recovered by the executor, the plaintiff may declare in his own right, and not as executor; *Crawford* v. *Whittal, H.* 13 *G.* 3. *B. R. Dougl.* 4. *n.*—So an executor may maintain an action in his own name against a sheriff for the escape of a prisoner who was in execution on a judgment obtained by him as executor; *Bonafous* v. *Walker*, 2 *Durnf.* & *E.* 126. (contrary to *Glover* v. *Kendal*, 1 *Lutw.* 893; *Reynell* v. *Langcastle*, *Cro. Jac.* 545; *Brookes* v. *Cooke*, 1 *Show.* 57; and *Wate* v. *Briggs*, 1 *Ld. Raym.* 35.)—So where an executor pays money which be was not obliged to pay, and afterwards brings an action to recover it back, he may declare in his own right; *Munt* v. *Stokes*, 4 *Durnf.* & *E.* 561.—And if an executor bring trover on a conversion in his own time, or assumpsit for money received after the testator's death, and fail, he is liable to pay costs though he name himself executor; *Atkey* v. *Heard*, *Cro. Car.* 219; *Anonymous*, 1 *Ventr.* 109; *Harris* v. *Hanne*, *Rep. temp. Hardw.* 201; *Goldthwaite* v. *Petrie*, 5 *Durnf.* & *E.* 234; and *Bollard* v. *Spencer*, 7 *D.* & *E.* 358. in which last case a contrary determination in *Cockerill* v. *Kynaston*, 4 *D.* & *E.* [illegible] was overruled

paid no costs, because there was no *new cause* of action, but a new action ascertaining the ancient cause, which is still a debt of the testator's. And in the case of *Jenkins* v. *Plombe*, as appears from *Salkeld*, this distinction of insimul computasset is also taken; and it was said that if the defendant received this money by the appointment of the plaintiff, it was assets immediately, if without his consent yet the bringing of the action is such a consent that upon judgment it shall be assets immediately before execution, which otherwise it would not be until after execution; and the reason is because it is recovered against a person who never was indebted to the testator, and the original debt was discharged.

To apply this to the present case; here is money received by the defendant since the testator's death, and therefore it could not be received to the use of the testator, but must be received to the use of the executor. The executor has consented by bringing the action, and the money is assets immediately upon the judgment. It is quite a new debt created from the defendant to the executor since the death of the testator, and a new cause of action which was not subsisting before. The defendant was never indebted to the testator for this money, and the original debtors, the tenants, are discharged. No doubt had the action been brought against the tenants, it must have been brought against them by the plaintiff as executrix, because it was a debt as to them subsisting in the testator's life-time, and no new cause of action arising to the executrix.

It is said that, as this case of *Jenkins* v. *Plombe* is stated in 6 *Modern*, *Powell* J. and *Gould* J. doubted: but whatever they might have done on the first argument, it is plain they were satisfied afterwards; for in page 182 it appears that the judgment was given per totam curiam.

It is said that the defendant had an authority by letter of attorney to receive the testator's rents, that this authority did not determine with the testator's death, and that therefore as the defendant received it by the authority of the testator it is money had and received to his use, and it shall not be presumed to have been received by the consent of the executor. But I think, as this is a naked authority and not coupled with any interest, it could not subsist after the testator's death. In *Combe's* case, 9 *Rep.* 76. *b.* it was resolved that where a person has authority as an attorney to do an act, he must do it in the name of him who gave the authority; for he appoints the attorney to be in his place and represent his person; and for that reason the attorney cannot act in his own name, nor do it as his own act, but in the name and as the act of him who gave the authority. And if this be so, it is impossible to say that this defendant received this money as attorney for the testator or that he represented his person, in regard that the testator was dead; it is the executrix only who represents the person and stands in the place of the testator.

This has been likened to the case of an assignee of a bankrupt, of whom it is said that though the property of the bankrupt's goods or debts be vested in him, yet he must sue as assignee; and no doubt he must for all debts due to the bankrupt. But if goods be taken from the assignee, or money received from a debtor of the bankrupt after the assignment, I do not know that it has been any where adjudged that an action brought in his name would be ill. But be that as it will, this is the case of an executrix and not of an assignee of a bankrupt, and it was (I think) plainly and clearly adjudged in the case of *Jenkins* v. *Plombe* that an executor in such case may bring an action in his own name; and I do not find that it was ever adjudged to the contrary.

With regard to the case of *Chapman* v. *Darby*, *Carth.* 232, where it was holden that, where the plaintiff brought assumpsit for so much money had and received to his use as administrator, the promise was not ill laid; no doubt it is so, and so allowed in *Jenkins* v. *Plombe* that the plaintiff may bring the action either way; so that this case of *Chapman* v. *Darby* does not prove that the administrator may not bring the action in his own name, but only that he may do it as administrator; and no doubt he may do it either way. As to the case of *Curry* v. *Stephenson*, *Carth.* 335. *Holt* Ch. J. took exception to the declaration that it was not well, because the money was received after the death of the intestate, and then it was received to the use of the plaintiff generally, and not as administratrix; and the point was, that though it was received by the defendant after the intestate's death, yet it was before administration granted; and this is the reason on which the book seems to go why it was disallowed, which is not the present case.

As to the set-off; we cannot consider the convenience or the inconvenience on one side or the other, but must go according to the act; for the stat. 2 *Geo.* 2. *c.* 22. *s.* 13. says, or *if either party sues or is sued as executor or administrator* where there are mutual debts between the testator or intestate and either party, one debt may

Collins v. *Collins*, *T. T.* 32 *Geo. II. A. D.* 1759. 2 *Burr.* 820.

THIS was an action of debt upon bond.

The condition appeared, upon *Oyer*, to be, "to pay the plaintiff an annuity of "10*l.* a year during his life; and likewise to *maintain* him in meat, drink, washing "and lodging, in the dwelling-house at Crundall-End, for and during his *life*."

To this declaration, the defendant pleaded (by leave) several pleas.

As to the payment of the annuity of 10*l.* *per annum*.—There was a plea of a *set-off*; (viz. that only 60*l.* is due to the plaintiff on account of the said annuity; and that the plaintiff owes him more than 60*l.* viz. 500*l.*)

As to the *maintaining* the plaintiff, &c.—There was a plea that the plaintiff left the house voluntarily, and did not board and lodge *in* the house: so that he (the defendant) was *not obliged* to board, wash and lodge him. But the defendant avers that he was always ready to maintain him, &c. AT and IN the house. [*V. infra.*]

The plaintiff demurs: and the defendant joins in demurrer.

The latter plea depended upon the words of the condition; which was—"That "if *Joseph Collins* the younger, his heirs executors or administrators, do and shall "well and truly pay or cause to be paid unto *Joseph Collins* the elder, and his as-"signs, yearly and every year during his life, one annuity of 10*l.* of lawful money "of Great Britain, clear of all taxes, &c. on the 25th of March and 29th of Septem-"ber yearly; and if the said *Joseph Collins* the younger, shall find, provide and allow "to and for the said *Joseph Collins* the elder, good and sufficient meat drink wash-"ing and lodging IN *the dwelling house at Crundall-End* aforesaid; then this obliga-"tion to be void; but if default shall be made in the payment of the said annuity "of 10*l.* or any part thereof, at or upon any or either of the days abovementioned "for the payment thereof; *or if* he the said *Joseph Collins* the younger, shall *ne-glect or refuse* to maintain and keep the said *Joseph Collins* the elder, during his "natural life as aforesaid; then, and in *either* of the said cases, to be and remain "in full force and virtue."

The defendant (having leave to plead several pleas &c.) pleaded a set-off (as is before mentioned) to the former part of the condition, which was for payment of the *annuity*. And as to the latter, he pleaded that the *house at Crundall-End* was the house where the said *Joseph Collins the younger, dwelt*, and ever since has dwelt, with his family; and that he did admit the said *Joseph Collins* the elder, and receive him into the said house; and did *until his departure* aftermentioned, find provide and allow to the said *Joseph* the elder, meat, drink &c. [in the words of the condition:] but that he the said *Joseph* the elder, *of his own accord*, departed from the said house at *Crundall-End*, and has *never yet returned*, to be there provided with meat, drink, &c. (*ut supra;*) nor hath *ever required* to be provided with any, or to have any allowed, THERE. And the said *Joseph* the younger, has *al-*

---

due from the testator to the defendant cannot be set-off against this plaintiff in an action brought by her in her own name, and not as executor. And supposing this to be so, it was urged as one reason why the action here ought to have been brought by the plaintiff as executrix; but this statute will not alter the law as to that point from what it was before; and if the statute has not remedied all the inconveniencies, we must take it as it is, and cannot (I think) extend it further.

So the postea must be delivered to the plaintiff, and she must have her judgment." MS. Mr. Justice *W.* (then Mr. Baron) *Fortescue*.

To the above Mr. B. *Fortescue* afterwards added this note; "N. B. The court of B. C. on a case made were of the same opinion as to both points." (1)

(1.) The same point, relative to the set-off, has been since determined by the court of King's Bench in two cases, *Kilvington* v. *Stevenson*, *East.* 1768, on demurrer; and *Tegetmeyer* v. *Lumley*, *Tr.* 25 *Geo.* 3. on a motion for a new trial. *Vid. post.* 261. But a debt due to the defendant *as surviving partner* may be set-off against a demand on him in his own right; *Slipper* v. *Slidstone*, 5 *Durnf.* & *E.* 493, & e converso a debt due from the plaintiff as surviving partner to the defendant may be set-off against a debt due from the defendant to the plaintiff in his own right. *French* v. *Andrade*, 6 *D.* & *E.* 582.

ways been ready to have provided the said *Joseph* the elder, with meat, drink, &c. *(ut supra)* AT *and* IN *the said dwelling-house*, if he had *not departed*, or would have returned THITHER: but that he always has refused and still does *refuse to return*; but has continued *absent from* THENCE. *Therefore* he could not provide him with meat, drink, &c. *(ut supra)* AT *or* IN *the said dwelling-house.*

To this plea the plaintiff demurred; and the defendant joined in demurrer.

Mr. Serjt. *Poole*, on behalf of the plaintiff, argued that this case of an *annuity* or *yearly payment* does not fall within the statute of 8 *G.* 2. *c* 24. § 5. concerning set-offs; because the action is not brought for a sum *complete* and *certain*, but for a part of a growing sum payable *for life*; whereof *future* payments will be continually be coming due.

Now if the judgment be here entered for the remainder (as that act directs,) it passes *in rem judicatam*; and the plaintiff cannot recover any more, on any *future* default of payment upon the same bond.

By sec. 4. of this act, the provision for setting mutual debts one against the other, was looked upon as highly just and reasonable at *all* times: it is therefore provided that the clause in 2 *G.* 2. *c.* 22. "for setting mutual debts one against the other" shall be and remain in full force *forever*.

Section 5. of this act of 8 *G.* 2. *c.* 24, provides "that by virtue of the said clause "in 2 *G.* 2. *c.* 22. (which is thereby made perpetual,) mutual debts may be set "against each other, either by being pleaded in bar, or given in evidence on the "general issue, in the manner therein mentioned, *notwithstanding* that such debts "are deemed in law to be of a *different nature*; unless in cases where either of the "said debts shall accrue by reason of a penalty contained in any bond or specialty; "and in all cases where either the debt for which the action hath been or shall be "brought, or the debt intended to be set against the same hath accrued or shall "accrue by reason of any such penalty, the debt intended to be set-off shall be "pleaded in bar, in which plea shall be shown how much is truly and justly due "on either side: and in case the plaintiff shall recover in any such action or suit, "*judgment* shall be entered for NO MORE than shall appear to be *truly and justly* "*due* to the plaintiff, after one debt being set against the other as aforesaid."

This is not a bond conditioned for performance of covenants or agreements contained in any deed or writing: it contains a quite different and distinct condition. The present action is an action of debt upon a bond conditioned to *pay an annuity* and *maintain a parent*.

Mr. Serj. *Hewitt contra*—This is a new case.

The setting-off of mutual debts arises on 2 *G.* 2. *c.* 22. *sec.* 13. (which was a temporary act,) and on 8 *G.* 2. *c.* 24. *sec.* 4, 5. (which makes the former perpetual.)

This last section (§ 5.) provides, generally "That *wherever* the debt arises upon "a *bond or specialty with a penalty*, and accrues by reason of such penalty, a set-off "may be pleaded." My brother *Poole* says, "It extends *only* to cases where the "debt is a *sum certain*." But the words of the act are *general*; and are not at all confined to sums certain. And the plaintiff *may* afterwards recover, for *subsequent* defaults; notwithstanding the prior judgment: for the *penalty* will *always* remain a duty.

Our plea covers the whole demand.

Mr. Serj. *Poole* was beginning to reply. But an observation having been made by Mr. Just. *Denison*, upon the latter part of the condition;

Mr. Serj. *Hewitt* desired it might stand over till next paper-day; (intending to make a motion, in the interim, for leave to amend.) To which request the court agreed.

ULTERIUS CONCILIUM.

On the next paper-day, (26th *June*,) Mr. Serjeant *Poole* proceeded in his reply: (Serjeant *Hewitt not* having moved to amend.) He argued that a set-off could not be pleaded under *this* act: for this act is general, and has no such provision as there is in the act of 8, 9 *W.* 3. *c.* 11. *sec. ult. viz.* "That the judgment shall "*stand as security*." And therefore if the plaintiff should now recover judgment, there would be an *end* of the bond; and there would remain *no* security at all for *future* payment of the annuity.

And he agreed with Mr. Serjeant *Hewitt*, that this is a *new* case.

Mr. Serjeant *Hewitt* insisted, that this act of 8 *G.* 2. *c.* 24. differs materially from 8, 9 *W.* 3. and from 4, 5 *Ann. c.* 16. *sec.* 13. for bringing in the money, and having the bond discharged. The present act says " That the plaintiff shall recover the sum truly and justly due, and *no more.*" And my brother *Poole* says, " That after the matter is passed *in rem judicatam*, the plaintiff *cannot afterwards* " recover any more upon the same bond." But I answer, that the plaintiff *would be* at liberty to bring an *action for any further breach* : for the present judgment (upon the set-off) would not be for the *penalty*, but only for the *sum truly and justly* due, and no more.

Lord MANSFIELD—These clauses in 8, 9 *W.* 3. *c.* 11. and 8 *G.* 2. *c.* 24. are extremely *beneficial to the subject.*

Therefore his lordship chose, he said, to consider of it ; and did not mean to give his opinion at present. However, by way of breaking case, he entered into an explication of the acts , which he thought ought to be considered *all together*, as being made in *pari materia.* So that *stoppage* or *setting-off* must have the same effect, under the 8 *G.* 2. as *payment* had under 8, 9 *W.* 3.

Therefore he thought, (at present,) that it was most beneficial to the subject, that in the case now before the court, the set-off *should* be allowed. But he assured Serjeant *Poole*, that if they should be of that opinion on deliberation, he should not, as it was a new case, be caught by his demurrer ; for that they would give him leave to withdraw it, and reply.

CUR. ADVIS.

Lord MANSFIELD now delivered the resolution of the court ; *viz.* That they were all (upon deliberate consideration) unanimously and clearly of opinion (as it struck him before) that this is a case within 8 *G.* 2. *c.* 24. *sec.* 4, 5. Where mutual *debts* may be set-off, just as much as actual *payment* of the money might have been *before.*

He said he would consider how the law stood, before the acts of 2 *G.* 2. *c.* 22. and 8 *G.* 2. *c.* 24. and under the act of 8, 9 *W.* 3. *c.* 11.

The act of 8, 9 *W.* 3. *c.* 11. is entitled " An act for the better preventing frivolous and vexatious suits." The last clause of it is a provision intended to meet the case of non-performance of covenants and agreements secured by bonds or indentures ; and which covenants or agreements are to be performed at *different* times, or the monies paid by *instalments*, &c.

Before that act, a plaintiff could only assign *one* breach, upon such bond or indenture. And if the defendant could prove that the *whole* debt was *paid*, there was an end of the matter. But if the defendant had only paid *part* of the debt, and *not the whole*, then the judgment was taken for the *whole penalty* : and this judgment for the *whole penalty* stood as a security for the *residue* of the demand which remained unpaid. So that the judgment stood for the *whole* penalty, though only *part* remained due ; and the plaintiff was justly entitled only to *that*, and *no more* : which often forced the defendant, in such a case, into expensive suits in equity for relief.

To prevent which, the last clause of this act of 8, 9 *W.* 3. *c.* 11. provides " That in all actions, in any of his majesty's courts of record, upon any bond or " bonds, or on any penal sum, for non-performance of any covenants or agreements " in any indenture deed or writing contained, the plaintiff or plaintiffs may assign " as many breaches as he or they shall think fit ; and the jury shall assess damages " and costs on so many of them as the plaintiff shall prove to have been broken : " and the like judgment shall be entered on such verdict, as had been usually done " in such like actions." Then there is a suitable provision for suggesting several breaches, where the judgment passes by default, confession or on demurrer. Then the act provides, " That if after judgment and before execution executed, the " defendant shall *pay* into court all the damages and costs on the several breaches " assigned and found, a *stay of execution* on the judgment shall be entered upon " record : or if, by reason of any *execution executed*, the plaintiff shall be *fully paid* " *and satisfied* all such damages and costs, and the charges of such execution : then " the body, lands or goods of the defendant shall be discharged of such execution : " which shall likewise be entered upon record. But yet, in each case, the JUDGMENT shall *remain as a further security*, to answer damages to the plaintiff for " *future* breaches ; upon which the plaintiff may have a *scire facias* on the judg-

"ment, suggesting *other breaches*; whereupon there shall be the like proceeding as "was in the action of debt upon the bond, for assessing damages on *such* breaches; "and on payment or satisfaction, as before, of such *future* damages costs and charges "as aforesaid, all further proceeding shall be AGAIN *stayed*; and so *toties quoties*; "and the defendant, his body lands or goods shall be discharged out of execution, "as aforesaid."

A very beneficial remedy, and a very just one to the subject, this is. The JUDGMENT is to be for the *whole penalty*, and is to *remain* as a *further security*; though EXECUTION is to be stayed on payment of the sum due, &c. So that the *penalty* is a *security* for the debt interest and costs, upon any *future* breach.

Before this statute, the ACTUAL PAYMENT of money in discharge of the demand, was exactly upon the same foot, as the SET-OFF *of a debt* is *now* put upon; and a *plea of* PAYMENT of a sum of money sufficient to discharge the *whole* demand was just the same *then*, as a SET-OFF *of a debt* large enough to balance the *whole* demand, is *now*: that is to say, it was a *full answer* to the plaintiff's demand; and he could have no *judgment at all* against the defendant.

But if it had come out, that there had been a failure of *payment* of *any part* of the plaintiff's just demand, the plaintiff would have been entitled to take his JUDGMENT for the *whole penalty*; (Though EXECUTION was to be stayed on payment of the *damages already incurred* and *costs*:) and this judgment for the *whole* penalty was to stand as a *security*, to answer *future* breaches.

But the payment here intended was to be an ACTUAL payment. For *stoppage*, or *setting-off* debt against debt, was not *then* equivalent to actual payment: but cross actions must at *that* time have been brought, for the respective mutual debts.

Since these two very beneficial acts of 2 *G*. 2. c. 22. and 8 *G*. 2. c. 24. *stoppage*, or *setting-off*, of mutual debts, is *become equivalent to actual payment*: and a *balance shall be struck*, as in equity and justice it ought to be.

At *common law*, before these acts, if the plaintiff was as much, or even more indebted to the defendant than the defendant was indebted to him, yet the defendant had no method to strike a balance: he could only go into a court of *equity*, for doing what is most clearly *just* and *right* to be done.

The 2 *G*. 2. c. 22. was made to answer this just and reasonable end; and enacts generally, "That where there are mutual debts between the parties, one debt may "be set against the other." Upon which act of 2 *G*. 2. doubts about the *different natures* of debts have arisen; the 8 *G*. 2. c. 24. was thereupon made: the 5th section whereof is a *general* provision *without exception*. So that the objections which have been here made, on the part of the plaintiff, are made by *construction* only.

It is objected, first, "That this is *not* an action brought upon a penalty for non-"performance of an agreement or covenant *contained* in any *indenture deed* or "*writing*."

This is an *agreement between* the parties, and an agreement *in writing*: the *condition of the bond* is an *agreement in writing*; and people have frequently gone into courts of equity upon conditions of bonds, *as* being agreements in writing, to have a *specific performance* of them.

It is said that if the plaintiff should take his judgment upon this act of parliament, it would *not* be a *judgment* for the PENALTY, but a judgment *only* for the *sum due*, and NO MORE; and that after the matter has once passed *in rem judicatam*, the plaintiff *cannot afterwards recover any more* upon this bond, whatever may become due by future non-payments; for that here is *no provision* "that the judg-"men shall *stand as a security for future payments*," as there was in the act of 8, 9 *W*. 3. c. 11. made for the better preventing frivolous and vexatious suits.

The judgment is indeed by this act of 8 *G*. 2. directed to be entered "for no "more than shall appear to be justly and truly due to the plaintiff:" But it is clearly *within the words and meaning* of the act, that the *penalty* is to *remain* as a security against future breaches, in this case of a *set-off* pleaded, as much as it would have done upon the act of 8 9, *W*. 3. c. 11. if *payment* had been made agreeably to the directions therein contained.

But as this has not been before settled, "That a set-off may be pleaded in such a "case as this, where the condition is for the payment of an *annuity* or *growing sum*." It would be hard to bind the plaintiff down strictly to his demurrer. Therefore my brother *Poole* may move to *withdraw the demurrer*, and to reply in a proper manner;

which will give the plaintiff an opportunity of disputing the debt pleaded by way of set-off, if he thinks proper.

Which Mr. Serj. *Poole* moved accordingly: and the court granted it; but added that it should be *upon payment of costs*.

Stacey Ross & al. v. *Decy. M.* 1789. *Esp. Cases*, 469.

IT was an action for goods sold and delivered: Plea of set-off.

It appeared in evidence, that the plaintiffs had entered into a partnership as grocers; and it was agreed that *Ross* should keep the shop in his own name only; under those circumstances he dealt with the defendant for the partnership goods, for which this action was brought.

The defendant had done business for the plaintiff *Ross* on his own account, and not on account of the partnership, to a greater amount than the demand now made against him by the partnership, and this he offered to set-off.

It was opposed on the ground of the demands accruing in different capacities, that so it was inadmissible.

Lord KENYON was of opinion, that the set-off was good; his lordship said, the plaintiffs had subjected themselves to it, by holding out false colours to the world, by permitting *Ross* to appear as the sole owner; that it was possible the defendant would not have trusted *Ross* only, if he had not considered the debt due to himself as a security against a counter-demand.

Erskine observed, that the defendant had thereby a double advantage; for, if he dealt with *Ross* as the only partner, and had had a demand against the partnership account, he might have maintained an action against them all; yet here he was permitted to consider *Ross* as the only partner.

Lord KENYON admitted this consequence to follow from the fallacy held out to the world by such as stand in the situation of sleeping partners, but allowed the set-off to the extent claimed; and the defendant had a verdict.

Jaques v. *Withy*, *H. T.* 27 *Geo. III. A. D.* 1787. 1 *T. R.* 557.

CASE for money had and received, money lent and advanced, &c. Plea set-off 340*l.* upon a judgment recovered in *Trinity* term, in the 22d year, &c. by the defendant against the plaintiff in this court, which is still in force and unsatisfied.

The plaintiff in his replication admitted the judgment, &c. but said that the defendant in *Michaelmas* term in the 23d year, &c. in order to obtain satisfaction of the said judgment, charged him in execution of the said judgment in the custody of the marshal of the *Marshalsea*, &c. and kept and detained him in such custody, and in execution of the said judgment, until the 6th of February 1783, when he was by and *with the consent, privity, authority, and licence of the defendant, and by his order and direction, released and enlarged from and out of the said custody*, and wholly discharged from the said execution at the suit of the defendant of and upon the said judgment.

Rejoinder, That the plaintiff on the 28th of February, 1783, at his instance and request, was by and with the consent, privity, authority and licence of the defendant, and by his order and direction, released and enlarged from and out of the said custody, &c. and discharged from the said execution of the said suit of the defendant of and upon the said judgment so recovered, &c. for and in consideration of the plaintiff's then and there making and delivering to the defendant a certain writing obligatory, bearing date the 28th of February, 1783, in 681*l.* with a condition to satisfy the judgment either by instalments or by an annuity, and also for and in consideration of a warrant of attorney, executed by the plaintiff on the 28th of February 1783, given to the defendant to confess judgment on the said writing obligatory in the court of our lord the king of the bench. That afterwards and within twenty days of the execution of the said writing obligatory, and warrant of attorney, (to wit,) on the 18th day of March, 1783; the defendant, according to the form of the statute, caused a memorial to be enrolled in chancery, of and concerning an annuity secured by a bond and warrant of attorney to confess judgment thereon in his majesty's court of King's Bench, executed by the plaintiff, in the penal sum of 681*l.* in consideration of the sum of 340*l* 10*s.* paid to the plaintiff by the defendant for one annuity of 50*l.* to be paid to the defendant by the plaintiff during his life. That the plaintiff, after the granting of the said annuity to the defendant, made default of payment therein. And thereupon the defendant, by virtue of the said warrant of attorney in *Hilary* term, in the 26th year, &c. signed judgment upon the said writing obligatory against the plaintiff in the court of Common Pleas. And afterwards in the said *Hilary* term sued and prosecuted out of the same court a writ of *fieri facias*, directed to the sheriff of Middlesex, who executed it. That afterwards in *Easter* term, in the 26th year, &c. the plaintiff obtained a rule in the court of Common Pleas, to show cause why the judgment signed by the defendant against the plaintiff, and the writ of execution issued thereon and executed, &c. and all proceedings in that cause subsequent to the said judgment, should not be set aside, and the bond and warrant of attorney brought into court and delivered up to the plaintiff to be cancelled, and the goods &c. levied under the execution, restored to the plaintiff, and why the defendant should not pay the costs of all these proceedings; which rule was made absolute in the same *Easter* term. That the said court of Common Pleas so ordered the said writing obligatory and warrant of attorney to be delivered up to be cancelled *by reason of a mistake, informality, and irregularity, in the said memorial*, that is to say, by reason of the said warrant of attorney being therein expressed to be a warrant of attorney to confess judgment in his majesty's court of King's Bench, instead of his majesty's court of Common Pleas, and by reason of the consideration of the said writing obligatory and warrant of attorney being expressed to be for 340*l.* 10*s.* paid to the said plaintiff, instead of expressing it to be in consideration of the said judgment for that sum.

To this rejoinder there was a general demurrer, and joinder in demurrer.

Morgan was to have argued in support of the demurrer, but the court desired to hear the other side.

Wood, contra, admitted as a general position, that where a person is once taken in execution and discharged, he cannot be sued again for the same debt. But he contended that that was not universally true, and that under the particular circumstances of this case, the debt due from the plaintiff to the defendant was not extinguished. An execution against the person of a defendant is not in all cases a satisfaction of a debt: for if he escape out of custody when charged in execution, it is clear that an action may be maintained on the judgment, because it is by the defendant's act only that he obtains his discharge. The same rule likewise holds if that discharge be obtained by fraud. Now in this case the discharge granted by the defendant was not voluntary, but it was on a consideration which has failed; and therefore the discharge cannot operate as a bar, or extinguish the debt. This is like the case where a judgment on a simple contract is reversed by a writ of error, the simple contract still remains, and an action may be maintained on the *assumpsit*. So if an execution be set aside for irregularity, the plaintiff may sue out another.

Ashhurst, J. There must be judgment for the plaintiff in the present case; I cannot pretend to say how far a court of equity would interfere in this case; and indeed the defendant seems to have some ground for claiming relief. But at all events, the discharge from the execution is certainly a discharge at law. I know of only one case where a debtor in execution, who obtains his liberty, may afterwards be taken again for the same debt, and that is where he has escaped; but the reason of that is because he was not *legally* out of custody. But where a prisoner obtains his discharge *with the consent of the party* who put him in execution, he cannot be retaken. In the present case, the plaintiff trusted to the other security, and therefore he cannot resort to the first security again.

Buller, J. The counsel for the defendant has relied only on the equity of the case; and that advantage has been taken of a mere slip. It is not material for us to consider whether a conscientious man would have taken this advantage; the truth is, there is a flat objection under an act of parliament(*a*) of which the plaintiff is entitled to take the benefit. The facts are, that the plaintiff, being in execution at the suit of the defendant, was discharged by him on giving a bond and warrant of attorney, which security, at the time it was given, was good. Therefore the plaintiff was not guilty of any fraud. But the objection is, that the

(*a*) 17 *Geo.* 3. *c.* 6.

requisites of the act not having been complied with, the security is void. That however arose from the neglect of the defendant himself, in not complying with the directions of the statute. If the security were good at the time of the discharge, the defendant cannot have recourse to the judgment again, because that was waived; and the debt having been once extinguished, cannot be revived again. This is not a new question. The case of *Vigers* and *Aldrich*,(a) goes the whole length of this; for it shows, that if a defendant has been once discharged out of execution upon terms which are not afterwards complied with, the plaintiff cannot resort to the judgment again, or charge the defendant's person in execution. So here, if the defendant has neglected to avail himself of the advantage of the security, it is his own fault, and he must take the consequences.

Judgment for the plaintiff.(b)

Percevall Hutchinson v. *William Sturges*, *T. T.* 14 & 15 *Geo. II. A. D.* 1741. *C. P. Willes* 261.

[H. 14 Geo. II. Rol. 444.]

A DEBT on a bond for 8*l*. given by the defendant to the plaintiff one of the bearers of the virges of the King's household and an officer and minister of the King's Court of his palace at *Westminster*; dated the 25th of July, 1740.

The defendant pleaded that the plaintiff was indebted to the defendant in 10*l*. for work and labour, &c. in 10*l*. for goods sold and delivered, &c. and in 5*l*. for money had and received, &c. amounting in the whole to the sum of 25*l*. which exceeds the debt of the plaintiff, and which the defendant offered to set-off, &c. according to the statutes, &c.

The plaintiff prayed that the condition of the bond might be enrolled, and then demurred to the defendant's plea. The condition of the bond was for the appearance of *S. Daniel* before the judges of the King's Court of his palace at *Westminster* at the next Court of the King of his palace to be holden at *Southwark* in the county of *Surry* on Friday the 25th of July to answer *T. Squier* in a plea of trespass on the case, to his damage of 99*s*.

This case was argued on the 7th of February, 1740, by *Bootle* Serj. for the plaintiff, and *Agar* Serj. for the defendant; and now the opinion of the court was given as follows, by

Willes, Lord Chief Justice. "The question is whether these debts which the defendant sets forth in his plea can be set-off against the plaintiff's demand. There are two statutes(c) in relation to this matter; and it will be proper to consider under which statute this falls, and how the determinations have already been in the construction of them.

The words of the first statute, which is the 2 *Geo.* 2. *c.* 22. *s.* 13. are "where there are mutual debts between the plaintiff and the defendant, or if either party sue or be sued as executor or administrator where there are mutual debts between the testator or intestate and either party, one debt may be set against the other, and such matter may be given in evidence on the general issue or pleaded in bar as the nature of the case shall require; and if intended to be given in evidence, notice shall be given, &c. Upon the construction of this statute several questions arose before the making of the stat. 8 *Geo.* 2. *c.* 24.

1st. Whether debts on simple contract could be set-off in common cases against a debt on speciality?

2dly. If in common cases, whether they could where an executor or administrator is plaintiff?

And 3dly. Whether in the case of a bond the penalty was to be considered as debt? &c.

In *Kemys* v. *Betson*,(d) *Tr.* 6 *Geo.* 2. in *B. C.* it was holden in the case of an executor that simple contract debts cannot be set-off against debts on specialties; for that the debts must be of an equal nature; otherwise such a construction might occasion a devastavit. I should have been of the same opinion before the stat. 8 *Geo.* 2. but not for the same reason. For if a statute orders it to be so, it will justify the

(a) 4 *Burr.* 2442. (b) *Birch* v. *Sharland*, *post.* 715. (c) See 2 *Burr.* 824; 1024, 5; 1230; and 4 *Burr.* 2221. (d) 8 *Vin. Abr.* 561. *pl.* 30.

executor, and it will be no devastavit in him; and of this opinion was Lord HARDWICKE in the case of *Brown* v. *Holyoak*, which I shall mention by and by. The true reason is that this was only substituted in the room of an action, to prevent circuity or a bill in equity. It was therefore held that you cannot set-off a debt barred by the statute of limitations, because you cannot recover it by action. This judgment was never reversed. And in the case of *Joy* v. *Roberts* in the Exchequer *M.* 6 *Geo.* 2. there was the same resolution. But in the case of *Stevens* v. *Lofton*(a) *M.* 6 *Geo.* 2. this court carried it further, and held in the case of an action upon a bond between common persons a debt upon simple contract which was pleaded could not be set-off, go ng upon this reason that there ought to be the same construction on every part of the act; but in this I think they were mistaken; for where the cases are different the construction ought to be different too. And of this opinion were the Court of King's Bench, when it came before them on a writ of error,(b) and would have reversed the judgment but for another objection, the debt pleaded being less than the penalty though more than the money due by the condition; and this being a case before the stat. 8 *Geo.* 2. they held, and I think very rightly, that at law the penalty must be considered as the debt. And in the case of *Brown* v. *Holyoak*,(c) *P.* 8 *Geo.* 2. *B. R.* on a writ of error out of this court, the court of King's Bench reversed the judgment of this court which had determined that a debt on simple contract could not be set-off against a debt due for rent; and I think that the judgment was rightly reversed for the reasons I have already mentioned. In that case Lord HARDWICKE said it would not work a devastavit, and seemed a little to doubt how it would be in the case of executors. But his doubt was removed by the statute 8 *Geo.* 2. *c.* 24. passing just at that time. By that statute it is enacted that mutual debts may be set against each other either by being pleaded or given in evidence on the general issue, though such debts are deemed in law to be of a different nature, unless in cases where either of the said debts shall accrue by reason of a penalty in the bond, &c. in which case the debt intended to be set-off shall be pleaded in bar, in which plea it shall be shown how much(d) is truly and justly due on either side; and in case the plaintiff recovers, judgment shall be entered for no more than is truly and justly due to the plaintiff after one debt is so set-off against the other. This statute has solved all the difficulties before mentioned.

But as this is not a bond with the condition for the payment of money, we are all of opinion that the case is not within this statute, but must stand on the stat. 2 *Geo.* 2. For we are of opinion that the debts pleaded cannot be set-off in the present case, this being a bail-bond, and the plaintiff not suing in his own right but in the nature of a trustee for *Squier*. If this were otherwise, all bail-bonds might be defeated. But it might be as well said that when a man sues as executor the defendant may set-off a debt due from the plaintiff to the defendant in his own right,(e) as that the defendant can set-off in the present case; and yet that is contrary not only to common sense but also to the plain words of the statute. If indeed this had been a bond to the sheriff assigned over to the party according to the statute, we should have thought otherwise, and that the penalty must be considered as the debt, this not being a case within the statute 8 *Geo.* 2. But the bond here being sued by the officer himself, we are all of opinion that the debt due from the officer cannot be set-off, and that judgment must be for the plaintiff.

(a) 8 *Vin. Abr.* 562. *pl.* 31. (b) Vid. Sir *W. Kel.* 139: 2 *Barnard*, 338; and 8 *Vin. Abr.* 562, *pl.* 33. (c) *Barnes* 290; 8 *Vin. Abr.* 562. *pl.* 32, and 35; *and Bull. N. P.* 179.

(d) The defendant in pleading a set-off, to debt on bond, must set out the sum justly due on the bond; and that averment is traversable. *Symmons* v. *Knox*, 3 *Durnf. & E.* 65. even though laid under a videlicet, *Grimwood* v. *Barrit*, 6 *D. & E.* 460.

(e) Nor, when an executor sues for a cause of action arising after the testator's death, can the defendant set-off a debt due to him from the testator. *Shipman* v. *Thompson*, *T.* 11 & 12 *Geo.* 2. *C. B. sup.* 103; and *Tegetmeyer and another*, executors, v. *Lumley*, *T.* 25 *Geo.* 3. *B. R.* The latter was an action of covenant for rent, part of which became due in the testator's lifetime, and part since his death. The defendant at the trial, before Lord *Mansfield* at the sittings after *Easter* term 25 *Geo.* 3. set-off a debt due from the testator to him, and the plaintiffs were nonsuited. *Erskine* moved for a new trial, on the ground that this could not be set-off; and cited

Evans v. *Prosser*, *E. T.* 29 *Geo. III. A. D.* 1789. 3 *T. R.* 186.

THIS was an action upon the case for work and labour, care and diligence, as an attorney, with the common money counts, and the declaration was entitled of *Hilary* term, 29 *Geo.* 3. Pleas, first, *non assumpsit*; 2dly, that the plaintiff *before and at the time of the plea pleaded* was and still is indebted to the defendant in a larger sum than is due and owing from him to the plaintiff, *sc.* in 25*l.* 9*s.* on a promissory note of the plaintiff dated 30th July, 1787, made payable to *P. H. Cecil*, and by him on the same day and year indorsed to the defendant, &c. and in other sums, &c. Replication (protesting that the plaintiff exhibited his bill against the defendant on Tuesday next after the morrow of *All Souls in Michaelmas* term, in the 28th year, &c. protesting also that the indorsement was made to the defendant, and that the several sums by the plea supposed to be due to the defendant accrued and became due to him after exhibiting the plaintiff's bill.) That, notwithstanding the defendant's plea, to wit, on Tuesday next after eight days of *St. Martin* in *Michaelmas* 28 *Geo.* 3. the defendant brought an action in this court against the plaintiff upon the same note, in which action, and after the defendant's pleading in the present action, to wit, on *Wednesday next after fifteen days of St. Martin*, in *Michaelmas*, 28 *Geo.* 3. the plaintiff paid the amount of the note into court, under a rule of court: with an averment that the plaintiff was not, at the time of the pleading in this action, indebted to the defendant upon the several causes or considerations in his plea mentioned in any sum xceeding 25*l.* 13*s.* so by him paid into court, &c. in that action.

To this replication there was a general demurrer, and joinder.

Morgan, who was called upon to support the replication, contended that the defendaut could not bring an action on the note, and plead the same note by way of set-off: and that, by the plaintiff's paying the amount of it into court in that action, he had done away the defendant's set-off. But the defendant's plea is also bad, and may be taken advantage of on the demurrer to the replication. For it is not stated that the debt on the note which is the subject of the set-off, was due and owing from the plaintiff to the defendant at *the time of exhibiting the plaintiff's bill.* Its being a debt at the time of *the plea pleaded* is no answer to the plaintiff's demand. If such a plea could be supported, the plaintiff would be deprived of those costs to which he was entitled when he brought this action; and perhaps the note may have been indorsed to the defendant after the action was brought for the very purpose of defeating it.

Lane, contra, cited *Brown* v. *Baskerville*,(*a*) to shew that the defendant might bring his action on the note, notwithstanding his plea of set-off. And in support of the plea, he relied on the authorities of *Sullivan* v. *Montagu*,(*b*) and *Reynolds*

Rydout assignee v. *Brough*, *Cowp.* 133. *Shipman* v. *Thompson* (1) *Bull. N. P.* 180, and *Kilvington* executor v. *Stevenson*, which he read from a note of Mr. Justice *Yates*. "Assumpsit as executor for goods of his testator. There were two pleas; 1st. Non-assumpsit; 2dly. A set-off for a debt due from the testator to the defendant. To this the plaintiff demurred. And *Wallace*, in support of the demurrer, insisted that the plea was bad, and that the defendant could not set-off a debt owing to him by the testator in satisfaction of the present demand, as that would be altering the course of distribution, and he might by that mean be paid before creditors of a superior nature. Mr. *Solicitor-General*, who was to have argued on the other side, mentioned the stat. 2 *Geo.* 2. *c.* 22. *s.* 13. *Per Curiam.* The plea is clearly bad. This is not an action for goods that were in his hands at the testator's death, in which case he might set-off; but for goods he has taken possession of since his death, in which case to allow the set-off would be altering the course of distribution. Judgment for the plaintiff."

Cooper showed cause against the rule; here the executors unite both their demands; and this case differs from those cited. The balance only ought to be paid. And as to the inconvenience of altering the course of administration, the executors have put themselves in this situation.

Erskine, who was going to argue in support of the rule, was stopped by

Lord *Mansfield*, Ch. J. who said he was satisfied on the point, on the authority of the case of *Kilvington* v. *Stevenson*.

Rule absolute.

(1) *Sup.* 103. S. C.

(*a*) 2 *Burr.* 1229. (*b*) *Dougl.* 108.

v. *Beerling*;(a) in which it was expressly decided that *actio non* goes, in every case, to the time of plea pleaded, not to the commencement of the action. And he observed in answer to the argument, that the note might have been indorsed to the defendant after the action brought; that it appeared on the record that the note was given in July, 1787, and on the same day and year indorsed to the defendant; whereas this action was not brought till *Hil.* 29 *Geo.*3. so that in this case the set-off was of a debt due at the time of bringing the action.

The court were clearly of opinion that the replication was ill, on the authority of *Brown* and *Baskerville*; adding that, if the set-off were proved to the jury, and the defendant also succeeded in his action on the note, the plaintiff in this action might bring an *audita querela*, or have some other remedy. But they wished to look into the cases cited in support of the plea.

On the next day BULLER, J. said he had looked into the case of *Reynolds* v. *Beerling*, and found that it could not be supported. One question, which arose there, was whether a judgment could be pleaded by way of set-off pending a writ of error; which the court were of opinion might be done: and so far the judgment was right. On the other point there ruled, namely, that a judgment recovered after the action was brought, and before plea pleaded, might be pleaded by way of set-off; perhaps the court did not consider the strict law, so much as the justice, of the case. But this point cannot be supported. On which

Judgment was given for the plaintiff.

Baskerville v. *Brown*; *et e contra.* *T. T.* 1 *Geo. III.* 2 *Burr.* 1229.

BROWN brought an action against *Baskerville* upon two promissory notes amounting (both together) to the sum of 30*l.* The cause was entered and tried before Lord *Mansfield* at the sittings: and the plaintiff took a verdict for the *whole* of his demand.

Baskerville had also brought an action against *Brown*, for 11*l.* 18*s.* for taylor's work done by him for *Brown*; and this cause was likewise entered and tried at the very same sittings; but it happened that the former cause (wherein *Brown* was plaintiff,) was first entered and first tried.

In the latter cause (wherein *Baskerville* was plaintiff,) the therein defendant (*Brown*) had given notice of a *set-off* of *so much* of the before-mentioned two promissory notes, as would suffice to answer *Boskerville's* demand against him; and he was ready, at the trial, to have done so, notwithstanding his having taken a verdict for the whole 30*l.* in the cause wherein he was plaintiff: but *Baskerville's* counsel opposed this; and insisted that *Brown* had *estopped* himself from making this set-off, by having taken a *verdict* for the *whole* of his demand; whereas he ought (as they insisted,) to have *left out* so much, in taking his verdict, as was equal to *Baskerville's* demand upon him.

Lord MANSFIELD, at the trial, inclined against allowing the set-off; but he thought it a matter that deserved consideration.

It was accordingly brought before the court, for their consideration, in the form

(a) REYNOLDS v. BEERLING. *M.* 25. *G.*3. *B. R.*

Assumpsit. Plea, set-off on promises, and also on a judgment recovered by defendant against the plaintiff after the action brought and before plea pleaded. Replication, error pending on that judgment. To this there was a general demurrer and joinder.

Shepherd, for the demurrer, insisted that the replication was no answer to the defendant's plea; that the circumstance of the writ of error being pending was no bar to the defendant's setting off the judgment. And in support of the plea he cited *Sullivan* v. *Montagu*.

Lane, *contra*, said that as the writ of error was a *supersedeas* to an execution, it ought to be so to every other mode of obtaining the effect of the judgment. And contended that the plea itself could not be supported, because it was not only contrary to the settled mode of pleading, but also contrary to justice, for the plaintiff might be thus deprived of the costs of the action to which he was entitled. And as to *Sullivan* v. *Montagu*, the principal question was, whether the judge could certify after the cause was over. But

The court said, on the authority of *Sullivan* v. *Montagu*, that the plea was good; and that the replication was no answer to it.

of a motion made on the part of the defendant, *Brown*, for a rule upon *Baskerville*, the plaintiff, to show cause why the verdict (which had been found for *Baskerville*) should not be set aside; and why the defendant, *Brown*, should not have the costs of a nonsuit.

Mr. *Norton* and Mr. *Yates*, on behalf of the plaintiff, *Baskerville*, now shewed cause against this rule. And, besides urging what they had insisted upon at the trial, they added further, That the statute only says "that the defendant *may* set-"off the debt due to him from the plaintiff;" but does *not compel* him to do so: and here the defendant, *Brown*, had actually made his election "not *to do it*," by taking a verdict for his *whole* demand in the cause wherein he was plaintiff. And they insisted that the *nature* of the debt is *changed*, and the former debt *extinguished* by the verdict; so that it *cannot* be set off, in an action tried *after* that verdict had been given.

To this, it was answered by Mr. *Morton* and Mr. *Stowe* (in support of the rule), that the debt remains *unchanged* in its nature, and *unextinguished*, notwithstanding the verdict. And it might have been still set-off, they said, in the present action, without any inconvenience: for if *Brown* should attempt to take out execution for the *whole*, in the other action wherein he was plaintiff, *after* a set-off in this action, either the court would set the matter right, (even with costs,) or *Baskerville* might have redress by an *audita querela*. But *Brown* was *obliged*, they said, to take his verdict for the *whole* of his demand: for he could not be sure that *Baskerville* would try his cause at all: and then *Brown* would have entirely *lost* this sum of 11*l*. 18*s*. *Brown* did all he could to come at a fair balance: he could do no more than plead it, or give notice to set it off, *as it stood* at the *time* of the plea pleaded. The *fault* was in *Baskerville*. He ought to have set off his demand upon *Brown* of 11*l*. 18*s*. against *Brown's* demand upon him of 30*l*. And then complete justice had been done easily and at once. He *ought not* to have brought his action against *Brown at all*.

CUR. ADVIS.

Lord MANSFIELD now delivered the resolution of the court.

The meaning of the act of parliament, he said, was, that in all cases of mutual debts, the less sum should be deducted out of the greater, *if the defendant desires it*.

But *Brown could not compel Baskerville* to set-off his less demand upon *Brown*, against *Brown's* greater demand upon him nor could *Brown* have safely taken his verdict for less than his *whole* demand. Yet *Baskerville* himself might have done this without prejudice, and with perfect safety: and he ought to have done it.—But he declined doing it; and at the same time brings his action against *Brown*, for what he might, without prejudice, have set off against *Brown's* demand upon him.

Therefore it was litigious and vexatious in him not to do it, when he might safely and easily have done it; but chose, instead of it, to commence an action against *Brown*.

Both actions stood together for trial: but it happened that the cause of *Brown* v. *Baskerville* stood first. *Brown* took his verdict for the *whole* demand upon the two notes; there being no plea nor notice of any set-off in *this* cause wherein *Brown* was plaintiff.

Then came on *Baskerville's* cause, in which he was plaintiff, and *Brown* the defendant; in which cause, *Brown* had given notice to set-off so much as was equal to *Baskerville's* demand upon him. This he would have done: but it was opposed; and the objection seemed specious.

But we are all clearly of opinion, upon full consideration, "that the debts might "be set off one against the other in this latter cause, notwithstanding *Brown's* hav-"ing taken a verdict in the former for his whole demand." For if at the *time of the action brought*, the defendant may set off one debt against the other, or plead (if a larger sum be due from the plaintiff to him, than from him to the plaintiff;) in bar of the plaintiff's action; *Brown* had a right in the cause wherein he was defendant, to give this notice of a set-off, *at the time* when he gave it. And *Baskerville* might, in the cause wherein he was defendant, have set off such part of the larger sum due from him to the plaintiff *Brown*, as was equal to the debt due to him from the plaintiff, if he had thought proper. And *Brown's* notice to set off against *Baskerville's* demand, told him, that *Brown* was *ready to strike a balance* between the mutual debts, and to be *content with the difference* between them: and it specified the nature of *Brown's* demand upon him, as the act requires,

Thus it stood *before* the verdict: the debt due to *Brown* was a mutual debt and notice was given of it, and upon what account it became due, and that it was intended to be insisted on. And *after* the verdict, it still REMAINED *a mutual debt*, as it did before. The verdict did *not* annihilate or extinguish the debt; nor change the nature of it, or the rule of law: it only amounted to *conclusive evidence* of it. So that *Brown* had the same right to set it off *after* the verdict, as he had before the verdict.

We are of opinion, this right to make the set-off still remained in *Brown*, both within the *words*, and *reason*, and *intent* of the act of parliament: and that the debt was *neither extinguished*, nor its *nature changed*.

Baskerville was the only person in fault: and he ought not to have brought his action.

Brown was right all along: he could not have taken his verdict for less than he did, with safety. He may now *remit* so much of the sum he has recovered, as will bring the mutual debts to a just balance: and this he *ought* to do.

But it would be strange, if the mere accident of the priority of trial should, by his cause happening to stand first in the paper, preclude him from taking the benefit of the act, according to his notice rightly and truly given at the *time* when it was given.

Per Cur. unanimously. VERDICT set aside; and the defendant to have costs of nonsuit: and *Brown* to remit so much of his damages recovered in the other action, as exceed the balance of the mutual debts.

Symmons v. *Knox*, *H. T.* 29 *Geo. III.* 3 *T. R.* 65. *A. D.* 1789.

DEBT on bond in 11619*l.* 13*s.* 4*d.* dated the 14th *July*, 1784. The defendant (after praying *oyer* of the bond and of the condition, which was that the bond should be void on payment of 5089*l.* 11*s.* 8*d.* with lawful interest, on the 25th of *March* then next) pleaded as follows: that at the time of exhibiting the bill of the said *John there was justly and truly due and owing to the said* John, *on the condition of the said writing obligatory*, for principal and interest, the sum of 5809*l.* 11*s.* 8*d.* *and no more*, to wit, at *Westminster* aforesaid in the county aforesaid; and that the said *John* now is, and on the day of exhibiting the bill of the said *John* was indebted to the said *William* in more money than is remaining due to the said *John* by virtue of the said writing obligatory; and concluded with a set-off in the common form. The plaintiff replied, that at the time of exhibiting the bill of the said *John* there was and *yet is juslty and truly due and owing to the said* John *from the said William*, upon and by virtue of the said writing obligatory and the condition thereof, for principal and interest, *a larger sum of money* than the said sum of 5809*l.* 11*s.* 8*d.* in the said plea mentioned, to wit, the sum of 6930*l.* 3*s.* 9*d.*; concluding to the country.

To this replication the defendant demurred: and showed for cause that the plaintiff in and by his replication attempted to put in issue a matter wholly immaterial, and therein traversed a fact, whereon no certain or material issue could be taken; and hath not in and by his replication traversed, or denied, or confessed, the only fact in the plea whereon a certain or proper issue could be taken; and because the replication was in various other respects defective, informal, &c.

Baldwin, in support of the demurrer. This question arises on the 8 *Geo.* 3. *c.* 24. *s.* 5. which gives the plea of set-off where the demand on either side accrues by bond; and which directs that judgment shall be entered for no more than shall appear to be due to the plaintiff after one debt is set against the other. The material issue, therefore, to be tried is, whether the plaintiff's demand on the defendant exceeds that which the defendant has on him: and it is immaterial to take issue on the exact sum due from the defendant to the plaintiff. For if the parties were to go to trial on such an issue, and the plaintiff proved that only one shilling more was due to him, the defendant would be deprived of the benefit of the statute, even though his demand exceeded that of the plaintiff. And no inconvenience can arise from this practice, because the act directs that judgment shall only be entered up for so much as is really and justly due.

Dampier contra. The statute expressly requires that the sum which is justly and truly due shall be pleaded in bar, in which plea shall be shown how much is truly and justly due *on either side*. If then it be necessary to aver that something is due on the bond, the particulars of that averment are necessary. And the meaning of the statute is that, in case the defendant sets off a bond debt, the plaintiff may know the amount of the defendant's claim; or that, in case the defendant sets off to a debt due to the plaintiff arising on a bond, he may know how much the defendant admits. If the defendant were not to set forth the true sum, the plaintiff would go to trial ignorant of what was to be proved by the defendant, which was the very thing against which the statute meant to provide. Then if this be a material averment, it is traversable; for if the plaintiff were not to traverse it in his replication, he would be taken to have admitted it. And it is so material, that, unless the defendant avers what is truly and justly due, he is not entitled under the statute to set off at all. But whatever may be the general construction of this statute, the particular manner of pleading this plea has made the averment material, and consequently traversable. The plea states that the defendant was indebted to the plaintiff, on the bond, in 5809*l.* 11*s.* 8*d.* *and no more*, without laying it under a *videlicet*; in consequence of which it became necessary to deny it in the replication, otherwise the plaintiff would have been bound by that precise sum. In *Durston* v. *Tuthan* (*a*), where the declaration stated that, in consideration that the plaintiff would buy of the defendant 45 sheep for 54*l.* 11*s.* 6*d.* the defendant undertook and promised that they were sound, the plaintiff proved the price to be 54*l.* 12*s*, 6*d.* *Buller*, J. held the variance to be fatal, because the sum was not laid under a *videlicet*; and non-suited the plaintiff. The defendant in this case has also added the words "and no more," which the statute does not require, but which make the traverse the more necessary.

Lord Kenyon, Ch. J.—I own I form an opinion on this subject with great diffidence. This is an action brought on a bond, in which case the statute says that, if the defendant wishes to set-off a cross demand against the plaintiff, he must first state in his plea what is really due on the bond; the defendant then in this case, being furnished with the means of ascertaing the extent of the demand upon the bond, states that such a sum only is due; and having thus complied with the requisition of the statute, sets off a cross demand. And the question is, whether the plaintiff is bound to admit that that is the extent of his demand. Now if he does not deny it in his replication, he admits it: it therefore became necessary for the plaintiff to traverse it; for, if the plaintiff were to go to trial only on the issue, whether his demand did or did not exceed the defendant's great injustice might be done. And it seems to me that there is reason in requiring that the exact sum should be pleaded, because the purpose of pleading is to reduce the matter to a point. Here, too, the sum is not pleaded under a *videlicet*: and it has been long settled that where any thing is laid under a *videlicet*, the party is not concluded by it; but he is, where there is no *videlicet*. It would therefore be very hard on this plaintiff if he were bound by the sum, which the defendant has stated not under a *videlicet*, without having an opportunity of traversing it.

Ashhurst, J.—There is a manifest distinction between this statute and that of the 2 *Geo.* 2. c. 22. For this act expressly requires that the defendant shall set forth the precise sum which is due on the bond, before he can be permitted to set off his demand. And therefore we are precluded by the statute from considering this on the same footing with simple contract debts. The form of pleading under a *videlicet*, where the party does not mean to be concluded by the sum stated, shows that, where it is not so pleaded, he is bound by the precise sum pleaded. Now here the defendant pleaded that a certain sum was due to the plaintiff on the bond, *and no more*, which would have concluded the plaintiff, if he had not traversed it in his replication.

Grose, J.—(*b*). If the two statutes 2 *Geo.* 2. c. 22. and 8 *Geo.* 2. c. 24. be considered and compared together, there will be found to be no difficulty in this question. By the former act the defendant was permitted to set off his demand against the plaintiff, either by pleading it, or by giving it in evidence under the general issue with notice. But as it was conceived that the words "mutual debts" mentioned in that act did not extend to cases where the demand arose on a penalty, the 8 *Geo.* 2. c. 24. was passed, which enacts that, where

(*a*) *Taunton Sp. Ass.* 1788. *cor. Buller*, *J.*
(*b*) Mr. Justice *Buller* was sitting for the Lord Chancellor.

either the plaintiff's or the defendant's demand accrues by reason of any penalty, the debt intended to be set-off shall be pleaded in bar, in which plea shall be shown how much is justly and truly due on either side. So that under this act the defendant cannot give a notice of set-off with the general issue: but he is required to plead it in bar, in which plea he must state what is really due on the bond. And as far as my experience goes, the plea in this case is warranted by the usual form of pleading: it has not been usual to plead that a large sum of money, *to wit*, so much is due, *but that a specific sum is due and no more*. And this mode is certainly consonant to the 8 *Geo.* 2. *c.* 24. Then, as the defendant set forth what was really due without a *videlicet*, the plaintiff would be taken to have admitted it, if he had not traversed it in his replication.

Demurrer overruled.

But as *Baldwin* suggested that it had not been the practice to traverse this averment in the replication, the court gave the defendant leave to amend on paying the costs.

Hankey and others, Assignees of John & Benjamin Vaughan, v. *Smith and others, E.* 29 *Geo. III. A. D.* 1789. *B. R. in Notes* 3 *T. R.* 507.

TO this action upon the case for goods sold and delivered by the bankrupts the defendants pleaded the general issue, and gave notice of set-off applicable to the bill of exchange hereafter mentioned. At the trial at the sittings after *Michaelmas* term 1788, at *Guildhall* before Lord *Kenyon*, the jury gave a verdict for the plaintiffs, damages 520*l.* 16*s.* subject to the opinion of this court on the following case:—

On the 26th of *July* last a commission of bankrupt issued against the *Vaughans*, who on the 29th of the same month were declared bankrupts. *John Vaughan* committed an act of bankruptcy on the 22d, and *Benjamin Vaughan* on the 23d of *July*. The plaintiffs on the 5th of *August* were duly chosen assignees, &c. On the 3d of *July* the bankrupts, who were sugar-refiners, sold the defendants sugar and molasses to the amount of 452*l.* 2*s.* 8*d.* and on the 21st of the same month sold other sugars to them to the amount of 68*l.* 13*s.* 4*d.* making together 520*l.* 16*s.* for which this action was brought. One *William Broadhurst*, on the 6th of *June*, 1788, drew a bill of exchange on the bankrupts for 600*l.* payable to his order two months after date for value delivered to him in raw sugar; which bill was duly accepted by the bankrupts, and indorsed by *Broadhurst*, and delivered by him to *Towgood* & Co. who on the 2d of *July* last, and after the bill was accepted and indorsed, discounted it with the defendants, and delivered the same to them. The defendants on the 5th of *August* last proved under *Vaughan's* commission, 79*l.* 4*s.* as the balance due to them on the bill of exchange, after deducting 520*l.* 16*s.* On the 10th of *September*, 1788, one of the defendants, *Francis Kemble*, was examined before the commissioners named in the commission against the bankrupts, when he deposed, That he, together with *Jos. Kemble*, *Smith*, and *Travers*, the other defendants, carried on the trade and business of grocers; that on the 2d of *July* last, *W. Towgood* applied to him to discount the bill in question; that he had before that time heard that *Vaughans'* house was in difficulties, but he knew that *B. Vaughan* was a partner with *J. Vaughan*, and he thought him a good man; that *W. Towgood* said there had been rumours of *Vaughans'* stopping, *and that as the house of him (this examinant) was engaged in the sugar trade they could buy goods to cover the bill;* that he said he did not care what rumours there were, as he believed the house of *J. Vaughan* & Co. to be perfectly safe, and that they only wanted time; *that at the time he took the bill he meant to buy sugars to cover the bill; that accordingly some sugars and molasses were bought on the next day;* and that between that time and the 22d of *July*, sugars and molasses to the amount of 520*l.* 16*s.* were bought by their (this examinant's) house of the bankrupts; that he had never discounted a bill for *W. Towgood* before, and that he knew that *Towgood's* father was a banker. The defendant, *Joseph Kemble*, was also examined before the commissioners, who deposed that he was the person who bought the abovementioned sugars of the bankrupts, and that at the time he bought the same he did not inform them of their house being in possession of the bill; *that one reason of his going to the house of* Vaughan *& Co. to purchase the sugars and molasses was their being in possession of* the bill; and that at the time when the bill was discounted for *Towgood* he did not indorse the same, but by a memorandum in writing agreed to indorse it when he should be thereunto required; that he accordingly indorsed it a few days afterwards and after he had heard that *Vaughan's* house had stopped payment; that the reason why the bill was not indorsed was that if *Vaughan* & Co. had stood their ground it might be presented for payment without the indorsement of *Towgood, Danvers*, and Co. (the house in which *William Towgood* is a partner,) as *W. Towgood* did not choose that their names should appear.

Russel, for the plaintiffs, contended that, abstractedly from every circumstance of fraud, the set-off could not be maintained, because there were neither mutual debts or mutual credits between the parties within the 5 *Geo.* 2 *c.* 30.(*a*) *Prescot's case* shows that there was no *mutual debt*, because the bill was not due till after the bankruptcy. Neither was there any *mutual credit;* for at the time of selling the goods the bankrupts did not know that this bill was in the hands of the defendants. They, in taking the bill, gave no credit to the bankrupts; they took it merely to accommodate *Towgood* and Co. But

The court were clearly of opinion that there was *mutual credit*.

Lord KENYON, Ch. J. said—The mutual credit was constituted by taking the bill on the one hand, and selling the sugars on the other. Though if the bill had come into the defendants' hands *ex post facto*, as after the action(*b*) was brought, it would have been otherwise.

BULLER, J.—In order to constitute mutual credit, it is not necessary that the parties mean particularly to trust each other in that transaction. For if a bill of exchange, which is accepted, be sent out into the world, credit is given to the acceptor by every person who takes the bill: now that constituted the credit on one side in this case; then, on the other, credit was given to the defendants by the bankrupts for the goods.

The case was also argued on the ground of *fraud*: but the court, not considering the transaction to be fraudulent, gave judgment for the defendants. But on a subsequent day in *Easter* term they observed that there were circumstances to be left to the jury, on which they ought to exercise their judgment, whether or not fraud to the defendants could be imputed; and for that reason they ordered it to be sent down to another trial.

Holroyd, for the defendants.

Hancock and others, Assignees of Edensor, a Bankrupt, v. *Entwisle and others, M. T.* 30 *Geo. III. A. D.* 1789. 3 *T. R.* 435.

THIS was an action on a bill of exchange; and, the plaintiffs having proved their case, the only question was whether the defendants were entitled to a set-off arising from an agreement, made in *March*, 1788, between the defendants of the one part, and the bankrupt of the other, by which, (after reciting that a loss had been sustained by the defendants in consequence of the purchase of some cotton by the bankrupt as their broker, for reimbursing which they made a claim on him,) in order to put an end to all controversy concerning it, it was *agreed that the loss*, though exceeding 1900*l. should be fixed at that sum, and no more*; and that in payment or satisfaction of that sum the bankrupt should, from time to time, within the space of four years recommend parcels of cotton, not exceeding 150 bags at one time, to the defendants for their purchase, and that the defendants should purchase them, paying for them in notes at three month's date. *And the bankrupt undertook that the clear profits on such sales should in the course of four years be sufficient to discharge the* 1900*l. but if the same should not be paid within that time, then the bankrupt agreed immediately after the expiration of the four years, in case he should be then living, to pay them the difference.* And if the purchases should occasion a loss to the defendants, the bankrupt undertook to make good such loss. Lord *Kenyon*, before whom the cause was tried, being of opinion that the defendants were not entitled to set-off, the plaintiffs obtained a verdict.

On a former day a rule was obtained to show cause why a new trial should not be granted; against which

Erskine and *Marryat* were now to have shewn cause: But

Law and *S. Heywood*, in support of the rule were desired to begin. The set-off may be allowed, because these were liquidated damages, by the agreement; and therefore this is not like the case of *Howlet* v. *Strickland*(*c*) When the party became a bankrupt, he was incapable of performing his contract; and then a right of action to the amount of 1900*l.* attached. This then became a debt which the defendants might have proved under the commission, the parties having previously

(*a*) *Atk.* 230. (*b*) *Vid. Evans* v. *Prosser, ante* 150. (*c*) *Cowp.* 56.

agreed as to the *quantum* of satisfaction to be paid by the bankrupt to the defendants; and if they might have proved the debt under the commission, they may also set it off in this action brought by the assignees.

Lord KENYON, Ch. J.—If this deed had never been entered into, the claim which the defendants had on the bankrupt could not have been set-off in this action, because it rested merely in damages; it arose from the misconduct of the bankrupt, and might have beeen settled in an action. But by this deed the damages are liquidated, and the parties agreed on certain things to be done in the course of four years, as the means of making a recompense to the defendants to the amount of that sum. If a certain sum of money had been payable at all events, by instalments, and one of the payments had become due before the bankruptcy, the whole might have been proved under the commission. But it is clear that the bankrupt was not discharged by his bankruptcy from the operation of this deed; for when he obtains his certificate, he may be enabled to perform the stipulations contained in it. Then if he were not discharged from his covenants by his certificate, this debt could not be proved under the commission, nor can it be set-off; for it had no existence as a debt at the time of the bankruptcy. The distinction has been well settled in a variety of cases, as in those of *Ex parte Grome*(a) and *Ex parte Winchester*,(b) that if the demand be payable *at all events*, though at a future day, it may be proved under the commission: but where it depends on a *contingency*, whether it will be paid or not, it cannot be proved, unless it be secured by a penalty which is *forfeited at law*: in which case the court will take hold of the legal right to give the party a remedy under the commission. But in this case there was no legal demand at the time of the bankruptcy.

Rule discharged.

Ryall, Knt. and others, assignees of Harvest, a bankrupt, v. *Larkin, B. R. M. T.* 20 *Geo. II. A. D.* 1746. 1 *Wils.* 155.

ACTION on *assumpsit*, that the defendant was indebted to *William Harvest* and *Jonathan Stevens* deceased, whom the said *William Harvest* survived, in 20*l.* for goods sold and delivered by the said *William Harvest* and *Stevens* in his life-time, and before the said *William Harvest* became a bankrupt, to the said *William Larkin quantum volebant* for other goods, and an *insimul computasset* with *Harvest* and *Stevens* in his life-time, whereupon defendant was found in arrear 13*l.* 5*s.* 6*d.* and being so found in arrear promised payment, and concludes that the defendant hath not paid the said *Harvest* and *Stevens* in the life-time of the said *Stevens*, and before the said *Harvest* became a bankrupt, or to the said *Stevens* in his life-time since the said *Harvest* became a bankrupt, or to the said plaintiffs, the assignees, since the death of the said *Stevens*, to the damage of the said assignees of 20*l.*

Defendant pleads *non assumpsit*, and thereupon issue is joined; and further the defendant by leave of the court says, that the said assignees ought not to have or maintain their said action against him the said defendant, because he the said defendant says that the said *William Harvest* before he became a bankrupt, that is to say, on the 21st day of *April*, 1740, at *Westminster*, in the county aforesaid, by his certain writing obligatory called a bond, sealed with the seal of the said *William Harvest*, and shown to the court of the said Lord the King now here, the date whereof is the day and year last mentioned, acknowledged himself to be held and firmly bound to the said *William Larkin* in 100*l.* of lawful money of *Great Britain*, to be paid to the said *William Larkin*, when he should be thereunto required; and the said *William Larkin* in fact saith, that there is now due and owing to him the said *William Larkin* from the said *William Harvest*, upon account of the said writing obligatory, for principal and interest the sum of 64*l.* of lawful money of *Great-Britain*, to wit, at *Westminster* aforesaid in the county aforesaid, which said sum of 64*l.* by the said *William Harvest* owing as aforesaid, exceeds the money from the said *William Larkin* due to the said assignees of the said *William Harvest* as aforesaid, to wit, the sum of 13*l.* 5*s.* and 6*d.* by occasion of the promises mentioned in the said declaration, namely at *Westminster* aforesaid, and out of which said sum of 64*l.* he the said *William Larkin* is willing and offers to pay the said assignees the whole of the said money due to them as assignees aforesaid, by reason of the pre-

(a) 1 *Atk.* 115. (b) 1 *Atk.* 116.

mises according to the form of the statute in such case made and provided; and this he is ready to verify, wherefore he prays judgment if the said assignees ought to have or maintain their said action thereupon against him, &c. To this the plaintiff demurred generally, and the defendant joined in demurrer.

This case was argued by Serjeant *Bootle* for the plaintiffs, and by Mr. *Lawson* for the defendant. For the plaintiffs it was insisted, that the act of parliament for setting-off one debt against another did not extend to assignees under a commission of bankrupt, and that in the present case there were not mutual debts, for wherever there are mutual debts there must be mutual remedies, and the defendant could have no action on his bond against the plaintiffs; and of this opinion was the court, and gave judgment for the plaintiffs.

Smith and others, Assignees of Lewis and Potter v. *Hodson, H. T.* 31 *Geo. III. A. D.* 1791. 4 *T. R.* 211.

ASSUMPSIT for goods sold and delivered to the defendant by the bankrupts, before, and also by the assignees since, the bankruptcy. Pleas *non assumpsit*, and a tender of 131*l.* 7*s.* 6*d.* which the plaintiffs took out of court. There was also a set-off. At the trial at *Guildhall* before Lord *Kenyon*, a verdict was found for the plaintiffs, subject to the opinion of this court on the following case.

In *August*, 1787, *Lewis* and *Potter* sold goods to the defendant to the amount of 42*l.* and on the 4th of *March*, 1788, they drew a bill on him at two months for 442*l.* payable to their own order, although at that time he was indebted to them in 42*l.* only, which bill the defendant accepted. *Lewis* and *Potter* made the following entry in their books: "4th of *March*, 1788, received from *James Hodson* an acceptance due 7th May, 442*l.* to bills and notes; to provide 400*l.*" On the 26th *April* several bills were refused payment by *Lewis* and *Potter*, some of which were presented by bankers on behalf of the indorsees. On the 28th *April*, 1788, the defendant went to the house of *Lewis* and *Potter*, and bought goods to the amount of 531*l.* 7*s.* 6*d.* which were sent to him with a bill of parcels the same day; the goods were sold to the defendant at six months credit. On the 29th of *April*, 1788, *Lewis* and *Potter* committed acts of bankruptcy. On the 9th of *May* the commission issued, and they were duly declared bankrupts, and the plaintiffs chosen assignees of their estate and effects. The bill for 442*l.* drawn by the bankrupts, and accepted by the defendant, became due the 7th of *May*, 1788: the defendant did not pay it on that day, but in *September* following paid to *Gibson* and *Johnson*, the holders thereof, 200*l.* on account of the bill; and in *October* following, before the six months credit upon the goods was expired, he paid the residue with interest. The jury thought the bankrupts gave an undue preference to the defendant in the sale; and gave a verdict for the plaintiffs, damages 400*l.* The questions for the opinion of the Court are; 1st. Whether the plaintiffs can support this action for the price of the goods? 2dly. If they can support this action, whether the defendant cannot set-off against it the money paid by him on the above-mentioned bill for 442*l.*

Russell, for the plaintiffs, was desired by the Court to confine himself to the second point, as they entertained no doubt upon the first. As to which he contended that though the sale were good to charge the defendant in this action, yet he was not entitled to support his set-off under the 5 *Geo.* 2. *c.* 30. *s.* 28. (*a*) The words which will be relied on are *mutual credit*: But they were by no means intended to be used in so extensive a sense as the one now put on them by the defendant. The giving of *credit* is merely giving a future day of payment for a pre-existing debt; and to entitle a defendant to set it off, it must exist previous to the act of bankruptcy. As where goods are sold to be paid for at a future day, the

(*a*) Which enacts that where "there hath been *mutual credit* given by the bankrupt and any other person, or *mutual debts* between the bankrupt and any other person, at any time before such person became bankrupt, the commissioners, &c. shall state the account between them, and one debt may be set against another; and what shall appear to be due on either side on the balance of such account, and on setting such debts against one another, and no more, shall be claimed or paid on either side respectively."

vendee becomes a debtor for the value upon the delivery, though payment cannot be exacted from him till the day arrives: In the mean time the vendor is his creditor to that amount; and in that sense only is the word *credit* to be understood in the act. This appears further from the subsequent words of the statute; for the commissioners are directed to *state the account* between the parties, and claim or pay only so much as shall appear *due on the balance of such account.* In order therefore for a party to set-off any demand, it must be such as may be made an item in the account, and either certain or reducible to a certainty at the time of the act of bankruptcy committed. The act itself says, that the balance of the account is to be made appear "on setting *such debts* against one another;" which plainly shows that nothing more was meant by the word *credits* than such *debts* as were payable at a future day. Then how does the statute apply to this case? There was no debt existing between the bankrupts and the defendant at the time of the bankruptcy; nor was it certain there ever would be one; for in case of the defendant's bankruptcy or refusal to pay, the holder might have proceeded against the estate of the drawers and recovered the amount; and that perhaps after the defendant's acceptance had been admitted as an item of account between him and the bankrupts. And at all events no debt could arise till after payment by the defendant, which was long after the bankruptcy, and therefore could not be set-off; for at that time the bill was outstanding in the hands of third persons, and was therefore the subject of mutual credit, if at all, between them and the bankrupts. But in *Groome's* case(*a*) Lord *Hardwicke* was clearly of opinion that a debt arising on a contingency after the bankruptcy, could not be set-off. And it has been determined that though a note indorsed after an act of bankruptcy may be proved under a commission against the drawer,(*b*) yet it cannot be set-off against an action by his assignees.(*c*) The cases *Ex parte Deeze,*(*d*) *Ex parte Prescot,*(*e*) and *French,* assignee of *Cox* v. *Fenn,*(*f*) were all of them cases where the bankrupts were actually indebted to the defendants, before the bankruptcies, in the sums which they set-off against the demands of the assignees; which differs them materially from the present. But even supposing this were such a demand as could in a fair transaction be set-off in a court of law under the statute, yet it cannot avail the defendant in this case, where the whole is vitiated by fraud. It therefore becomes material to examine what part of the transaction may be substantiated, and what is void. There is no fraud in the mere act of sale; and the defendant must be bound by that so far as he made himself liable for the amount of the goods: that would have been the case had the sale been made to a person who was no creditor of the bankrupt's. But the objection arises to the fraudulent use now attempted to be made of the sale. No party is entitled to set-off a demand against the assignees of a bankrupt, for which he could not have maintained an action, or which he could not have proved under a commission. Now if the defendant could not have done either in the present instance, before the bankruptcy, he shall not be permitted to recover the amount indirectly in this manner; for that would be to permit him to avail himself of his own fraud.

Gibbs, for the defendant, insisted, first, that if the whole were to be considered as a *bona fide* transaction, the defendant was entitled to set off the sum paid under his acceptance; and, 2dly. That the finding of the jury, as to the undue preference, could not vary the case in favour of the plaintiffs in *this* action. The first question depends on the stat. 5 *Geo.* 2. *c.* 30. *s.* 28; the true construction of which is, that wherever there is *mutual credit* between the bankrupt and another person before the bankruptcy, the debts may be set-off against each other, although one of them may accrue after the bankruptcy, and although that one debt could not form an item of an account, so as to enable the bankrupt and such other person to strike a balance. The plaintiff's argument, that nothing can be set off under the statute, but that which may form an item of an account at the time of the bankruptcy, and the payment of which is only postponed for a time, directly militates against the decision of *French* v. *Fenn*. If that case be law, the construction now attempted to be put on this statute by the plaintiff's counsel cannot prevail. In that case *Fenn*

(*a*) 1 *Atk.* 119.
(*b*) *Ex parte Thomas,* 1 *Atk.* 73.
(*c*) *Marsh* v. *Chambers,* 2 *Str.* 1234.
(*d*) 1 *Atk.* 228.
(*e*) *Ib.* 230.
(*f*) *Tr.* 23 *Geo.* 3. *Co. Bk. L.* 2d ed.

owed nothing to *Cox* previous to the bankruptcy: so here *Lewis* and *Potter* owed *Hodson* nothing previous to their bankruptcy; but *Fenn* had been intrusted by *Cox* with that, upon which he probably would become his debtor, namely the sale of the jewels, in which *Cox* was interested one-third part; so *Lewis* and *Potter* had been entrusted by *Hodson* with that upon which they probably would become his debtors, *ss.* with his acceptance for 442*l.* he having effects to the amount of 42*l.* only; There, *Fenn*, upon the credit of the jewels intrusted to him, trusted *Cox* on another account; so here, *Lewis* and *Potter*, on the credit of the acceptance intrusted to them, trusted *Hodson* on another account, namely, for the goods in question;—There, after the bankruptcy of *Cox*, *Fenn received* a sum of money upon the sale of the jewels intrusted to him, which became due to *Cox's* estate; so here, after the bankruptcy, *Hodson paid* a sum of money upon the acceptance intrusted to them, for which he has a claim upon their estate. In that case the court allowed the set-off; and yet at the time of *Cox's* bankruptcy no balance could have been struck between the parties, because the defendant's claim arose from the produce of the pearls afterwards. What that produce would be could not be known at the time of the bankruptcy, and consequently could not then form an item in an account between the parties. Secondly. The finding of the jury, as to the undue preference, is either nugatory as to the plaintiffs, or it operates as a ground of nonsuit. The plaintiffs have an option either to affirm or disaffirm the contract; if the former, the defendant is entitled to set-off his demand; if the latter, though the plaintiffs might recover in trover, they cannot maintain this action. The jury found that there was a fraud *in the sale*: the plaintiffs cannot therefore contend that the fraud is confined to the *use* made of the sale. If the defendant had obtained his defence by fraud, it would not have availed: but it does not follow that, because there was a fraud in the sale of the goods, from the bankrupt to the defendant, the latter shall not set-off a cross-demand against the price of the goods. The fraud (if any) was in the sale of the goods; and the effect, which it has, is this,(*a*) that the bankrupt conveyed no property in the goods to the defendant, and that it was a naked delivery; if so, the plaintiffs should bring trover, not assumpsit.

Russell in reply. With respect to the case of *French* v. *Fenn*, which seems to have been principally relied on by the other side, there are two very material distinctions between that and the present case; there did exist mutual debts between the parties in that case, though the precise amount was not actually ascertained at the time of the bankruptcy; but still it was capable of being reduced to a certainty at any time by the sale of the jewels. And if *Fenn* had become a bankrupt instead of *Cox*, it cannot be denied but that *Cox* might have come in under *Fenn's* commission for a third of the value of those jewels. Again, in that case the jewels were in the hands of the party between whom and the bankrupt the account was to be settled and the mutual debts and credits allowed: whereas here the acceptance was in the hands of third persons at the time of the bankruptcy, without any certainty that they would ever be discharged by the defendant. *Cur. adv. vult.*

Lord KENYON, Ch. J. now delivered the opinion of the court. His Lordship, after stating the facts, said, We have considered this case, and are of opinion that the defendant has made a sufficient defence against the action in its present form, and consequently that a judgment of *nonsuit* must be entered. It is expressly stated in the case that the goods in question were delivered by the bankrupts to the defendant with a view to defraud the rest of their creditors; and therefore an action might have been framed to disaffirm the contract, which was thus tinctured with fraud; for if the assignees had brought an action of trover, they might have recovered the value of the goods. The statute *5 Geo. 2. c. 30. s. 28.* enacts that where it shall appear to the commissioners that there hath been *mutual credit* between the bankrupt and any other person, or mutual debts between the bankrupt and any other person, before the bankruptcy, the commissioners or the assignees shall state the account between them, and one debt may be set against another; and the balance only of such accounts shall be claimed and paid on either side; in the most extensive words. And therefore we are perfectly satisfied with the cases *ex parte Deeze*,(*b*) and *French* v. *Fenn*. But if an action of trover had been

(*a*) *Cook B. L.* 2d ed

(*b*) 1 *Atk.* 228.

brought, instead of assumpsit, this case would have differed materially from those two; because in both those cases the goods had got into the hands of the respective parties prior to the bankruptcy, and without any view of defrauding the rest of the creditors; and therefore, according to the justice of those cases, whether trover or assumpsit had been brought, the whole account ought to have been settled in the way in which it was, because the situation of the parties was not altered with a view to the bankruptcy: but here it was; and if trover had been brought, the defendant would have had no defence, and those cases would not have availed him. But this is an action on the contract for the goods sold by the bankrupt. And although the assignees may either affirm or disaffirm the coutract of the bankrupt, yet if they do affirm it, they must act consistently throughout; they cannot, as has often been observed in cases of this kind, blow hot and cold; and as the assignees in this case treated this transaction as a contract of sale, it must be pursued through all its consequences; one of which is, that the party buying may set up the same defence to an action brought by the assignees, which he might have used against the bankrupt himself; and consequently may set-off another debt which was owing from the bankrupt to him. This doctrine is fully recognised in *Hitchins* v. *Campbell*,(*a*) and in *King* v. *Leith*.(*b*) Now here the assignees, by bringing this action on the contract, recognised the act of the bankrupt, and must be bound by the transaction in the same manner as the bankrupt himself would have been; and if he had brought the action, the whole account must have been settled, and the defendant would have had a right to set-off the amount of the bill. Therefore, on the distinction between the actions of trover and assumpsit, we are all of opinion that a judgment of nonsuit must be entered.

Judgment of nonsuit.

Atkinson and others, Assignees of Hodges, a Bankrupt v. *Elliot and another*, *M. T.* 38 *Geo. III. A. D.* 1797. 7 *T. R.* 378.

ON the trial of this action of assumpsit for money had and received, the following case was reserved for the opinion of this court.

On the 2d May, 1796, the defendants sold to *Hodges*, the bankrupt, 300 barrels of tar for 430*l.* at 6 months' credit, and on the 3d of the same month they drew a bill on him at six months' date for the amount, which *Hodges* accepted On the 2d *September*, 1796, *Hodges* also purchased at 6 months' credit of the defendants 200 barrels of tar for 230*l.* for which he gave the defendants his acceptance to their draft dated 6th *September*, 1796, at six months' date. The first mentioned bill for 430*l.* became due on the 6th *November*, 1796, which *Hodges* was not able to pay, but on the 9th of the said month he gave the defendants a bill upon *Walpole* and Co. for 100*l.* due the 11th of *December* following, and on the following day (*November*, 10th) indorsed and gave defendants a bill of exchange drawn by him on and accepted by *Bullock* and Son, dated 27th *October*, 1796, at six weeks after date for 500*l.* and the defendants gave him the following memorandum or undertaking:-
"Memorandum; I promise to pay to Mr. *N. Hodges* 170*l.* when his bill on Messrs.
"*Bullock* and Son is paid, which bill I received *November* 10th, 1796, (signed)
"*Thomas Elliot* and Co.—Bill dated *October* 27th, at 6 weeks, for 500*l.*" It was not in the contemplation of either party to do more than take up the first mentioned acceptance of *Hodges* with the bill of *Bullock* and Son, and therefore after payment of what was due on that acceptance, so given as aforesaid, for the first mentioned parcel of goods, the residue was to be returned to *Hodges*.—The acceptance by Messrs. *Bullock* and Son for 500*l.* became due on the 11th of *December*, 1766, and was then duly paid by them to the defendants, the holders thereof; and the abovementioned bill on *Walpole* and Co. for 100*l.* was likewise paid on that day. On the 13th of *December*, 1796, a commission of bankruptcy issued against *Hodges* who was duly declared a bankrupt, and the plaintiffs were chosen assignees of his estate and effects. They immediately applied to the defendants for payment of the 170*l.* they had been overpaid in the said bill for 500*l.* on *Bullock* and Son, pursuant to their undertaking above stated, when they objected to it alleging

(*a*) 2 *Bl. Rep.* 827. (*b*) *Ante* 2 *vol.* 141.

that they then held *Hodges'* acceptance for 230*l.* above mentioned, and claiming a right to retain the said 170*l.* in part payment of the same, though it did not become due and payable till the 9th of *March* last, when the six months' credit for the goods sold to *Hodges* (which was their usual credit and customary mode of dealing) expired. The action was commenced on the 12th of *February* last.

Reader for the plaintiffs, after stating the question to be whether the defendants were entitled to set-off the bankrupt's acceptance, or rather to retain the 170*l.* the remainder of the bill for 500*l.* towards satisfaction of their demand on the bankrupt for 230*l.* the price of the goods sold by them to him on the 2d of *September*, 1796, argued in the negative. This question depends on the contract between the parties made on the 10th of *November*, 1796. Now the deposit of the bill for 500*l.* with the defendants on that day was not a general deposit to answer all demands that they might have on the bankrupt, but for the specific purpose of securing to them the 230*l.* the remainder of the value of the first goods sold by them to the bankrupt; and by that memorandum the defendants expressly agreed to return the overplus of 170*l.* to the bankrupt as soon as the bill for 500*l.* was paid. The attempt, therefore, on the part of the assignees, to retain this in satisfaction of another debt is in direct opposition to their agreement; it being stated as a fact in the case that nothing more was in the contemplation of the parties, when the bill for 500*l.* was deposited with the defendants, than to secure to them the amount of the bankrupt's first acceptance for the first parcel of the goods. As between the original parties to this contract it is clear that the defendants could not have had any lien on the bill for 500*l.* for any other demand than that expressed in the memorandum; and the bankruptcy of *Hodges* cannot put the defendants in a better situation than they were in before. It will be contended, however, on behalf of the defendants that it is immaterial by what means they got this money into their hands, but that having got it they are entitled to set-off their second demand against it by virtue of the stat. 5 *Geo.* 2. *c.* 30. *s.* 28.(*a*) And it cannot be denied but that some debts may be set-off under this statute that were not due at the time of the bankruptcy on the ground of there being mutual credit between the parties; as in the cases *Ex parte Prescott*, 1 *Atk* 230; *French* v. *Fenn*, *Tr.* 23 *Geo.* 3. *B. R.* and *Smith* v. *Hodgson*, *ante* 4 vol. 211. But on examination it will be found that this case does not come within the meaning of the statute respecting "mutual credit;" for that only applies to cases where mutual credit has been given in the ordinary course of commercial transactions: whereas this is not a case of that description, the bill for 500*l.* having only been deposited with the defendants for a particular purpose. The property in that bill was never in the defendants for a single moment: they held it merely as trustees for the bankrupt. But even if this were a case of mutual credit, the defendants are not entitled to retain the overplus of 170*l.* by reason of their express stipulation. Suppose the defendants had undertaken to pay this surplus to a third person, instead of the bankrupt, there would have been no pretence to say that they could have retained it on the ground of their having another demand on the bankrupt; and if not, they cannot retain it as against the assignees of the bankrupt.

Gally, contra, was stopped by the court.

Lord KENYON, Ch. J. The statute 5 *Geo.* 2. *c.* 30. *s.* 28. enacts, that where there are either *mutual credits or mutual debts* between the bankrupt and any other person, one debt may be set off against another, and only the balance claimed. Now in using those words the legislature must have intended something more than would have been expressed by "mutual debts" only; and the decisions referred to show that this construction has been put upon this act. I agree to what was said by Mr. J. *Buller* in one of the cases, that where there is a trust between both parties there is a mutual credit. Justice also requires that the whole account on both sides should be stated; and that the balance should be the only thing to constitute the

(*a*) Which enacts, that where it shall appear to the commissioners that there hath been mutual credit given by the bankrupt and any other person, or mutual debts between the bankrupt and any other person, at any time before such person became bankrupt, the said commissioners, &c. shall state the account between them, and one debt may be set against another; and what shall appear to be due on either side, on the balance of such account, and on setting such debts against one another, and no more, shall be claimed or paid on either side respectively.

debt. In my opinion the case *Ex parte Prescott* was properly decided; and that has since been followed by a series of determinations.

Grose, J. It has been objected that the defendants cannot set-off the 170*l.* because it is contrary to their express agreement: but consider that the bankrupt by his agreement was bound to pay his acceptance for 230*l.* at a future day, but that his bankruptcy disabled him; that was a credit on one side; and credit was constituted on the other by giving a bill which became due at a subsequent time. It is clearly therefore a case of mutual credit, and it is just that one demand should be set-off against the other.

Lawrence, J. This is directly within the authority of the case *Ex parte Prescott.*

Per Curiam. Postea to the defendants.

Grimwood v. *Barrit, M. T.* 36 *Geo. III. A. D.* 1795. 6 *T. R.* 460.

DEBT on bond for 1400*l.* dated *July* 20th, 1787. The defendant craved oyer of the condition, which was that the bond should be void on payment of 700*l.* on the 24th of *June*, 1788, together with lawful interest for the same from the 24th of *June*, then last; and then pleaded, first, that there was due from him to the plaintiff on the bond "a much less sum than 1400*l.* *to wit*, the sum of 735*l.* and no more;" and that the plaintiff at the time of exhibiting his bill was indebted to him (the defendant) in a much larger sum of money, to wit, 1200*l.* for goods sold and delivered, &c. which he is ready to set-off. He also pleaded that on the 20th of *July*, 1787, it was corruptly agreed between him and the plaintiff that the latter should lend him 700*l.* to be repaid on the 24th of *June*, then next, and that he (the defendant) should pay the plaintiff interest at the rate of 5*l.* *per cent.* from the 24th of *June*, 1787, to the 24th of *June*, 1788, namely, one year's interest, and give a bond for securing payment of the whole; and that in pursuance of the said corrupt agreement the bond in question was given.

To the first plea the plaintiff replied, that there was due on the bond more than 735*l.* namely 835*l.* 0*s.* 7*d.*; concluding to the country; and he traversed the corrupt agreement mentioned in the second plea. The defendant demurred specially; for causes of demurrer to the replication to the first plea, (he said) that the plaintiff had not by his replication given any answer to the plea, nor admitted or denied that the plaintiff was indebted to the defendant in manner and form as in the plea alleged. The causes of demurrer to the replication to the second plea were, that the plaintiff had not in his replication given any answer to the plea, or denied that by the condition of the bond there is expressly reserved above the rate of 5*l.* *per cent.* &c. for a shorter time than a year, &c.

Morgan, in support of the demurrer. First, the defendant, having pleaded that the sum of 735*l.* *under a videlicet* was due on the bond, was not bound to prove that that specific sum was due, but it was competent to him on that allegation to prove either a greater or a less sum; and therefore that averment was not traversable in the replication. In this respect this case is distinguishable from that of *Symmons* v. *Knox*,(*a*) where it was held that an averment that a precise sum only was due on the bond, was traversable; for there it was not laid under a videlicet. Secondly. This appears to be usury on the condition of the bond itself; for a year's interest is reserved on a particular sum, though the forbearance is stated to be for a less time than a year, namely from 20th of *July* to the 24th of *June* following. And even if the plaintiff had intended to show that the money was not lent on the day when the bond was given, according to the principle established in *Collins* v. *Blantern*,(*b*) he should have protested against the corrupt agreement, and pleaded that the money was lent on the 24th of *June*, 1787, for a year, but that the bond for securing it was not executed until the 20th of *July* following.

Dampier, contra. The case of *Symmons* v. *Knox* must govern this; it being immaterial in such a case as the present whether the sum be or be not pleaded under a videlicet. For though the want of a videlicet may in some cases make an averment material which would not otherwise be so, yet the addition of a videlicet cannot render a material averment immaterial,(*c*) or prevent the adverse party deny-

(*a*) *Ante* 3 vol. 65. (*b*) 2 *Wils.* 347. (*c*) Vid. 1 *Saund.* 169.

ing it. With respect to the other point: the corrupt agreement, which is stated in the plea, is denied in the replication; and there being a demurrer to that, the non-existence of any corrupt agreement is admitted on the record. Therefore, the defendant, to maintain this demurrer, must prove that the loan of money secured by a bond dated *July* 20th, and conditioned for the payment of a sum of money with interest at 5*l*. *per cent*. calculated from a past day, must necessarily have been made on the day when the bond was given, and that this is so necessary a conclusion of law that a denial of the fact, and that denial admitted on the record, cannot weigh against it. But that is in effect saying that the court are bound to infer corruption against the fact, when that fact is admitted on the record It might equally be said that in an action on the statute against usury for a penalty this bond would be conclusive evidence of usury against the plaintiff, notwithstanding he could prove that the money was in fact lent on the 24th of *June*, 1787. In *Collins* v. *Blantern* it was held that an unlawful consideration might be averred against a bond which was good on the face of it: then here the plaintiff may aver a lawful consideration consistent with and explanatory of the bond.

Lord KENYON, Ch. J. Where an averment is material, the addition of a videlicet does not render it immaterial. And on the other point there is not the least doubt; the defendant might have taken issue on the corrupt agreement, the existence of which was denied by the replication; on that issue the whole case might have been gone into before the jury. But on this record we must take it for granted that the money was in fact lent in *June*, though the bond was not given until *July*. And the justice of the case perfectly coincides with our determination.

GROSE, J. This plea being founded on the statute 8 *G*. 2. *c*. 24. *s*. 5. it was necessary for the defendant to show how much was due on the bond: he accordingly pleaded that the sum of 735*l*. and no more was due, and this was traversable according to the case of *Symmons* v. *Knox*. But it is said that the averment of the sum here is laid under a videlicet, which was not the case in *Symmons* v. *Knox*: but the rule is, that where any thing in pleading is material, it is not rendered less material by its being pleaded with a videlicet; it is still traversable; and therefore this case must be governed by that of *Symmons* v. *Knox*. With respect to the other plea of usury; the corrupt agreement is denied by the plaintiff. It is however contended that notwithstanding that denial it must be understood, from what appears upon the face of the bond, that there was an usurious agreement, because the court must infer that the money was lent on the day when the bond was given: but such an inference is contrary to the fact; it is not alleged that the money was lent when the bond was given; and on the contrary it is admitted by the demurrer that there was no such usurious agreement as is stated in the plea, and if so, the money was not lent on the day that the bond bears date.

LAWRENCE, J. As to the last point: the plea consists of two parts; it first states that there was an usurious contract between the parties, and then alleges that the bond was given in pursuance of that agreement. It was sufficient for the plaintiff to deny either of these parts in his replication, because both were essential to establish the plea: and the plaintiff having traversed the corrupt agreement, the defendant, if he had meant to rely on its existence, should have taken issue on it: whereas, by demurring to the replication, he has admitted that there was no such agreement. With regard to the other plea: it was necessary for the defendant to show the real sum due on the bond to entitle him to his set-off: and it was decided in *Symmons* v. *Knox* that the averment of that sum was traversable. The question therefore here is, Whether the introduction of the videlicet in this case makes any difference; but it certainly does not. That it does not render an averment immaterial, which, without the videlicet is material, has been decided in many cases. In *Johnson* v. *Picket* and another,(*a*) which was an action on the statute against usury, the agreement to forbear and give day of payment was stated in the declaration to be on the 14th under a videlicet, but it was proved that the money was not advanced until the 16th; on which Lord *Mansfield* nonsuited the plaintiff, being of opinion that the day from whence the forbearance took place was material, though laid under a videlicet; and on a motion for a new trial this court confirmed the decision at Nisi Prius. So in the case of *Pope* v. *Foster*,(*b*) which was an

(*a*) *E*. 25 *Geo*. 3. *B*. *R*. (*b*) *Ante* 4 vol. 590.

action for a malicious prosecution, the declaration stated that the indictment "afterwards, *to wit*, on the 25th of *February* 1791, came on to be tried;" by the record of that indictment it appeared that the trial was on a different day; on which the plaintiff was nonsuited; and on a motion to set aside that nonsuit, this court thought the objection fatal, "though it were laid under a videlicet, the day being material."

Judgment for the Plaintiff.

INDEX.

FINIS.

Spotted something that isn't quite right?

Let us know and we'll fix it for future reprints. And as a thank you for your diligence, we'll send you a free Sothis book of your choice.

publisher@sothis.press

This page intentionally left blank

Made in the USA
Monee, IL
05 November 2026

67808954R00081